THE WINDWARD ROAD

THE

Windward Road

Adventures
of a Naturalist on Remote
Caribbean Shores

ARCHIE CARR

University Presses of Florida

THE FLORIDA STATE UNIVERSITY PRESS
Tallahassee

00 99 98 97 96 95   6 5 4 3

First published January 23, 1956. The 1979 reprint edition was published with partial support from the Caribbean Conservation Corporation, which was founded as a result of the first publication of THE WINDWARD ROAD. The lines from "Kitch" on pages 118 and 120 are by Aldwyn Roberts (Lord Kitchener) and are reprinted with the kind permission of the Mechanical-Copyright Protection Society Limited.

University Presses of Florida, the agency of the State of Florida's university system for publication of scholarly and creative works, operates under policies adopted by the Board of Regents. Its offices are located at 15 Northwest 15th Street, Gainesville, Florida 32603.

Library of Congress Cataloging in Publication Data

Carr, Archie Fairly, 1909–
    The windward road.

    "A Florida State University book."
    Includes index.
    1. Zoology—Caribbean area.   2.   Turtles—Caribbean area.   3.   Caribbean area—Description and travel.
    I. Title.
QL134.5.C37   1980   639'.97'813   79–23624
ISBN 0–8130–0639–2

TO THE MEMORY OF

Thomas Barbour

Contents

Illustrations

Maps

All photographs not otherwise credited are by the author.

Foreword

*T*he *Windward Road*, first published in 1956, has made history. As Dr. Carr reveals at the outset of the book, the main purpose behind the Caribbean roving that he tells about was to collect information on sea turtles—primarily on the green turtle. The record of the things he saw, learned, felt, and thought during his wandering makes the reader's skin tingle and his blood surge. It is not often that a book entertains, instructs, and drives people to action. This one did, however, and does, and it leaves one with spiritual urge and grace.

I first heard of the book when I visited William M. Pepper, Jr., publisher of the *Gainesville Sun* and a devoted member of the Inter-American Press Association. I told Bill that I had been reading a remarkable book, *High Jungles and Low*, written by a naturalist from the University of Florida. Bill said, "*High Jungles* is a great book, all right; but wait till you read *The Windward Road*, in which Archie walks the windward beaches of the Caribbean islands and tells of the coming destruction of the great turtles that used to abound there."

When, finally, I read the book, I understood what Bill meant. The story was engrossing, humorous, and deadly serious. One day in New York, after a meeting of the executive committee of the Inter-American Press Association, we had finished our business and sat down to lunch, and I started talking about green turtles. The little group around the table listened politely. They were amused at my fantasies, but the conversation soon turned to more familiar themes.

When I returned to my office I asked my secretary to buy 20 copies of *The Windward Road*. I mailed these out to 20 friends, with a letter to each announcing that he or she had been elected a member of The Brotherhood of the Green Turtle. The response was almost unanimously quick and interested.

Until then I had never spoken to, or been known to, the writer whose message I was spreading, so I wrote him, apologizing for using his name without permission and asking for guidance. He was happy about the development, and so our campaign to save the green turtle began. I visited Costa Rica and asked the Minister of Agriculture to approve our research and protective efforts at the Tortuguero nesting ground. He did this. I also enlisted the aid of my friend Jack Fendell in San José. In 1959, at a luncheon in New York, the Brotherhood of the Green Turtle was formally launched. John H. Phipps took over responsibility for the direction of its sister organization, the Caribbean Conservation Corporation, and Dr. Carr took charge at Tortuguero and directed the serious research on which the rescue program had to be based.

Now, twenty years later, the work at our modest camp in the cocal has inspired Costa Rica to create a national park at Tortuguero, and this draws tourists and scientists from distant places. The work there has revealed a great deal about the life of the green turtle, and everything learned has reinforced the movement to save *Chelonia* from the destruction it once was facing.

1979   *Joshua B. Powers*

Preface
to the 1979 Reissue

In SETTING out to write this preface to the new printing of
The Windward Road, what I mainly wanted to do was to
tell about water that has passed under the bridge since the
book was first published two decades ago. The world has
changed drastically since then, however, and so, inevitably,
have I. Every page and paragraph tempts me to expand,
expound, or justify myself. But it would take more than
an 18-page preface to bring the diverse themes of *The
Windward Road* up to date after 22 years. So I shall just
leaf through the book, briefly relating some sequels and
laying bare some of the anachronisms that readers of a
present-day printing are sure to find.

As for how I came to write *The Windward Road* in the
first place, the germ of the idea had been generated long
before when I was working on *Handbook of Turtles.* In
putting that book together I saw how little was known
about the natural history of turtles that live in the sea.
They seemed wonderfully colorful creatures, bound to be
doing exciting things in remote places it would be pleasant
to visit. From the beginning I was inclined to accept the
folk belief that green turtles were long-range migrants, and
therefore navigators; and if they were, investigating their
ecological geography seemed sure to be scientifically re-

warding. Besides those attractions, *Chelonia* had been an important source of food for Caribbean people from time immemorial, and had even influenced the European colonization of America. Along the way, however, its populations had been sadly reduced from their primitive levels. The appeal of marine turtles for me thus had several facets, and I decided to learn everything I could about them. *The Windward Road* was just a compulsive recounting of things I saw and pondered, including the fascinating Caribbean people I consorted with during the first exciting years of that quest after *Chelonia*.

One hope I had for the book was that it might improve the melancholy survival outlook of the Caribbean green turtle. As a conservation document *The Windward Road* had a good start in its public relations. In 1952, the last chapter, which was written first, was presented as an address at the annual meeting of the American Institute of Biological Sciences. Another chapter—"The Black Beach" —appeared separately in *Mademoiselle* and was selected for the O. Henry Award (*Best Short Stories of 1956*). Then the book itself, published in 1956, received the John Burroughs Award and began to appear in foreign-language editions, including an unauthorized 30-kopek edition in the Soviet Union, to which a new chapter calling attention to the proletarian leanings of the author had been editorially added.

But before that a portentous thing had happened to *The Windward Road*. Joshua B. Powers, a New York publishers' representative, happened to read it. To Josh the book suggested a way to show his affection for Latin America by helping Caribbean countries save a part of their natural heritage. He sent copies of the book to twenty influential friends who he hoped would share his interest. They did, and the Brotherhood of the Green Turtle was promptly formed with the aim of "restoring green turtles to their native waters, and insuring to Winston Churchill his nightly cup of turtle soup." John H. Phipps of Tallahassee, Florida—"Ben" to his friends—was a charter member, and so was Jim Oliver, then director of the American Museum of Natural History. Ben provided financial stability for the organization, and Jim's naval connections later helped enlist support of the U. S. Navy for research and conservation work. Grants from the American Philosophical Society and the National Science Foundation helped set up and staff a seasonal turtle tagging camp at the Tortuguero, Costa Rica, nesting ground.

Later developments I have told about at length in *So Excellent a Fishe* and elsewhere. The Brotherhood incorporated under the name Caribbean Conservation Corporation (CCC), with its headquarters in Tallahassee and John H. Phipps as its president. (John's son Colin Phipps is president of the corporation today.) At Tortuguero some old United Fruit Company field survey buildings were acquired as quarters for our turtle tagging project, and negotiations with the Costa Rican government resulted in legislation that prohibited commercial turtling on the nesting beach—the dismal *velador* system described in the book. The tagging program that we established at Tortuguero in 1956 has been under way ever since.

The first venture of the CCC, or of anybody for that matter, in international sea turtle conservation was a spectacular exercise that we called Operation Green Turtle. Operation Green Turtle aimed to rehabilitate previous nesting grounds around the Caribbean wherever government surveillance could be insured. The working hypothesis of the venture was that Tortuguero hatchlings released on a distant shore would not go back to Turtle Bogue to nest when they matured, but would return, as salmon do, to the place where they had been released. A million eggs or more were being deposited on Tortuguero Beach each year, and it seemed justifiable to take a few thousand a year for Operation Green Turtle.

So every October for eight years we hatched thousands of little turtles and flew them away to ten or a dozen places in an amphibian airplane sent down by the U. S. Navy from Roosevelt Roads, Puerto Rico. By the time the Vietnam war took away our Navy transportation and ended the program, we had transported tens of thousands of hatchlings to beaches in 19 different localities in Colombia, Trinidad, St. Vincent, Grenada, St. Lucia, Puerto Rico, Belize, Yucatan, Inagua, Bimini, Antigua, Nassau, Bermuda, Barbados, and in Florida at Cape Sable, Indian River, Dry Tortugas, Islamorada, and Cape Canaveral.

Operation Green Turtle continued for eight seasons. In those days our estimate of the age of a green turtle at sexual maturity was based on scraps of growth data from captive turtles, and we started out believing that five or six years was a conservatively high estimate. So when five, six, and seven years passed and no nesting had been reported on any of our beaches, we began to get uneasy. When the eighth season of distribution flights was finished and still there was no nesting, we decided to stop the program.

Except at Bermuda. During the last couple of years of the effort, we began to realize, with some chagrin, that our project had another possible hole in it. If baby turtles were imprinted with the smell or taste of the water they first swam in, and grew up with an urge and ability to go home to such water when they were ready to breed, then our transplanted turtles would try to go back to Tortuguero, because we usually kept them in tanks of sea water for a few days before the airplane arrived to distribute them.

So belatedly, during the sixth season of Operation Green

Turtle, we began sending out eggs instead of hatchlings. One of the places the eggs went to was Bermuda. When two years later the program ended, the Bermuda deliveries were continued by the Clay Frick family until in 1977 international permit problems interfered.

It cannot be proved that Operation Green Turtle restored any green turtle colonies, but it brought about two important advances. One was the first glimmering of international concern over the outlook for *Chelonia mydas* as a Caribbean resource and species. The other was Jane Frick's research into the earliest stages of the "lost year" of green turtle ecology. Nobody knows where little sea turtles spend the first year or so of their lives. One theory is that they get into floating mats of Sargassum weed, finding food and shelter there and going where the rafts go until they are able to move into the coastal habitats in which they reappear at sizes a little bigger than a saucer. At most nesting shores, the surest way for a newly hatched sea turtle to get into Sargassum weed would be to steer a course directly toward the open sea after passing through the surf. Until recently, nobody knew anything about the behavior of hatchlings after they pass the breakers. To investigate this, Jane adopted the beautifully direct and somewhat heroic technique of swimming after the little turtles. With face mask and flippers, she swam for hours eight or ten feet behind hatchlings, a mile or more out from Nonesuch Island, in water half a mile deep. A boat attended her at a distance and plotted her positions from landmarks on shore. In this straightforward way she proved beyond any doubt that the little turtles were somehow able to maintain constantly nonrandom open-sea headings. Later on she found that they do the same thing down at Tortuguero, holding their headings at least as far as 30 or 40 miles from shore. Jane's results thus opened up a new area of research into the lost-year mystery. If Operation Green Turtle had produced nothing else, that advance of Jane Frick's would have made it worthwhile.

The most dramatic sequel to any story told in *The Windward Road* is the latter-day history of the ridley—the elusive subject of the first chapter. During the first years the book was in print, the thing readers used to ask me about most often was how the ridley mystery turned out. Even though the solution of the mystery of its breeding place was narrated in detail in my later book, *So Excellent a Fishe*, and in many other places, people still ask about it. The bare bones of the story are that the nesting place was finally revealed by a film made by a Mexican architect named Andres Herrera, who in 1947 filmed a fantastic assemblage of turtles nesting, in the daytime, on a short section of the Gulf coast of Mexico. The circumstances under which the film was made and the way it was brought to light after 18 years of neglect are almost unbelievable. What it revealed was a monstrous conclave of nesting ridleys, later estimated to be composed of at least 40,000, gathered on a single mile of the Gulf coast near the town of Rancho Nuevo between Tampico, Mexico, and Brownsville, Texas. Thus, when the ridley nesting aggregation—*arribada*, the Mexicans call such gatherings—was finally found, it turned out to represent the most intense concentration of reproductive effort ever recorded for any vertebrate animal.

I went into paroxysms over all this in *So Excellent a Fishe*. Coming as the discovery did after the long frustration related in "The Riddle of the Ridley," I believe my excitement was justified.

But almost at once, Kemp's ridley revealed that even then it was not going to let anybody relax. Immediately it became apparent that the huge *arribadas* of the 1940s no longer occurred, and before long it began to seem clear that the ridley was facing extinction. Reacting to letters from concerned turtle people, the Mexican government in 1966 began sending biologists down to Rancho Nuevo to monitor the *arribada,* and armed marines began patrolling the shore to scare off poachers and coyotes. The International Union for the Conservation of Nature (IUCN) declared Kemp's ridley an endangered species, and all around the world more people began writing worried letters about the situation. During each successive season, reports from Rancho Nuevo grew more dismal. My own uneasiness came to a peak in 1977. A letter I wrote to Sir Peter Scott, chairman of the Survival Service Commission of IUCN, sounds the tone of my panic:

Dear Peter:

This is not the first time I have written you a panicky letter about the plight of *Lepidochelys kempi,* Kemp's ridley, but it seems likely that it may be the last time. Since the IUCN last made representations to the Mexican government in respect to the plight of *kempi,* the situation has degenerated so badly that I must again beg you to bring the circumstances to the attention of the Survival Service Commission, at it April meetings. I deeply regret that I can't be there to say more on the subject, because it is a grave and complicated one.

Last week, while preparing to write a popular article on the ridley for a magazine, I carefully went over all available records of breeding population levels at Rancho Nuevo, the only nesting ground of the species, and I realized that we really do have a crisis on our hands. Accordingly, I went to Brownsville, Texas, for four days to gather more information. I discussed the current status of the nesting *arribada* with Ila Loetscher, Dearl Adams, Kavanaugh Francis, and others of the corporation that has been formed on South Padre Island to save the ridley. I spent two afternoons with the Port Isabel shrimp fleet, the biggest shrimping exercise in the world. Going from trawler to trawler, I plied every shrimper who was willing to talk with exactly the same set of questions that I had asked at the same docks 16 years earlier, back in the days when the trawlers, their nets, and the periods for which the trawls stayed down were all about half what they are now; when the price of shrimp was one-eighth its current price; and when ridleys were being abundantly caught not just in Texas and Mexico but in Florida waters and northward all along the Atlantic coast.

On that first visit to the shrimp docks, there was evidence of incidentally caught ridleys everywhere. Every crewman I spoke with knew the ridley well, said it was the only abundant sea turtle in the area, and deplored the damage it did to the shrimp in their trawls. Last week, almost none of the shrimpers I spoke with even knew of the existence of ridleys. I was careful to indicate that my only interest was in collecting tags and paying rewards for them, and for the most part I was able to dispel apprehension that I might be an enforcement officer of some kind. I am thus quite sure that the contrast in catch frequencies that I saw is real; and it is just the same all along the ridley migration route in Florida and beyond. Few ridleys are caught anywhere now, simply because few remain.

Besides the hours I spent on the shrimp boats, I attended the convention of the Texas Shrimp Association, to try to soak up an impression of their attitude toward the incidental catch problem. Then I spent a long time conversing with René Márquez and others in

Mexico City agencies, to get all existing figures on the size of the 1976 nesting aggregation.

What has happened to *kempi* can be graphically shown by comparing successive sizes of the Rancho Nuevo breeding population, as indicated by counts or estimates of *arribada* size during past decades. I'll list only three of these here, but the figures are representative, and we are working up a more complete record. *Arribada* sizes, and calculated total mature breeding population for the successive periods since the nesting ground was discovered, are shown below (I'll explain our method of converting *arribadas* to total mature population later, if desired):

Year	Estimated Nesting Arrival	Total Mature Population
1947	40,000	162,400
1970	2,500	10,150
1974	1,200	4,872

The figures speak for themselves. The species is clearly on the skids, and if present conditions continue it will shortly—in two years perhaps, or three, or five— be gone. The dramatic drop during the 1950s was caused by overexploitation combined with very heavy natural predation pressures. The terminal decline now in progress has been brought about by incidental trawler catch. When ridleys were many and shrimping was less intensive that factor was negligible. Today it is wiping out the species.

Lepidochelys kempi can possibly be saved, but it will surely disappear unless drastic action is taken. I hope therefore that the Survival Service Commission will be willing to write the new Mexican president, explaining the crisis and imploring him to take the only steps that could possibly save the Atlantic ridley from early extinction. I also hope you will solicit similar letters from other groups or individuals who might be willing to write. I enclose notes for the sort of letter that might be written.

With best wishes for a successful meeting, and with my sincere regrets that I won't be able to attend.

By the time that letter was written, protecting the Rancho Nuevo beach alone seemed insufficient to keep the ridley from sliding into limbo. The burgeoning shrimp industry was making increasing inroads. Shrimp boats were multiplying, their nets were growing in size, and dragtimes were lengthening beyond the suffocation thresholds of the turtles. With the ridley population already decimated, the effect of this incidental catch by trawlers, once a bagatelle, had become a major factor in the survival plight of *kempi.*

The climax of this concern was reached when in the fall of 1975 an international group including the Mexican Instituto Nacional de Pesca and four U.S. agencies arranged a series of meetings to develop a rescue program. The U.S. agencies represented were the National Marine Fisheries Service, the U. S. Fish and Wildlife Service, the National Park Service, and the Texas Park and Wildlife Service. The first meeting was held at Matamoras, just across the Mexican border from Brownsville, Texas. One phase of the project decided on was to establish a new ridley breeding colony on Padre Island National Seashore, between Corpus Christie and Brownsville. The island has good beaches but they are almost devoid of turtles. The hope was that a ridley nesting population might be planted. If so, it obviously would vastly improve the survival outlook of the ridley. Ila Loetscher and her colleagues had been bringing Rancho Nuevo ridley eggs to Padre Island for years with the same aim but without demonstrable success. In fact, no such effort had ever been successful anywhere. Another phase of the program was to provide the Mexican government with assistance—personnel and vehicles—for their surveillance of the Rancho Nuevo nesting beach at *arribada* time.

The transplantation program decided on was complicated. To make sure the hatchlings were appropriately imprinted, it was decided to hatch 2,000 of the eggs in Padre Island sand, let the little turtles crawl down the beach and swim through the surf, and then catch them in nets. They would be sent to the National Marine Fisheries Service Laboratory in Galveston, Texas, reared for eight months, and then released in places ecologically appropriate for their size class. This procedure has been called "head starting." Its aim is to circumvent the host of predators that newly hatched turtles are plagued by.

Neither head starting nor hatchling transplantation are proved management techniques. No head-started turtle has ever demonstrably been launched in a successful career. None, in fact, has ever been seen after reaching sexual maturity. And no new sea turtle colony has ever been provably established anywhere. So both these procedures are in an experimental stage. However, either or both might work, and the ridley situation was so desperate that the agencies decided to take the risk of failure. As recompense to Mexico for the introduction stock, another thousand hatchlings imprinted with the aura of Rancho Nuevo sand and water would be head started in Galveston.

As to the urgent need for the other phase of the Rancho Nuevo project—U. S. participation in the surveillance of the beach—there can be no doubt at all. The gringo collaboration is being supervised by Peter Pritchard, who did a part of his doctoral research at Rancho Nuevo in the early 1960s and has kept closely in touch with the colony ever since. In carrying out the U.S. agreement to help with the beach work, Peter mobilizes teams of able young people from the University of Central Florida, who go down to walk with the Mexican biologists and Marines. This unique mission has had one successful season of collaboration with the Mexicans, and the second beach watches are in progress as this is being written.

Also, at the time I write, the first season's yearling ridleys from the Galveston nursery have been tagged and released in the Gulf of Mexico. Little radios were fastened to the shells of some of them, and the paths they took after release were tracked from an airplane. So a lot of well-grown yearling ridleys have journeyed off to whatever their destiny may be. One can only hope that some day some of them will colonize Padre Island, and that others will reinforce their dwindling kin at Rancho Nuevo.

Back in the days before *Silent Spring*, when *The Windward Road* was being written, people were still naive about the durability of the wild world. The exhaustibility of nature was known, of course, but the pace at which species and landscapes were being obliterated had not sunk deeply into the public mind. I was a professional zoologist with great affection for wilderness and wild creatures, but you can easily see the rudimentary state of my own conservation conscience in my lighthearted attitude toward eating wildlife. Nowadays, some people who read the book are bothered by the zest with which I used to eat wild animals, some of them now endangered or threatened species.

I recently found evidence that even in those days I had transitory pangs of conscience about this paradoxical attitude of mine. While looking through a file of old notes for *The Windward Road* I came across this inscription:

> Looking over the parts of this book now in legible shape, I see plainly that it is rife with subjective passions and callow opinions, and that my emotions sometimes conflict in ways that could be confusing to readers. I regret this, but it was inevitable. For example, every time I set out to write about sea turtles in a level-headed, impersonal way I start giving myself a bit of rein, and then pretty soon emotions appear, and then conflicting emotions, like those I referred to. One trouble of this kind is the way I appear to be at one moment dejected over the precarious survival state of sea turtles, and at the next, drooling over the thought of eating them.

So even then I was uneasy over my inconsistency. But I went ahead and ate the turtles. I ate a lot of other kinds of animals as well and won't try to rationalize this, beyond saying that today I try to do better.

For example, we never eat green turtle at Tortuguero, even when someone offers to share one that has been killed on the legal village quota. This is a gastronomic and logistic deprivation for us, because turtle is good and meat is scarce at the Green Turtle Station. But our abstinence is good public relations for the unpopular law against killing turtles at the nesting beach; so when we pass the window of a kitchen where some lady is stewing turtle fin, we merely drool.

It isn't eating just turtle that readers of *The Windward Road* have berated me about. It is all kinds of animals. I have always been a catholic victualer and in traveling have exploited any opportunity to try out a dish that local people esteem. Along the Caribbean coast, with its diverse human races and edible wildlife, there is always something new to try. To get an idea of the diversity of wild meat with which people of Miskito Coast have always pieced out their diet of rice, yuca, plantains, and coconut oil, consider the following menu, based wholly on the vertebrate fauna of coastal Nicaragua. The menu and introductory paragraph are from *Dottings on the Wayside*, by Captain George Pim.

> Subjoined is the bill of fare of an entertainment given by the officers of a detachment of the 3rd Regiment (Buffs) at their station on the Mosquito Coast. It will give some idea not only of the progress of civilization in that part of the world, but also of the delicacies in the highest estimation there at the end of the eighteenth century.

BILL OF FARE

Calipash.

Manati soused.	Guana fricasseed.	Waree steaks.

Turtle Soup.

Armadillo curry.	Monkey barbequed.	Parrot pie.

Antelope Roasted.

Peccary smoked.	Indian Rabbit boiled.	Hiccatee stewed.

Calipee.

Captain Pim recorded that menu as a bizarre bit of local ethnozoology with which to bemuse Victorian English readers. Actually, however, by Tortuguero standards, there is nothing at all peculiar about the meal—except, of course, for the redundance of entrees. At one time or another—though never at a single meal—we have eaten every item on the list at Tortuguero and have rejoiced in them all.

Except the parrot. We only tried to eat one parrot at Tortuguero, and that was a failure. It was a parrot I had bought in San José for seven dollars. That was a high price in those days, but I willingly paid it because the parrot could say quite a few things, which, though mostly irrelevant, were very well pronounced. We ate it because it was killed by an ocelot. The wonder was that the parrot didn't kill the ocelot. Shefton cooked the corpse for six hours and finally gave up and converted it into a form of hamburger.

All the other items on the officers' menu are very worthwhile, some of them superlative.

Manati (manatee) is of course sea cow, an altogether admirable creature that happens to be too good to eat for its own good. Manatee meat was never a staple at the camp, but hunters brought it in regularly and, until we began to realize how sad its survival outlook was, nothing we got from the markets in San José was ever more welcome. In 1964 we stopped eating manatee meat. Today the species is in bad shape almost everywhere in Central America and is in need of far better protection than it gets anywhere.

Guana is iguana, a big herbivorous, arboreal lizard. It is the female that is eaten and only when she is full of eggs. There is a nesting ground on Tortuguero beach up near the boca. Every March when the females swim over from the forest to nest in the beach sand, posses of little boys go up to the boca every day and drag the poor iguanas out of their nesting burrows and take them to the village to eat or sell. Stewed with their eggs they are elegant, but the Tortuguero nesting colony is small, and unless the iguana boys are soon curbed the rookery will disappear.

Waree is white-lipped peccary, a piglike animal that roams in herds of up to a hundred or more in the Caribbean lowlands. It is excellent meat and once was a mainstay in the local diet. It is now diminishing wherever it is accessible to the spreading coastal population, including the area near Tortuguero.

Armadillo is not much esteemed at Tortuguero. Although it is very popular in the interior of Nicaragua, most coastal people disdain it. The meat is bland and almost without taste. If well seasoned with garlic, cilantro, and chile, however, it is acceptable. It is significant that the armadillo dish on the menu was a curry.

The monkey at the officers' dinner was almost certainly *mono colorado,* the spider monkey, which is excellent eating. My current feeling about monkey cookery is that only a fiend would eat one, but I have not always felt that way. Fortunately all monkeys are now very strictly protected in Tortuguero Park, and they are moving back close to the village.

The smoked peccary on the list was a collared peccary, a very widespread animal, a little smaller than the waree, and never found in bands as huge as those the warees usually travel in.

Indian rabbit is tepescuintle, Nelson's paca, a rodent related to the agouti and capybara but vastly more savory than either. One of these played a major role in my chapter "Tiger Bogue."

The *hiccatee* (*jicotea* in Spanish) is a freshwater turtle of the genus *Chyrsemys* (*Pseudemys*). The big females, especially, are excellent eating. Perhaps because of that the species is much less common than other freshwater turtles in the Tortuguero area and all along the coast.

The animal referred to in the list as antelope is a little spike-horned forest deer, called "goat" by the Creoles and *cabra de monte* in Spanish. The officers at the dinner would have been better served with the local white-tailed deer. Its meat is better, but the brocket is more available in the selva.

As to the green turtle dishes on the menu, calipash is the upper shell, with the adhering meat and fat, and calipee is the lower shell, or plastron. The turtle soup they had that night, if it was properly made, was the best soup in the world. In fact, I will say without hesitation that clear green turtle soup is the finest gastronomic contribution of the English people. Giving it up was my greatest sacrifice to the religion of turtle preservation. I have almost completely given it up, and this very clearly illustrates the complexity of my attitude toward eating turtles. For example, despite the complaints I have directed against the traffickers in sea turtle products, I am still not above going to the supermarket, counting the cans of illegal green turtle soup on the rack there, berating the manager for selling an endangered species, and getting his promise to desist—and then, on the grounds that the act would not generate continued traffic because there is no known source of supply, buying out his remaining cans of soup, to consume in secret self-indulgence. That behavior seems to me to epitomize the predicament of the conservationist devoted to eating the object of his concern.

Another thing I am often called on the carpet about is that in the book I seem to favor farming green turtles. The problem here is semantic. A form of "ranching" is what I had in mind—not farming. The turtle culture I thought of was just building up stock on natural turtle grass pastures and thus reinforcing populations and exploiting vast expanses of tropical submarine vegetation. That seemed a

way to help feed humans and at the same time relieve
pressure on natural colonies. Later on, when farming was
actually attempted, it proved easier to install expensive
plumbing and keep the turtles on shore in tanks, feeding
them on manufactured high-protein feed and amortizing
the huge investments by expanding international commerce in turtle products far beyond the extent of the traditional turtle soup trade. The technology involved is far
beyond the reach of most aspirant farmers, so glutting the
new markets is clearly impossible. To me it seems clear
that until excessive exploitation of natural sea turtle stocks
can be stopped all over the world, the main hope for saving
them is to stop international commerce in products derived
from them. There has been much disagreeable controversy
over turtle farming, and vast amounts of time have been
wasted debating the issues involved. I wish I had never
mentioned the subject in *The Windward Road*.

Personally, I consider the most distressing failure of *The
Windward Road* to be the miscarriage of my vigorous move
to excise from the language the revolting neologism *juke*.
You can read about the problem in "The Mouths of the
Bull." In that effort I was completely unsuccessful. I don't
intend to restate my case at this time. I had my day in
court. Nevertheless I was right—a humble, usually rustic,
beer joint with a record player and a few amiable girls is a
"jook." But the outlanders won out, and their word got
into the dictionary as "juke." And anyway, it would be
beating a dead horse to renew the struggle because the
term has lost its currency. Hardly anybody uses it any-
more, and I hope it will just fade away.

When I look back to the time when the ideas recorded in
The Windward Road were accumulating, it is pleasant to
see how much folklore we later turned into working hy-
potheses, and how correct most of the local beliefs turned

out to be. Since the days when I was searching for the Tortuguero nesting grounds we have tagged 17,000 turtles there, and the 1,400-odd long-distance recoveries that have been made confirm the folklore of the early 1950s in astonishing detail. In those days, when zoologists even doubted that *Chelonia* was a migratory animal, Captain Allee Ebanks and the other Cayman turtlers knew that green turtles made regularly scheduled long-distance journeys between their feeding and breeding grounds, and they knew the routes and schedules of the migrations. Both the Cayman turtle captains and the people at Turtle Bogue knew that Tortuguero was the place where the Nicaraguan turtles went to breed. They, and some of the Colombian fishermen, were aware that Colombian and Panamanian turtles also migrated north to Costa Rica at breeding time. It was also widely known that there was only one other big Caribbean nesting assemblage, located at Aves Island in the far eastern Caribbean, a hundred miles off the island of Montserrat. On Turtle Bogue everybody knew that when turtles migrate to Costa Rica they nest more than one time during their season there. Some said they nest three to six times, and that also appears to be pretty solid fact. The site-tenacity of the turtles—their tendency to re-nest close to previous nest sites—was also common knowledge, although it was thought to be sharper than it actually is.

And so on, and on. Of the things we have learned during our 22 years at the tagging beach, only the curious rhythms and shifts in the migratory periods were not already known to the people. A green turtle almost never nests in consecutive years. Most frequently she returns after three years, but two- and four-year intervals are common. The local sages, even Captain Allee Ebanks, had not dug out that trait, much less the fact that an individual turtle may change the length of her migratory period, and then perhaps change back again. Nobody prepared us for that, and tag returns have revealed it very slowly.

In one important way the wisdom of the Caribbean people seems to go unaccountably awry. That is in the widespread belief that the green turtle is an inexhaustible resource. My first season at Tortuguero, when I asked Sibella how long the turtles could stand the slaughter then going on at the nesting beach, she said, "Dey never finish don Archie. The tet-tel never finish." Every year thereafter—until she finally moved to Limon to care for her grandchildren, leaving her daughter Junie to cook for us at the station—Sibella's pronouncement was the same. "The tel-tel never finish. Dey *can't* finish."

When I asked her why not, she said, "Because they have the whole sea to come from." I told her they only live around the *edges* of the sea, but she was not convinced. Then 1978 came. The beach piled up with more turtles than we had seen in two decades at Tortuguero, and our insight was not deep enough to explain the jubilee. I knew I was in trouble with Sibella; and sure enough, one morning toward the end of the season when I went in to breakfast Junie said, "My mother write I should chide you." When I asked why—knowing all the time—Junie said: "Because you always say the tet-tel finish. She tell me I must ask you what you can say now."

All I could say was, I was happy so many turtles were coming in.

Gainesville, 1979   *AC*

THE WINDWARD ROAD

Preface

Down in the Caribbean the trade wind blows so honestly that in some of the islands you rarely hear the cardinal directions used, but people speak instead of living to leeward or of going to windward to visit an aunt. On all but the smallest or most rugged or least populated islands there are roads that lead to or run along the upwind coasts, and these are known as windward roads. I got to thinking in these terms and liked it, and then it occurred to me that the book I was writing grew mostly out of the hundreds of miles I had walked along the beaches of the Caribbean, where the good beaches are the windward ones built up high and clean by the driven surf. These beaches were the road I walked, and it is a good road. If you are in the tropics and have trouble seeing the good in where you are, work your way to windward where the trade comes in to land.

Leave your car at Maracas Bay, say, in northwestern Trinidad, and walk off into the marvel of the land-edge there; or travel the heights of north-coast Jamaica, past scenes I never believed in the old stereopticon days. Follow the windward road in Tobago from Scarborough to Speyside, through the West Indies as they used to be, and if the sea is not angry, take a boat out to Little Tobago and look for the birds of paradise there. Go west out of

Havana, turn into the wind to Baracoa, and stop at the little restaurant by the inlet for *rabirrubias* panbroiled in olive oil, and find the part of town where little houses have clear pools hewn out of the rock of the yards and loggerheads living there, with the people, like confident hens. Get out of Puerto Limón in Costa Rica and climb the stacks and spurs to search out the slips of palm-edged beach set like jewels among the tall rocks.

Or on Grand Cayman—if it is July and the broad scrub inside the island claws down the breeze before it gets to Georgetown and looses the mosquitoes in the shade and leaves the open land in the hard grip of the sun, and it is no longer a pleasant place to be, there in the lee of the land—take the road to windward and see the change.

Take a taxi for it. George Potter has one and there is another driven by a blonde woman named Honeysuckle. Flip a coin and say it comes out George. His wife just got back from the Bay Islands on the *Cacique,* and it was one long storm the whole way home and they threw out the cookstove to ease the little ship. George will want to take his wife along—he won't say to keep her in reach, but that is what he means. And then the young will set up a dinning to go, and you wind up sharing the car with a family of six. But they are all cheerful and none of them minds the crowding.

Now take it easy. You have a goal in mind—to get cool —but keep it in the background till you can do something about it. Forget the solid heat and take the quiet charm of this place so few outsiders ever see. You have to take it— nobody is going to sell it to you. Nobody tries to sell you anything in Grand Cayman.

So, stop twice before you ever leave the Iron Shore, as they call the rust-brown fossil reef of the downwind edge of the island. Stop first by the graveyard, where the sea sucks and bulges in a little tank cut out of the rock, and fish up the chicken hawksbills they keep there and hold them in the sun and see how you have to turn your eyes away from the five-colored fire from their rayed shells. Stop again to see how the old Cayman glory grew, how the old tradition hangs by a thread in the little shipyard, in the strong slim sculpturing of a mahogany hull. Look hard, because it is the last of something great.

Then start the seven-mile drive to windward, but keep your pace down, and when you hear the hoot of a blown conch, stop for an image to take away, when a bicycle crunches by on the white rock road, pedaled by a gangling tan man with long bare feet and a wide straw hat, who raises the shell twice a minute and blows one long note to cry the conchs and goatfish in his saddle basket. It is that sort of thing you will see if you are willing; and the little store beside the incandescent road out where the town wanes, with the chalked sign in big letters like train-times at the depot, and the sign says:

Just arrive

Sweet potatoes
Skellion
Fresh bullas
Chochoes
Cocoes

When you get there, don't just go on by—make the Potters stop and tell you what just arrived. They will enjoy the trip a lot more for it.

Then when you are still hardly under way, ask George which house belongs to Rosabelle Byrd, whom they call the best cook in Georgetown, which is saying a great deal. When he points out the gnome-hut, the only one nearby with a thatch roof, go in and tell Rosabelle you always

liked to eat, and hide the wince when she pokes you in the
ribs for love of you, and listen to what she says about Cayman fish stew, which is what happens to bouillabaisse in
the islands, or about codfish-and-akees or black crab
stuffed, or the things they do with green turtles to make
Caymanians strong and unafraid of the sea. Get a firm
commitment for her to cook you a meal and then head on
into the rain-hungry island, and after a while come out on
the windward shore. You see it first in the streaming trees,
and then the live air is in your face and you see the waves
of the upwind ocean and some old stone walls where hurricanes scattered a settlement ages past, and you say this
is the place. You get out there and ask George whether
he will wait for you or come back, but he is already necking and the kids are chasing crabs and you leave them
alone. It is the windward shore you are on now and the
burden of leeward heat is gone, the trade wind tilts the
slack feathers of the long, black smooth-billed anis in
the bushes, and only the rocks are still. You walk through
a grove of whistling casuarinas, sown all at once, they say,
when a storm spewed up the seeds from somewhere years
ago, and come out at a whitewashed house set by itself in
a clean-swept shady yard. Beside the house is a little
restaurant, a roof with three tables and bottled drinks from
Tampa and Blue Mountain coffee; and you go to a table
as if it were what you came for. A Negro girl makes coffee
for you and then sits down to talk, not troubled by your
being white, talking as anybody would who lived in lonesome country.

It may be that you'll want to stay on there for a long
time, in the shade with the coffee, hearing the wind hum
over the mimosa thickets, watching the crook-tailed beach
lizards all about the yard, each on top of its own log or
boulder or coco stump, seeing how two worlds can be on

two sides of one little island. But before George comes, ask the girl about the path through the thorn to a slant of different shore where Cayman Brac lies off in the unseen distance and no reef drags down the long waves, and the tawny sand stretches straight and smooth, as the green turtles want it. Go there as I did, for no good, practical reason, but full of a vague excitement, full of the wonder of the old travelers who sailed through the hordes of greens massed there from everywhere in Julys four centuries gone. Look off down the heat-blurred lane of untrailed sand and think of the lost fleets and the changing world, and then go back to the shade and wait in the wind till George is ready to take you home.

When I was growing into my leaning toward the tropics, it was the custom among sound scientists to inveigh against the having of what they spoke of as "adventures" in the field. Adventures on an expedition were a sure mark of incompetence, they said, or of chicanery—and there was something in it, too. In those days a regular rash of restless people of both sexes was dashing about the tropics cooking up sensational situations to write about and claiming to be doing it for the sake of science. It was only natural for honest men to bemoan such antics. But saying it was *adventure* that was the harm was nonsense.

The thing is—as you may know, but I had not discovered then—adventure is just a state of mind, and a very pleasant one, and no harm to anybody, and a great asset if you use it right.

In this book the real purpose behind the nosing around in the tropics that I tell you about was to collect information on sea turtles—primarily on green turtles, but also on the others: loggerhead, ridley, hawksbill, and trunkback. But it is not what you would call a book on turtles. The results of the investigation alone would not have made a book at all. Each of my trips to the Caribbean was just another installment in the piecing together of a puzzle. The result would be exciting eventually, but the piecing together was just a matter of repeated small discoveries, each of which seemed to add sadly little to the whole. It was just a slow saving up of odd little facts gleaned in long wandering, and a hope that they would mean a lot some day. And now the thing I want to show you is how a quest like that, or a trip of almost any kind, for that matter, goes better for whatever adventure—whatever extraneous stimulation—you are able to take along the way, so long as you take it passing and don't get really sidetracked. Prying about in strange places can either get on your nerves or be fun. If there is any one thing this book is about, that is it.

But I think you will like a sort of accounting on the sea-turtle stories, too, unfinished as they still are, and I have pulled out pieces that seemed to add up to something and put them together in the first chapter and in the last two. In between there are any number of other things.

THE WINDWARD ROAD

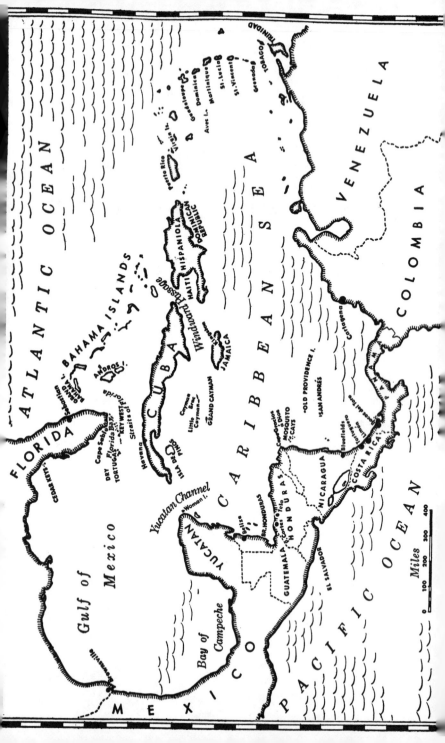

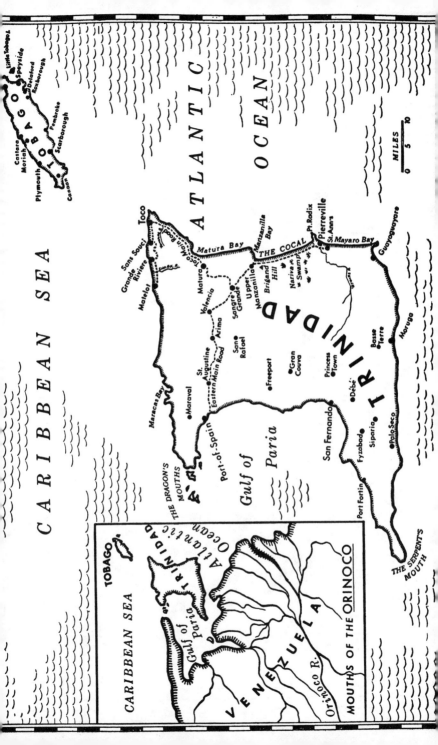

The Riddle of the Ridley

THE TWELVE-FOOT pole flew a high arc and struck true over the skidding shadow. It plunged quarter-down and stopped short against the hard shell of the turtle. Then it fell free and floated to the top.

"Missed him," I said. I should have known better. It was Jonah Thompson who threw the iron.

But how does anyone hit a target like that? The bow of the little launch was bucking and shying in a cross-channel chop. A gusty breeze kept throwing the surface of the bay into crowds of tight wrinkles that raced by and shot back the light in confused reflections. The water was milky white to start with, and the turtle was thirty feet out and a yard down and dodging like a rabbit. It was like trying to hit a scared pig from the bed of a truck lurching across a plowed field. Only the pig would be out in plain view, while the turtle was a dim blur in the cloudy water.

"He's carrying the iron," Jonah said. Then I saw the line snaking out of the bucket in the bow.

"How do you do it?" I said.

"I'm sixty-five and I started early. It's worse with green turtles; they run like a seagull. This here's a ridley."

He clawed in the pole with a boat hook. He took up the smoothly paying line and slowly closed both hands on it. The tension pulled us around a few points, and then a flipper broke water fifty feet out in front. Very carefully Jonah began to take in line, and the boat and the surfaced turtle drew together. When the gap closed he handed the tight line to his boy and deftly dropped a loop of rope over one of the flailing flippers. Then he heaved, and the turtle slid over the gunwale and fell back-down on deck, where it scraped and thrashed for purchase on the smooth planks.

"Stay clear of him," Jonah said. "He's mad. Ridleys is always mad."

I poked a rope end at the turtle's face. It seized the knot and crunched and then flew into a long frenzy of flopping and pounding about the deck.

"You can't keep a ridley on its back. Only a few hours. They're crazy. They break their hearts."

That was how I got to know the Atlantic Ridley. That was how the great ridley mystery began for me.

It is the sea that holds the great mysteries. There is still much to be learned in the land, to be sure, but it is the third dimension of the oceans that hides the answers to broad elemental problems of natural history. Somewhere out there young salmon lose themselves, and the Pribilof seals go there when they leave the rocks where they were born. Through chance concordance of cryptic forces, the Red Tide brews up and sporadically drifts in to the rich littoral of Florida, killing thousands of fishes, sending the tourists scurrying to flee the stink, and then sweeping away again, unchecked and uncomprehended. As long as man had had the wit to wonder, he must have puzzled over the new eels in his pasture pond; and being told they come from the sea where their parents went to spawn them is as preposterous as some theory of astrophysics. When J. L. B. Smith found a cœlacanth fish fifteen years ago, it was a living fossil, as stirring a discovery to a biologist, and quite as great a probing of the past, as finding a dinosaur would be. Who can trace the way of the great blue marlin or of Rhineodon, the whale shark, or tell anything worth hearing about the oarfish or the giant squid, or even say for sure where the homely mullet spawns its millions or where the gleaming hordes of tarpon come from?

And who can tell what the ridley is?

It was eighteen years ago when Jonah Thompson pulled in that first ridley out at Sandy Key in Florida Bay. I was there because of a letter from my friend Stew Springer, who is a gifted naturalist, versed in all sorts of seacraft. He was running a shark fishery at Islamorada on the upper Florida Keys at the time. He wrote to me to complain about a kind of turtle his fishermen brought in for shark bait. It was an evil-natured turtle, he said, flat and gray, with a big head and short, broad shell. Unlike the docile greens, which lie for weeks back-down on a ship's deck, or the formidable but philosophic loggerheads, this species made an unrestful, even dangerous, boatfellow. It snapped and fought, Stew said, from the moment it fell over the gunwale, biting the air and slapping its feet till it burned itself out from rage and frustration. The people on the keys called it ridley, and Stew said he could not even find the name—much less any information on it—in any of the books.

Neither could I. From the description I decided that Stew must be talking about a species that was first described some sixty years ago as *Lepidochelys kempi*, the specific name being taken from that of Richard Kemp of Key West, who sent the type specimen to Samuel Garman at the Museum of Comparative Zoology at Harvard. Practically nothing was known about the natural history of Kemp's turtle. Most people were unable to distinguish it from the loggerhead, and many even doubted that there really was such a thing. A scattering of herpetologists had published records of its occurrence or comments on its osteology, but the great majority of reptile students had never even seen one and the general attitude was that Kemp's turtle was a somehow inferior, if not altogether spurious form, not worthy of scholarly sweat. But Stew had a different opinion, and I had great respect for his perspicacity; I decided to go down and see his hotheaded sea turtle in the flesh. I suppose that one reason for my steadfast affection for ridleys is the memory of that trip to the keys.

My wife went with me. We were young then, and the keys were not yet real estate. A few outsiders were beginning to nose around, but most of the people living there were Conchs—descendants of the original English-Bahamian stock, the wreckers and turtlers of a hundred and two hundred years ago. You could still catch all the fish you wanted without a charter boat. The reefs were next to virgin, and the grouper and muttonfish would rise to a strip of your shirt tail; and even the mangrove snappers were still naïve. Around any pass or coral head you could cover the bottom of your dinghy with yellowtails or heap a particolored cargo of porkfish, queen triggers, rock hinds, and Spanish hogfish; or if rough weather sent you home you could always take back at least a mess of grunts to go with your grits. The grunts ran two sizes bigger then, and their mouths were more flaming scarlet; and they tasted far, far better.

If it was not something to eat but adrenaline in the blood you were after, you only had to drag a lure for a barracuda in the channel, or commune with the Bahía Honda tarpon train, or creep about the marl flats till you saw the tilted shadows of bonefish, foraging in their primitive peace; and if you made a proper approach you might hook one of these. After that your life would not be quite the same.

Over and above any mysteries of natural history they held, the keys were wonderful in those days. The overseas highway had just been built, but there was yet hardly a trickle of the stream that would one day make the islands a suburb of Miami. You could hardly notice it, but you knew it would come.

You knew the lovely bay would one day buzz with kickers, and the beaches be littered with people and their leavings, and the sunsets be dulled by neon. Among the first things to go would be the old crocodile in her hole too near the highway; and everywhere the fish would grow scarce or cynical. Even the ancient silvered logs of mahogany and princewood would be snaked off to cabinet shops and the gemlike tree snails snatched from the Jamaica dogwood limbs in the dim hammocks.

The lay and figure of the islands would not change. The indigo of the Gulf Stream would always lap the eastern rim of the arc, and inside, it would confine the incredible spectrum of the bay and its hot marl waters, swirled and banded with every shade from turquoise to green and milky jade. The thousand little mangrove-bordered islets would be there, and the big black niggerhead sponges; and new vast jewfish would move in to take the places of the ones the fishermen horsed out from among the piling at the old ferry slip.

Some things would last. But the year Margie and I went down to see Stew's ridleys, the keys were so fair and unplagued that we resented the existence of the road that led us there. No one else is so innately opposed to the more overt signs of human progress as a naturalist—especially a young one; and I remember well how bitterly we wished the keys might be left forever to the sun and wind, to the white-crowned pigeons and red coons and little key deer, and to a few quiet people with names like Lowe and Thompson and Sweeting. And to us, of course.

I remember Margie asked me if I would really be so callous as to deny to my fellow man the joy of conch soup; and I said I damn sure would—because there was only a certain amount of conch soup in the world, while the fellow man had no limits to his abundance. And now, these short two decades later, you can go lusting the length of the archipelago and never find a spoonful of conch soup anywhere. The conchs are gone—unless you live there and know the little secret caches—like the stone crabs, and the easy fishing.

But the ridleys are still there and we must get around to them.

We had hardly thrown our things on the bed in one of Stew's cabins when he herded us out again and into a launch with two Matacumbe men, a Mr. Jonah Thompson and his grown son, who looked just like him. Mr. Thompson had lost one side of his buttocks in the '35 hurricane—the one when the glass fell to 26.35 and a two-hundred-mile wind slammed a twelve-foot wall of water across the low islands, shattering and carrying away everything in its path. The official list numbered eight hundred dead, mostly from the camp of bonus-marching veterans of World War I who were living in tents on Lower Matacumbe, but everyone knows the counting stopped too soon. The survivors were mostly natives, who weathered the raving wind and seas in small, flush-deck boats heavily anchored among dense mangroves. The driving water wrecked a locomotive on the railroad and carried huge masses of reinforced concrete twenty miles to the tip of the mainland, but some of the people in the little boats got by.

Jonah Thompson got by, but he lost half of his buttocks when a flying timber nearly cut him in two. The injury would have made an invalid of an average man, but Jonah quickly dominated it and soon regained his place as the best boatman on the upper keys. He could handle an iron better than any man of any color I ever saw. He knew weather and water and fish and, what was most important of all, he knew turtles.

And so, when he contemplated the irate ridley he had just pulled up on deck and said: "Some say these ridleys is crossbreeds," I took notice and urged him on.

"We don't know where they lay," he said. "All the rest come up on the beaches one time or other, but you never see the ridleys there. We all say they are made when a loggerhead pairs with a green." He mumbled something else in an embarrassed sort of way. I thought I heard him right, but I didn't think my wife did.

"We think they're so damn mean owing to them not getting to coot none," was what I believe he said.

"What did he say?" asked Margie.

"Shut up," I said.

"Did he say they are mean because they don't make love?"

"That was the gist of it."

"Isn't that anthropomorphic?" Margie asked, in an unpleasant way.

"Could be," I said. I could see nothing wrong with the man's reasoning, provided he was right about the ridley's not breeding; but this assumption I did not like, and still don't.

It bothered me that the ridley should be such a distinctive and original-looking creature, with his traits his own and nothing about him that seemed intermediate between the other species. A mule is clearly a mixture of the ass that

sired him and the mare that bore him, but a ridley is his
own kind of animal. I nodded over Jonah Thompson's
theory, but I resolved then to get the straight of it somehow.

As I said, that was a long time ago, and I have made
very little progress. Indeed, the ridley mystery has grown
rather than shrunk, and I am farther from a solution than
I seemed then. The answer is so elusive that I have come
to regard the ridley as the most mysterious air-breathing
animal in North America.

First of all, there is the unimportant but vexing question
of the creature's name. Ridley! What kind of name is it
anyway, and where did it come from? I've traced it all
along the coast from Fernandina to Key West and out to
Pensacola and people only look vague or grieved when I
ask about the name. To most people it's like asking why
they call a mackerel a mackerel, or a dog a dog. Once in a
while I run into somebody who knows the ridley as "mulatto" or "bastard" or "mule-turtle," in reference to its
supposed hybrid origin; but most places the name is ridley,
and not a soul knows why. Maybe one out of a couple of
dozen fishermen pronounce it "ridler"; and it may be that
this form represents an earlier stage in the etymology of
the term, but it seems impossible to confirm this. Anyway,
compared to other things we don't know about the ridley,
the question of its name is a bagatelle; and our ignorance
here is exasperating, but not necessarily demoralizing.

A more unsettling eccentricity is the animal's range—the
territory in which it has been found to occur. All the other
sea turtles—trunkback, green, loggerhead, and hawksbill—
occupy pretty much the same area, each being found in
the Atlantic, the Caribbean, the Pacific, and the Indian
Ocean. Moreover, while the representative of each of these
species in the Indo-Pacific is isolated by land or by great

expanses of cold water from its counterpart in the Atlantic-Caribbean, the populations are remarkably similar. In fact, if you go to Colón, on the Caribbean side of Panama, and catch a green turtle, haul him across the Isthmus to Panama City, and compare him point for point with a green from the Pacific, you have to look very close indeed to see any difference at all. It is the same with a great number of other marine animals, both vertebrate and invertebrate, on the two sides of the Isthmus: they are separated by thousands of miles of alien territory but they nevertheless show very little of the divergence that such isolation usually brings. This is especially striking when you consider that the emergence of the isthmus that cut off the Caribbean animals from their eastern Pacific kin took place at least thirty million years ago.

The ridley partly fits this pattern; that is, there is an Atlantic ridley and a very similar one in the eastern Pacific. They are numerous only in the warmer parts of their ranges, and are apparently not in contact around the tips of either Cape Horn or the Cape of Good Hope, except perhaps as occasional, current-borne flotsam. But here the orthodoxy of the ridley stops. For some utterly unaccountable reason it is not found in the Bahamas or Bermuda, where all the rest are, or have been, abundant; and most peculiar of all, it is absent from the Caribbean.

It is not a simple matter to get a clear picture of the range of the ridley. You don't just go out and catch sea turtles on an afternoon collecting trip, and there are no really good sea-turtle collections in any of the world's museums.

Before Mr. Kinsey became preoccupied with sex, he worked on insects. At one time he wanted to learn all he could about a certain group of tiny wasps that make galls on twigs. In his spare time he went out and drove along the roads and stopped at hundreds of places where he collected the animals he was after. He caught seventeen thousand of them, and when he wrote a monograph on this material, it was a classic. This is the way to do a problem in animal distribution; but you can't do it with sea turtles.

Counting specimens I have begged or bought from fishermen or seen being butchered in fish houses, and the collections of the Museum of Comparative Zoology, the American Museum of Natural History, and the British Museum, I have managed to look at about a hundred ridleys in eighteen years. Add to what these show the small amount of information that has been published and the carefully sifted oral reports of fishermen, and there is still not a great deal to work with. But it is enough to give the outlines of the ridley story, and to show that it is a strange one.

There are two centers of abundance of ridleys: the Gulf coast of Florida from the Suwannee Delta to Florida Bay and the east coast from about St. Augustine to Melbourne. On the east coast, ridleys are best known by trawlers who work some distance off shore, perhaps indicating that even this far south the animals are being swept northward by the Florida Current—the headwaters of the Gulf Stream. I know a fisherman at Canaveral who claims to have caught a thousand ridleys during twenty years of fishing there. On the Gulf coast they are taken along with the green turtles that support the small turtle fisheries there, and are frequently sold with the greens to buyers who never know the difference. There they are caught in nets set across small channels among the flats, and like the young greens, they appear to be at home there. A single setting of a net will sometimes yield two or three of each species, while loggerheads are almost never taken.

Above: Kemp's ridley (*Lepidochelys kempi*), caught incidentally by a trawler, Cape Canaveral, Florida. *Below*: Kemp's ridley, four months old. The ridley shown here and in the next two pictures was raised by Archie Carr from an egg.

Above: Kemp's ridley, 18 months old. *Below*: Kemp's ridley, about two and a half years old.

Outside of Florida, ridleys occur all along the Gulf coast to Texas. At the Mexican border our information peters out; nobody knows what happens to the range of the ridley from there on. The few published articles on Mexican sea turtles mention the other four kinds, but not the ridley. On the Atlantic coast it seems to me that the distribution of the ridley is no true "range" in the zoo-geographic sense—an expanse of territory that an animal occupies or voluntarily moves across—but is a one-way, passive dispersal by the Florida Current and the Gulf Stream; an exodus with no return. Expatriate ridleys drift with the current with little more control over their ultimate fate than the plankton there. The ones near the edges may be able to move out into the coastal waters, reach shore, and live there more or less conveniently; but those deep within the stream go on. Where the Florida Current picks up its supply of ridleys is not known, for reasons that I shall reveal presently; but there can be little doubt that it is the northward sweep of this current just off the eastern shore that accounts for the occurrence in North Carolina and New York Harbor and Martha's Vineyard. Little as we know about ridleys, we can be sure they are not born in those places. They are carried there.

And they do not stop in Massachusetts. The Gulf Stream goes on, and they go with it. How they are amusing themselves all this time is hard to say, but they ride the great global drift out into the cold North Atlantic, where it travels its new easterly course at a reduced speed but glides on over the tail of the Grand Banks, pushes aside the arctic icebergs, and splits at last against western Europe, making it barely possible for human beings to stand the English climate, and stranding ridleys on such shores as Ireland, Cornwall, the Scilly Isles, southern France, and the Azores.

The range of the ridley, thus, is not an expanse of ocean or a strip of shore. Mostly it is the Gulf Stream. Ridleys are part of a vast planetary swirl that starts when the equatorial current and the easterly trades push water through the Yucatán Channel and pile it up in the Gulf of Mexico. The surface there rises six to eighteen inches higher than the Atlantic level and breeds the head that drives warm water clockwise around the eastern Gulf and nozzles it out through the Straits of Florida as the Florida Current. This soon meets the Antilles Current, and the two now form the "Gulf Stream" in the new strict sense, and this moves northward with an initial speed of about three knots. Somewhere along the line ridleys are fed into this system, to drift downstream to England through three thousand slow miles.

It would be wrong to give the impression that ridleys are of common occurrence in Europe. I recently looked at six English ridleys in the collection of the British Museum, which is the best sea-turtle collection in the world, and those six represent all the European specimens in that museum. These may represent half of all the English ridleys that have fallen into the hands of naturalists. Ridleys, and sea turtles of all kinds, are very rare in European waters. But even so, I wonder how many ridleys had to begin the voyage in America for each of the six that lodged at last in the British Museum!

Two features of the British waifs must be of some sort of significance in the cryptic life history of the animal: they are all small—none over eight inches long and one only four—and they have all washed up during the months from October to December. I suppose the small size merely means that baby turtles are swept away more easily than big ones; but the meaning of the seasonal occurrence of the strandings is unexplained.

If we suppose that the point of injection of ridleys into the Gulf Stream system is somewhere about the tip of the Florida peninsula—and the slim evidence that seems to support this assumption will come out shortly—then the trip to Europe might take as much as a year or even more. It seems unlikely that even a turtle could survive this period with no food at all. So, even though the ridley is characteristically a bottom feeder—a crusher of crabs and mollusks—we must conclude that it finds some sort of fare in the Gulf Stream.

It must have occurred to you some time back that the sensible way to go about finding out where ridleys get into the Gulf Stream would be to locate the beaches where the young hatch out. That makes sense, certainly. The only trouble is, the beaches can't be found.

In fact, I can't find any evidence that ridleys breed at all; at least, by any of the accepted methods. I am still just about where Jonah Thompson's folk theory left me. As far as I can determine, nobody ever saw a pair of ridleys courting or copulating. People are constantly catching and butchering sea turtles and looking about inside them for eggs, but no female ridley has ever turned up pregnant—not even with the beadlike, yellow eggs that other female turtles carry for most of every year. No ridley has ever been seen on a nesting beach, and no hatchling has been found. The smallest ridley known is a four-inch specimen that washed up in England. This one was at least several months old. A newly hatched one should be little more than an inch long, because the loggerhead, a turtle two or three times the size of the ridley at maturity, is only slightly more than an inch long at birth. Not only that, all hatchling turtles have a soft umbilical scar, marking the place where they were attached to the yolk in the egg; and at the tip of the snout there is a sharp spine

called an egg tooth that the little turtle uses in freeing itself from the shell. Turtles retain these signs of infancy for
several weeks after hatching. No little ridley has ever been
seen with them.

When Kemp sent the ridley to Harvard in 1880 he said:
"We know that they come out on the beach to lay in the
months of December, January and February, but cannot
tell how often or how many eggs." I don't think he knew
any such thing. When I made my first visit to Springer's
shark camp on the keys, I went armed with this observa-
tion; and since it seemed a bizarre reversal of the usual
nesting schedule, I went to some effort to authenticate it.
I had no success at all. I talked with people who knew
ridleys all the way from Homestead to Key West and
none had ever heard of a turtle nesting in the wintertime
or had seen a ridley nest or egg or baby at any time. Since
then I have heard the same story from something over 160
of the most knowledgeable fishermen I could find between
Cape Hatteras and the mouth of the Mississippi. I have
dissected every mature ridley I could get and have cross-
questioned the men who slaughter turtles for the market,
and I have begun to feel the real weight of the enigma.

When the turtlers and fishermen are pressed to account
for the facts of the case, they tell three different stories.
Most of them agree with Jonah Thompson that the creature does no breeding on its own but is produced when
two other species hybridize. The comment of an old pod
at St. Lucie Inlet was the sort of thing you hear:

"This yer ridley don't raise. He's a bastard, a crossbreed
you get when a loggerhead mounts a green—and a loggerhead will mount anything down to a stick of wood when
he's in season. This yer ridley don't have no young 'uns.
He's at the end of the line, like a mule."

A minority among the people I talk to say that ridleys

breed all right—bound to; everything does; but they do it somewhere 'way off, outside our field of responsibility. On some remote shore of the Caribbean, maybe, where they have yet to be observed by sapient man. Sapient gringo, anyway.

This kind of talk used to reassure me. It was something to fall back on when the thought of a parentless, childless animal weighed me down. It was no disgrace not knowing where the brute bred if it happened in some far corner of the Caribbean. The Caribbean is a big place, and I knew its shore only in a couple of spots. Ridleys were unknown in those spots, but this proved nothing at all.

Imagine my state of mind, then, when I had completed a carefully spaced series of visits all the way around the Caribbean and had found no sign either of ridleys or of people who knew them, anywhere in a dozen countries and islands. I went out with turtle-hunters and looked at turtles in crawls, and at shells on trash heaps, and at stuffed turtles on museum shelves. I walked some of the finest turtle beaches in the hemisphere. I saw a lot of things, but no ridleys. Everywhere I went the people knew four kinds of sea turtles, and none of them was the ridley.

This was a body blow. It threw the whole problem back into the Gulf of Mexico—into my lap. My ignorance became embarrassing again.

The third explanation I commonly hear is the opinion of a still smaller group that the ridley is out there each June laying, along with the other species, in the same places and at the same time. I have heard this seriously proposed by responsible parties five times. That is, five times people have named definite stretches of beach on which they believed ridleys laid. Four of these stories fizzled out under cross-questioning, proving to have been based either on pure hearsay or on erroneous identification of the turtle involved. In one case only, the battering system of interrogation I have developed through the years was unable to find the weakness in a man's claim that he had seen a ridley lay on a certain beach; and we parted at deadlock—he clinging to his memory of one lone ridley in moonlight twenty-five years old, and I sure without any proof at all that he was off his rocker.

I will admit that there is a slight possibility that each June ridleys lumber up at first full moon and dig their nests on the shoulders of State Road A1A, like the loggerheads; but I rest no easier for it.

That, then, is the riddle of the ridley: a big, edible, shore-water beast, abundant and well known to everybody along the east-Gulf littoral and around the tip of Florida, is swept up the Atlantic coast by the Florida Current and the Gulf Stream, through some whimsey never crossing to the eastern side of the current and being unknown in the Bahamas and in Bermuda. The drifting migrants trickle out of the stream into coastal waters as far north as Massachusetts, straggle across to Europe, and very rarely stick with the deflected drift as far as the Azores and probably farther. Nowhere in this vast territory has any hint of reproductive activity been seen.

What do you make of it? I used to think the solution would one day fall into my lap, but I believe this no longer. It will have to be worked for, and the campaign will require drive and imagination and patience. It will probably resolve itself into a systematic ransacking of ideas and places on a purely trial-and-error basis. It will not be settled on week-end field trips, and there is nothing to take into the laboratory. The solution will very likely turn out to be absurdly simple and obvious, once we get hold of it; but meantime it is a tough and nagging mystery.

While waiting for something else to happen, it is inter-

esting, if not really profitable, to take stock of the information at hand and see what can be done with it. Most of
the laws of science, as we call them, have started out as
theories; and theories are just figments of a disciplined imagination—until they can be proved. The scientific way
to formulate a theory is to examine every possible explanation for your facts that presents itself, however out-
rageous it may seem at the time. Some of the craziest notions turn out to be the best.

In the case of the ridley mystery, then, we have to weigh
without bias all the trial solutions at hand, whether con-
ceived by unlettered menhaden hands or by sadistic colleagues, or by my own troubled mind. We must list these
and evaluate each in its turn and then make an objective
choice; and this will then be the current, tentative answer
to the riddle of the ridley. It will probably be wrong, but
it will be the best we can do.

Of all the explanations that suggest themselves, the
simplest is that the ridley just doesn't reproduce, but arises
by spontaneous generation. This is the most direct answer,
in view of what we know, and in olden times it would have
been accepted as the only reasonable solution. But nowadays biologists are pretty insistent that everything alive
must have at least one parent, and this sets limits to our
imagination.

As a variant of that idea, we might toy with this one,
which has been suggested to me independently by several
acquaintances, some of whom at least are perfectly sane.
May not the ridley once have been able to reproduce its
kind, but have suddenly lost the ability—have become sterile through some sudden racial mishap? In such a case, the
ridleys we see today would be the last members of a line
on its way toward extinction. It is hard to put your finger
on the defect in this effort, but it seems a bit fey and irre-

sponsible. Quite frankly, I get no real comfort out of the notion and mention it at all only to be scientific.

We just about have to start from the assumption that the animal breeds—somehow, somewhere. It must be, then, that it is the place or the manner of the breeding that bewilders. There must be something about where or how little ridleys come about that it is just a bit beyond the scope of our imagining.

Maybe, for instance, this turtle lays no eggs, but bears its young alive, on the high seas, as a sea snake does. It is certainly conceivable, and it excuses our failure to find nests and eggs ashore. But don't forget the lack of pregnant females. You have to get just as pregnant to bear live young as to lay eggs. And not only that, an eggless turtle is too far out of character. Turtles are unwaveringly conservative. A live-bearing turtle would be almost as exciting as an egg-laying dog. No matter where they live—on dry land, in fresh water, or in the sea—all known turtles inflexibly dig holes and lay white-shelled eggs in them; and they have been doing this since the Cretaceous.

Suppose, then, that the ridley abides by the conventions of its kind and lays eggs, but lays them in the water—lays buoyant eggs so far from land that the young stop being young before we ever get to see them. If the laying place is very far away, maybe it takes the females a long time to get there, and we see them only when they are not carrying eggs. This is a variation of the preceding theory and a slight improvement on it, but is unacceptable on the same grounds. It just seems like too much of an innovation for a turtle suddenly to make, after fifty million years of making hardly any innovations at all. Besides, prolonged wetting with salt water kills the embryos in the eggs of other reptiles and other sea turtles, and we would have to propose a brand-new and very ingenious kind of egg for our theoretical pelagic ridley.

Perhaps, instead of a strange *way* of breeding, it is a strange *time* of breeding that has thrown us off. Maybe the laying season is very short or very oddly scheduled and restricted in time. Maybe they lay only on New Year's Eve or Twelfth Night, or on the shortest night or coldest night of the year. All the other Atlantic sea turtles have a laying season of several weeks in late spring and early summer; but the ridley may lay in midwinter when turtle-hunters are doing something else. Why not? Well, mainly because it again brings us up against the failure of the females to turn up pregnant. And not only that, even in the dead of winter there is traffic on most Florida beaches—people driving, hotrodding, surf fishing, courting, catching coquinas, even swimming. It is impossible to believe that winter turtle tracks, or tracks laid at any time however unlikely, could simply have escaped notice. This was Kemp's theory, you remember, but I think he was just repeating idle talk.

Next we might try the possibility that the ridleys in the United States originate somewhere else and either migrate into the Gulf of Mexico or are carried there by currents. This looks good at first, because there are the currents to do the job—currents that could, and almost surely do, bring ridleys clear across the Atlantic from Africa to the Antilles and very probably into the Gulf of Mexico. But if you look closely at the foreign ridley colonies that could lose turtles into these currents, you see that the ridley population in the Gulf could not possibly be derived this way. In the first place the Gulf form is too abundant to qualify as an accumulation of accidental waifs; and even more conclusive, there is a simple but constant difference between the ridleys in the Gulf and those in West Africa and on the Pacific coast of South America, which are the only stocks adjacent to the currents that bring foreign drift into Florida waters. All extra-Floridian ridleys everywhere in the world have two to six more scales in the upper shell than our Gulf ridley does. If we suppose that all those in the Gulf were brought in by the Equatorial Current, then we have to believe that each of them stopped over somewhere along the way and had its shell remodeled. It is possible that an occasional Gulf ridley does come into American waters on the Equatorial Current; but if so it is surely one that began its voyage three years before when it was swept away by the Florida Current and survived the world-wide circuit to return at last to its native waters. Any African ridley that turned up in the Gulf would be easily recognized as such. There is, thus, little point in looking to the ocean currents for a solution to the puzzle.

Why not just take it easy and accept the popular notion that the ridley is a hybrid after all, and, like many hybrids, sterile? This is what most of the fishermen and turtle-hunters believe, as I have said, and you can even read it in the *Riverside Natural History*. Mostly the responsibility for furnishing us with ridleys is laid to a loggerhead father and a green-turtle mother, but sometimes you hear the sexes switched. A few say the *mésalliance* involves a loggerhead and a hawksbill, and rarely you may be told that it is a hawksbill and a green.

This is where the pressure is, and where my skepticism has lost me friends and made me out, in the eyes of men I respected, a plain damn fool. Nearly everything we know, and everything we don't know, about this animal makes it easy to say it is a half-breed, with no more personal continuity than a medieval choirboy, or a mule.

As I have said before, there are also ridleys in the Pacific. And in the Pacific the males chase the females about, and catch them, and they mate, and the females go ashore and dig holes in the sand and lay round, white eggs in them. The eggs hatch and release baby ridleys with egg teeth and umbilical scars, like any other new turtle.

Now, what earthly sense would it make for the ridley to be a hybrid in one part of his range and a separate species in another—to do his own breeding at Acapulco but rely on other kinds of turtles to do it for him at Tampa? It is a distressing thought. In fact, it is untenable.

As I have pointed out, the Atlantic and Pacific ridleys are separated by a great deal of territory and are not exactly alike. But they are very nearly alike, and far more like each other than like any other kind of turtle. In fact, the only differences I have been able to make out are the extra scales in the shell of the Pacific form and sometimes a slightly greener color; and maybe a few trifling disparities in proportions. Certainly nothing that would lead a person with bat brains to believe that a ridley begot one of them and a loggerhead the other.

The problem would be simple if we didn't know about the Pacific ridley. My friends around the fish houses don't know about the Pacific ridley. They are at peace. I am not. It's what a Ph.D. in biology gets you. . . . The ridley breeds, like anybody else.

The same objections that make the hybrid idea unsatisfactory seem also to throw out the possibility that the ridley is some sort of sport—an occasional freak occurring among normal offspring of one of the other kinds of turtles, the loggerhead, for instance. Here again the almost identical Pacific ridley, with its orthodox breeding habits, stares us in the face and makes the sport theory seem just a shade too easy. It is possible, but only very feebly so.

Now, what can be said to the people who suggest that the nests have just been overlooked—that ridleys nest right along with the other turtles, at the same time and in the same places, and have simply escaped notice by a person competent to distinguish between them and the other species?

Well, as far as I'm concerned those are fighting words. Maybe my own hundreds of hours of unproductive beach-walking, and those of my zoological friends and correspondents, are not a valid test. But how about the lifetimes spent without seeing ridleys by professionals like Joe Saklin and Tony Lowe and Paco Ortega, and by the band of my consultants among the illegal east-coast turtle-hunters? These men spend three months of every year patrolling the beaches in turtle buggies—cut-down cars with oversized tires—dodging the far-spaced conservation officers and turning turtles by the yearly hundreds. They have always done this and they keep doing it at growing risk—slowly growing risk—because a few commercial bakers have learned what Savannah and Charleston housewives always knew about the keeping qualities turtle eggs give cakes, and will pay fantastic prices for them; and because the shoddier jooks and barbecue joints along the Dixie Highway like to cut their fifty-cent-a-pound hamburger meat with twenty-five-cent loggerhead. These men don't hunt turtles for fun. They are tough and practical. I know a game warden whom they threw into the sea just to show how tough they are. They know their business. They know ridleys and know the beaches and what goes on there during the long summer nights, and it is wonderful what goes on there, but it is not the nesting of ridleys. All these men have told me that ridleys never come ashore. By not moralizing on their ways, I have made friends among these poachers, and if a ridley ever comes up on one of the good mainland beaches in the turtle season, I bet I hear about it within hours.

But suppose she should not come ashore on one of the good turtle beaches. There is a lot of coast between Tampico and Beaufort, and there are still some unpatrolled, unbathed-on segments of shore not even shown as sand on maps. And as long as this is true, we can never be sure but that we have missed what we were after simply because we have not looked in the right place. Till every one of the unsearched beaches has been walked with ridleys in mind we can never be sure they do not nest on some rarely visited little island or cluster of keys or short, broken strand somewhere on the coast of the southeastern United States.

This, I believe, is the theory we must choose. It best fits the known facts and introduces the fewest wild assumptions. It is distasteful, because it proposes the laborious ransacking of every scrap of sand along hundreds of miles of coast. It seems unlikely, because no other turtle anywhere is so fanatically finicky in choosing a breeding ground as this explanation would imply. But the ridley has shown its disregard for tradition in other ways, remember. In spite of the drawbacks, this hypothesis seems the best of the lot.

So I guess we must go looking for a small, isolated stretch of shore as the answer to the ridley mystery. It must be some improbable place right under our noses. Cape Sable may occur to you, or Dry Tortugas, but it will not be so easy as that. People have been turning turtles on those shores for too many years. I believe it can't be any of the good turtle territory on the east coast—the strip from Palm Beach up to Melbourne: it is too well known, too continuously visited. It is not Sanibel or Bonita Beach or Naples, and it almost surely is none of the islands along the bend of the Panhandle. It barely might be outside

Florida—one of the Sea Islands of Georgia or South Carolina, or some place the Mexicans have somehow missed between Vera Cruz and Brownsville. But I doubt this; and I doubt that it is anywhere in all the island chain from Grand Bahama to Turks and Caicos.

As long as we believed the zoologists who kept quoting one another about there being ridleys in the Caribbean, we could just say, well, hell, the ridley must breed down there somewhere. But now there's no comfort there, for me at least. In all the poking about that I'm going to tell you of in chapters to come, the ridley mystery was right there with me. Stirred up as I may seem over other matters—over the green turtles I was mainly after down there, over the endless odd detours and distractions I relate—the one most exciting thing I found in all my wandering was no ridleys in the Caribbean.

What remains to be done, then, is slow, piecemeal searching. And before I look anywhere else I am going back to Florida Bay—to the shallow, island-set sea between the cape and the upper keys. There are dozens of little islands there like Sandy Key, and they have been little visited by naturalists with eyes open for ridley sign. The shores there are mostly mangrove thickets, where no turtle could nest; but in some the mangrove fringe is broken by sand; and while the strips of beach are short and narrow, they may be all the ridley needs. The bay is handy to both the Florida Current, which must be the agent that feeds the waifs into the Gulf Stream, and to the coastal waters of the peninsula of Florida, where ridleys are more abundant than anywhere else. It is at least possible that the natural secretiveness of sea-turtle hatchlings keeps baby ridleys out of sight, and that some local, seasonal migration of the egg-heavy females hides them from view.

All this seems unlikely, but it is the most possible solution at hand.

So I guess I should have stayed on there in the bay to look for the answer, where Jonah Thompson threw the iron so long ago. Perhaps all the Atlantic ridleys everywhere come from down there where the first one was, in the hot, white water with the sea cows and bonefish and the last crocodiles. Maybe the long questing will come full circle there on some first full moon of summer, and the riddle of the ridley will end where it began.

Nesting Olive ridley (*batali*), Surinam.

The Windward Road

You have still not heard all of the ridley story. What remains to be told is in some ways the most puzzling part of all. It happened only recently, long after I had decided that I knew at least the dimensions of the mystery. It happened away down in the southeastern corner of the Caribbean, a sea, you may recall, in which I have led you to believe there are no ridleys.

It was in Trinidad, up on the wild northeastern coast, out beyond the end of the windward road, where the forest comes down to the cliff edges and the big seas crouch and spring against ragged walls of schist. There is nothing between you and the world there; only the rushing wind and the dim loom of Tobago to eastward.

I was staying at Matelot, in the government rest house perched high on a rock that rises from the sea. One late afternoon I was taking my ease in a hammock in the deep shade of the veranda. I had spent the day climbing the steep trails back into the rain forest, catching frogs and snakes and trying to take impossible color pictures in the twilight under the mora trees; and accumulating the fatigue that makes a king of any man, even a college professor, who has a porch set square across the trade wind, and a hammock and a china cup of rum and lime. For the time, I envied no one anything. I just lay in the hammock and let the wind swing it, and propped my head to look at the sea.

The sea and the sky were framed by the hang of the roof and the handrail, like a Kodachrome—an underexposed one, with every color a bit too deep to be real. The far blue shadow of Tobago was piled over with towering pearly land clouds, and over the sea the little round wind clouds swept like close-set burst boles of cotton floating in on the steady air stream against the blue above. Into the land they came, not pausing, not crowding; and on the sea below, the ordered ranks of their shadows moved in with them.

Out among the whitecaps and the cloud shadows the Matelot trollers were working, maybe twenty of them—little twiglike dugouts with preposterous outsize lateen sails of sewn sugar sacks swelling out to leeward like racing spinnakers. From just under the cliff to nearly out of sight the little craft were strung out, rising and sliding on the burly seas, quartering, crossing, or plunging downwind with the sweeping trade.

Besides the marching field of cloud shades there were other patches on the water—black half acres that did not come in but stayed beyond the reef and moved longshore past the jutting promontory. I looked up to see what clouds were breaking rank to cast these shadows, but then I saw the gulls crying over them and the men-o'-war birds swooping, and the dark slashes and climbing jags of foam where kingfish ripped at the edges of the shadows and bigger things struck the kingfish.

I knew then that the clouds moving coastwise were little fish; and where the hosts were steadfast and took the shocks without sounding or breaking up in desperate unschooling the white-winged trollers came driving down from all directions to trail their baits of fish-belly and see

what kingfish or dolphin or wahoo might think pure fish-
belly white fancier than anchovies. And all the time the
big waves kept charging in, untamed to the last; raging
over the reef, one after one, crashing and spouting among
the towers and stacks of the shattered foreshore.

I was the only white man in the village, or for maybe
ten miles in any direction, and this was satisfying. Not
that I have anything against white men as such—some of
my best friends are white. But I have noticed that any
teller of travel tales who happens to find himself the only
white man for some distance around generally mentions
the fact with a certain satisfaction. I can understand this.

There was a big Ashanti woman in the little kitchen behind me, crouched over a six-pound mackerel. It was my
mackerel. It was in two pieces; the fore half was steaming
in a crock, half swamped among thumb-sized tomatoes
and garlic chips, and the after piece dripped Australian
butter on the mangrove coals beneath it. There was half
a breadfruit in a Birmingham roaster and I was at peace
with the world.

My chronic concern with sea turtles I had shifted for
the time to the back of the husband of the cook. He was
off down along the cliffs rousing out the local turtle-hunters. Three little boys were catching things for me—lizards
at thruppence and snakes at one and six. On the sodded
slope beneath the porch a she-goat and a donkey were
tethered. The goat kept rising on her hind legs to stretch
for guavas on some high twigs above her. The donkey was
a tiny, grizzled West Indian jack, an elfin creature full of
quiet force and long-eared calm, a strange little animal at
once ascetic and lecherous. Every now and then the mood
came over him and he gave voice to that most improbable
of all animal calls—the wild, sweet, fantastic, shocking ass-

song that always takes me back to misty Mexican dawns before the war.

Suddenly there was a step at the end of the porch. The turtle scout was back.

He told me the men who knew turtles best were in a village some nine miles westward up the coast. I thanked him and said I would go there in the morning. He told me how to keep the trail; and then I saw the first half of the mackerel on the table, and the conference was over.

Early the next morning I left my little English car at the end of the road and walked off down the foot trace above the cliffs. I made slow progress. I never saw scenery anywhere to equal the north coast of Trinidad, from Matelot to Maracas Bay. One moment the trail climbs through waist-high wind-pruned scrub on a towering promontory, and the next it threads among tall, smooth columns in tongues of jungle in quiet ravines, or drops to skirt an arc of palm-fringed beach at the head of a hidden cove; and you lose a half-hour trailing out turtle nests or looking into the blue pool where a fresh stream mingles icy water from distant mountains with the warm crystal of the bay, and little frogs meet crabs, and fingerling barracuda strike at whirligig beetles.

It was slow going; but at last I got far enough along to come upon a cluster of houses. They were tiny, sun-silvered shacks, tall and peak-roofed like Disney houses, and were set about the slope in clusters of palms and breadfruit trees. Below them a deep cove ended in a crescent of sand between spurs of granite. The cove was narrow as a fiord. I could see a dozen boats in various stages of getting under way to put out to sea. Some were just stepping the wide lateen sails, some clawing with slivers of jibs at the tag ends of wind that reached the cove-head or already gliding down between the high rock walls; and one was bobbing on the swells off the mouth of the inlet.

From the trail above the beach I could see one dugout still on the sand below me. Its three-man crew was preparing to slide it into the water. I leaned over the edge and yelled a greeting. I was an unlikely phenomenon up there on the trail, white, clay-smeared and strung about with sacks; but there is grace and tact in people like these. They get it from the sea, as poor people elsewhere get it from the soil. They only stared at me for a moment. Then one of them, an old man who was standing knee-deep in the water, said: "Good morning, sah."

"Does anybody here do any turtle-fishing?" I said.

They looked at me for a while. Then the man in the water said: "What that you say, sah?"

"Do you catch turtles here?"

"Tet-tel? Sometime we cotch them, sah."

"Well, tell me, how many kinds of turtles do you catch?"

It was routine. I had no premonition. I talk to all fishermen this way. I had heard nothing of the ridley for a thousand miles.

The three men muttered among themselves for a while in voices too low for me to hear above the surf, and made tentative tallies on their fingers. They had some trouble reaching an accord. Finally one of the two who had not spoken to me before looked up and called something loud enough to hear, but completely unintelligible.

"What did you say?" I yelled.

The man stared at me, then shrugged and grinned, then got very solemn. I don't know why.

" 'E telling you about the tet-tel, sah," the old one said.

"But what language was he speaking?" I said.

"Patois, sah," he said.

"What kind of patois?"

There was more muttering and low-voiced debate. Then the spokesman looked up at me again.

"French, sah. Speaking French," he said.

Instantly both the others clutched at his shoulders and started jawing at him with heat. Then they subsided and the three looked up and the man in the water spoke again.

"Careeb, sah. They say it careeb. I can' reely be shuah, sah. We call it patois."

I pondered this a moment.

"Well, O.K. But look, how about the turtles? You were going to tell me how many there are. Have you decided?"

"We cotch five kind tet-tel, sah."

"All right," I began—then it hit me like a rock and I yelled: "Five! Did you say five?"

This time the old man stared hard. They all did. I was behaving badly even for a white man. I tried to pass it off by hawking and spitting and getting very casual.

"All right. Five," I said. "Now let's see what the five kinds are. Most places they catch only four. What are the ones you get?"

"Only four we see often. We cotch oxbull. You know this, sah?"

"Hawksbill, yes. And you get leatherbacks?"

"What that, sah?"

"The big black one with ridges. The biggest one. Trunk-back."

"Yes, sah, trunkbock. We call this Orinook tet-tel."

"Sure, that's right. Then you get the green turtle."

"Right you are, sah."

"And the loggerhead."

"The logrit. Only in deep water we find logrit."

I drew a deep breath. There was nothing occult about it—you just get to know.

"All right," I said. "Now what else? What is the other kind?"

"Batalí, sah." And the other two nodded and their lips formed: "Batalí."

"Batalí?" I said. "What is a batalí? I don't know this one. What does it look like?"

Then he gave it to me.

"Smoll tet-tel, sah. Gray color; 'ave round shell and big head like logrit. This batalí come in only seldom, when the Orinook flood is slack and strong current come in from the sea. This bod tet-tel, sah; 'e's scrotch and bite and will not lie on 'is bock."

You see what the man was saying? He went on:

"Some people call this heartbreak tet-tel, since it heart break on deck. This tet-tel no good, can' resis' the voyage. We don't bring these home. Call them heartbreak tet-tel. We only cotch them sparing—three, four in a season, only when the current strong."

It was not just the sameness of words used a thousand miles and eighteen years apart. The old man in the water was bringing the ridley to Trinidad. Unless he was mistaken in some almost impossible sort of way, or was kidding me with a fabrication too elaborate for his resources, he was stranding ridleys on these shores as they strand in England. And since there is no south-trending current in the Caribbean, and no ridleys there either, the batalís could only be coming from Africa!

The current the old man spoke of is partly the North Equatorial Current, the tail end of the Gulf stream, and partly the South Equatorial Current, which is a continuation of the Benguela Current from southwest Africa. There are two ways in which ridleys might get into it.

They could simply stick with the Gulf Stream water when it is shunted southward against Europe, go on beyond the Azores, which is the last place we have been able to trace them, and then ride out the second ocean crossing when the current is shouldered westward toward Brazil by the African bulge. Or these Trinidad turtles may not be Gulf ridleys at all, but strays from a ridley race that lives along the west coast of tropical Africa. It would be easy to tell which. This African colony has a shell with six or seven big scales along each side, instead of five like the stock in the Gulf of Mexico. It would be easy to say which the Trinidad turtle is—if I could only see one.

These were the thoughts that came to me when I got back some composure on the cliff trail.

"I wonder if you could find me an old shell of this batalí," I said. "Lying around somewhere. Or a skull. Is there any way I could get to see one?"

The old man in the water looked apologetic.

"We don' bring them, sah," he said.

"Could we get them easily when they come up to lay?" I asked.

This made him look sad again, and I knew why.

"This tet-tel don' lay egg, sah," he said. "We don' see them on shore."

What can you do? Sweat. Harangue embarrassed clumps of fishermen. Join the buzzards picking over garbage heaps. Offer a reward for the next act of God. Swear, and wait.

I never found a scrap of proof to hold in my hand. I came home leaving a standing bounty and some interested friends among the people on the cliffs and among the fisheries men, but no heartbreak turtle has come to light.

If there *is* a batalí, and it *is* a ridley, then it almost surely drifts in with the African water. Some of the molecules of this water come from Florida—the long way round—and some come by way of Senegal; and one of these places is the home of the batalí, the heartbreak turtle, which comes in to the cliffs beyond Matelot, at the end of the windward road.

Matelot, northeastern coast of Trinidad.

The Lively Petes of Parque Vargas

I T WAS MIDDAY outside, but in Parque Vargas it was twi-light. On the hot streets around the plaza the people of Puerto Limón had given up for the day. There were a few bicycles still and an occasional taxi clattered by, and the little shoeshine boys still shrieked at intervals. Inside the shady park most of the sloths had given up hours before and hung quietly now, back down, from the high limbs of the Indian laurel trees. A casual observer would have said that *all* the sloths were sleeping; but I knew better, or hoped I did.

There was one sloth up there that I felt sure was, rela-tively speaking, seething with emotion. It was not the sort of emotion that stirs the surface appreciably, but I was certain it was there all the same. It was this sloth and its supposed emotion, and my suspense over the outcome of it, that held me in the dim interior of the plaza on that fifth day of my stay in Puerto Limón.

To walk into Parque Vargas from the searing sunshine on the streets around it was like diving into a deep spring. The light was the same and the feel of the air on your skin was too. The limbs of the tall trees interlocked so closely that only a stray splash of sunlight reached the ground, and so high that eddies of breeze, geared by the bay wind,

swirled and drifted among the trunks. It is hard to imagine
the appeal of such a place unless you have waited for time
to pass in a Caribbean town. For five days I had been doing a great deal of waiting here in midtown Limón, and I
should have been on a low limb indeed if it had not been
for the sloths and the shade and the wind-drift in Parque
Vargas.

The first day I entered the tiny office of Aerovías Costar-
ricenses, I was struck by the unpretentious scale of the en-
terprise. There was a counter across the single room and a
platform scale in front of it. Behind the counter there was
a table, a typewriter, and a girl, and the girl was pretty
like any Tica; but she seemed depressed when I asked if
I could charter a plane for the next day.

"Our plane is discomposed," she said in Spanish.

"Your plane?" I said. "Do you have only one plane?
What is the matter with it?"

"¿Quién sabe?" the girl said. "Paco is trying to find out.
He flew to San José Wednesday and the trip is high, over
the volcano; too high. He flies over 12,500 feet, and this is
bad for a plane like ours; and when he got back it was discomposed. All the passengers and freight for Sixaola and
la Barra are waiting. Lástima—a pity."

"Then you have no idea when I might be able to hire
the plane?"

"Where do you want to go?" she said.

"To Tortuguero. Maybe to la Barra."

"But we go to those places. Why hire the plane? Why
do you not just go as a passenger? It's all the same, only
cheaper."

"But I want to fly low and look for turtles."

"Paco likes to fly low and look for turtles."

"Well—would he circle when I asked him to?"

"That would cost more, I suppose. A little. But if you

will fly with the guaro you can go at almost the passenger rate."

"The guaro?" I said. "What guaro?" *Guaro* is a corruption of the Castilian word *aguardiente* and is used in most parts of Central America for locally made sugarcane rum. The girl held a hand out three feet above the floor. She held it knuckles-down, not palm-down as a gringo would.

"It is a big can of guaro for the company laborers," she said. "The Atlantic Trading Company at Tortuguero. The company employs a great many Mosquitos, and they need guaro. If Saturday night comes and the guaro lacks, they are sad; and they sometimes go away."

"All right," I said. "I don't mind riding with the guaro if we can fly low. When do you think the plane might possibly be ready?"

"This is all I can tell you: the first flight will have to be for Sixaola and the second for Barra del Colorado. You should be ready to leave the day after the plane is composed—or if it is finished late, the second day after. Where can I locate you, noontimes?"

I told her. Then I went away and waited five days. Mornings I hired a bicycle or a horse, and once, at prohibitive cost, a taxi, and went up the coast or back into the fecund hinterland catching frogs and lizards and snakes; or swam in the rock pools behind the reef at the point; or visited the turtle crawls and fish-landings across the river.

Every day at noon I came back to the plaza and waited and felt the coolness and watched the sloths in the trees. If you should ever have to do any waiting where there are sloths, I can recommend watching them as a way to pass the time. It is as good as reading *War and Peace*—it never gives out on you. You can while away a whole half-hour finding out whether a given sloth intends to reach for another twigful of leaves, or to scratch himself again. No matter which course he chooses, you can count on spending another half-hour watching him carry it out.

In Parque Vargas there are nine sloths. One man I talked to insisted that there are twenty-five, but I counted them every day for five days and always came out with nine. The consensus among the people I questioned was that this number was probably right and that it had remained about the same ever since they could remember. The nine sloths live in twenty-eight *laurel de la India* trees. The trees, which are a species of *Ficus* (fig), are wound about with philodendrons and their limbs sweep up and interlace to form a closed canopy that is a fine continuous roadway and pasture for the sloths.

The sloths in Parque Vargas are Gray's three-toed sloth, a race confined to Panama and Costa Rica and belonging to a genus that is found in lowland woods from Honduras to Bolivia. Sloths are among the strangest of all mammals. If you work at it you can make out a case for placing them in the order Edentata, along with the anteaters and armadillos. But no anteater or armadillo can begin to match the sloth for eccentricity.

In the first place, sloths *look* strange before they make a move of any kind. The mature animal weighs about twenty-five pounds and has a round, earless head on a long neck, bulging eyes, and long legs that seem to have no joints. Each hand and foot has three permanently flexed claws with which the creature hangs upside down beneath the limbs he lives on. The fur is coarse and bristly, and during the wet season green algæ grow among the hairs and give it a greenish color thought to be useful as camouflage.

But nothing in the appearance of this animal is anywhere near as curious as its incredible sloth. I use the term in its original sense of "slowness"—with none of its acquired connotation of *reprehensible* slowness. The sloth of these animals is one of the marvels of nature. It is a mockery of motion, an eerily mechanical, nerve-racking slowness that contractile protoplasm was never meant to support. The cytoplasm of an amœba streams faster than a sloth flees from a hungry boa constrictor. And besides being thus pointlessly, unbearably slow in everything it undertakes, the sloth is hesitant and vacillating in undertaking anything.

For example, a sloth may initiate some simple, straightforward move—like reaching for another handhold, say—and you may find that you must wait many minutes before it is clear whether he is carrying out the act or has stopped to reconsider the whole plan.

In spite of all this it seems to me unfair to brand the sloth as stupid and of "primitive mentality," as writers on the subject are inclined to do. It is quite possible that the animal is not stupid at all, and that its physical slowness is just that and nothing more, or even possibly a useful adaptation that we have not the wit to understand. Apparently no animal psychologist has turned his attention to sloths. They have never been put through a maze, for example, to get really reliable data on their learning ability. Putting a sloth through a maze would be quite a technical feat, I imagine, and very time consuming; but it must be done sooner or later, in fairness to the sloth. Meantime I shall go on wondering if the sloth may not be every bit as bright as its way of life calls for.

The slowness of sloths must be, in some way that I have never heard explained, part of a pattern of adaptation for life in the treetops. Some arboreal vertebrates are not slow, to be sure. Squirrels, for instance, are paragons of agility. But on the other hand there are three very different groups of backboned animals—sloths, chameleons, and the slow loris—that do live in treetops and that share the same odd retardation of motion and locomotion. Since these animals are not closely related, the loris being a kind of lemur—a primate like ourselves—the chameleon a lizard, and the sloth a climbing relative of the anteaters, and since their terrestrial relatives are not in any case notably slothful, the only sensible conclusion is that slowing down your muscles may be one way of fitting yourself for life in trees. The Pleistocene relatives of the modern tree sloths were ground-dwelling creatures, some of which were as big as oxen. We call them ground "sloths," but this does not mean that they were any more deliberate in their movements than, say, a bear. They are sloths only by a kind of reverse inheritance from their arboreal descendants.

Simply talking to people in the park, I was unable to find out either when the trees there were planted, or when the sloths came to live in them. Some said both had been there always. This is clearly a mistake, since the tree, as its Spanish name indicates, is native to Asia. Others said that a man who liked sloths put a pair there during the 1890's, and that the trees were already well matured then and formed the continuous canopy requisite to flourishing sloth life. An old woman sitting on a bench said that she remembered the time when a mayor of the town decided the sloths were a public nuisance and a menace to the future of the trees and should be shot. A policeman was detailed to kill them, with a military rifle that made a great *bulla* here in the center of the city. I told the woman that I had counted nine sloths only that morning.

"Exactly," she said with emphasis. "Now they are many. *Abundan.* It is my belief that the soldier missed two of them, or perhaps missed a pregnant female."

There may be records somewhere that would help establish the date of founding of the sloth-*laurel* community in Parque Vargas, but this is not essential. The important thing is that a native animal and an exotic plant have come together there and have worked out a natural equilibrium, with the sloth population completely dependent on the trees for food and yet not damaging them beyond the point of tolerance. It would be interesting to know exactly how the balance is maintained from one generation to the next. The sloths eat the leaves and fruit of the trees, and have no other food, and it seems safe to assume that the supply of food is the dominant factor controlling the size of the colony. Such uncluttered examples of population balance are easy to arrange among weevils in a flour bin or among protozoa in a jar of broth; but they are hard to find in nature, and especially among vertebrates. No zoologist of my acquaintance would have ventured to predict that two sloths placed in a grove of twenty-eight trees, of a sort untasted by sloths before and surrounded by city streets, would give rise to a population stabilized at nine individuals after thirty or forty years, or whatever the period has been.

It is curious how little this colony of extraordinary creatures intrudes upon the life of the city. Once in a great while a baby sloth, which normally clings spraddle-legged to its mother's upturned belly, falls out of a tree. Very rarely, for no discernible reason, a grown one descends and shuffles painfully across the bare earth among the plants and buttressed tree trunks. At such times a crowd of urchins and idle people gathers about the pitiful form. The boys shout and push one another toward the sloth, and when they try to stir up trouble between it and a jaded bitch more interested in sleep, the policeman strolls over from the sidewalk and tells them to stop molesting animals.

The only real excitement the sloths occasion comes when one of them swings from one handhold to another across the busy street on one of the electric wires that are strung through the trees. These are the times when everybody downtown stops to watch and talk about the sloths. "The lively Pete will be electrocuted," the Latins tell one another. The Castilian word for the sloth is *perezoso*, meaning about the same as ours; but in Central America it is everywhere known as *perico ligero*, "lively Pete," which is a fine example of vernacular irony. A windowful of Latin and creole girls across the street shrieks at the policeman at the corner of the park to stop the sloth before he gets to the insulator nailed to the angle of their building. A growing gang of boys leaning on bicycles howls and whistles with joy and mock lust.

"Yes, mon," one of them says. "I glod-ly walk this wy-ah upside down to get in that room. I do it fas-teah than the *perico!*"

After a while someone phones the power company, a truck comes with a ladder, and the sloth is plucked down and returned to the park. The people wander away or hang around in knots talking about the elections that are coming. The sloths are forgotten by everybody but me.

I was watching them still, as I said, on my fifth day in Limón. It was noon, and I was lying on my back and looking straight up to where two sloths were hanging in the deep shadows. There were several people on neighboring benches, but they had long ago got used to me and were paying me no attention. One of the sloths was scratching, dragging a foot across its shaggy side with the speed and regularity of the pendulum of a grandfather's clock. There was no likelihood that it would do anything else for hours. I had already lost interest in that sloth. But the other one, as I have said, excited me.

For fifteen minutes this second sloth had seemed to me to be moving nearer the first. If this was true, and the approach not just fortuitous, then perhaps the first sloth was a female and the second a male. It could be that I was at last to be allowed to witness what I had hoped for five days to see—the love-making of the lively Pete. Slow as the animal is, and upside down . . . I was intensely, perhaps even morbidly curious, and this approach was the first hint of sex that had crept into the activities of the sloths.

I waited longer. The advancing sloth—the supposed rutting male—had reached a point no more than two feet from what I hoped was his goal and he was still moving. I had every reason to feel that there was purpose in his advance, and to hope that within a few minutes I would learn whether his motive was really sex or just pugnacity or sociability instead. When the gap had narrowed to ten or twelve inches, the sloth stopped dead still, then unhooked one fore foot, moved it slowly to one side, and held it poised there. For a full minute he hung motionless. Then he began turning his head with barely perceptible motion —a slow swoop and swing to the left, then back one hundred and eighty degrees to the right, then forward again, where it stopped. He seemed to be staring fixedly at the sloth in front. I was not able to make out his expression, but I can tell you I was on tenterhooks. Something was bound to happen now.

It did. A little boy touched my shoulder. "*Señor*," he piped, "*está compuesto el avión*—the airplane is fixed!" His voice trembled with excitement at the news he bore.

"Wait a minute," I said. "Look up there. Look at those lively Petes." I pointed with tense concern, and the boy looked up into the dome of the grove and saw two sloths on a limb, one of them scratching itself rhythmically, the other hanging immobile from three legs.

"Yes, sir," he said. "You can see them any time. They live there."

"Sure, I know that," I said, still excited. "But what are they going to do?"

"Do?" the boy said.

"Yes. What are they going to do now?"

He hovered uncertainly, trying to pin down the joke that must be eluding him. "What are they going to do?" he said timidly.

"Sí, hombre!" I said. "What's the matter with you?"

He shrugged and spread his hands and rolled his eyes up toward the sloths and then back at me with mild reproach.

"They will hang there till it gets too hot. After that they will go to sleep." Then he tried once more to bring order into his world: "But, señor, the lady at the Aerovías says you must come now. Paco is making the Sixaola flight this afternoon and tomorrow you can have the airplane, but he has to see you now before he goes. Ahorita!"

With a sigh I rolled off the bench and onto my feet and found a coin for the boy.

"Bueno. Muy bien," I said.

But the boy was tough, really. He was going to try once more to get at the bottom of this thing.

"You are not content?" he said, eying me narrowly. "Though the airplane is composed?"

I was not content. I was cheated. Five days' waiting and hardly a foot between two sloths and their sex rites; and suddenly the wretched plane was composed.

"Well, yes and no." I said.

The little boy looked at me with widening eyes. He did not know whether it was being grown up or being a gringo that had warped my soul. But he was sure life was becoming a complex thing here in this city where he was born.

Three-toed sloth in a Cecropia tree. Although the lively petes of Parque Vargas eat mostly the leaves of the exotic *laurel de la India,* Cecropia is their chief natural food. (Photo by Brian McNab)

Tortuguero

T︎HE LITTLE engine skipped and spat, then caught with a roar. Paco leaned over and slammed the door on my side and twisted the ends of a loop of wire together to hold it shut. Then he reached behind us and tested the moorings of a fifteen-gallon can of guaro—the local cane rum—which filled the back third of the little cabin. He waggled his tail surfaces and revved the engine up to 1500 and let it warm there awhile. He tried one magneto alone, then the other one, and it was all the same sound. He held his brakes and opened her up and she took 2000 without quibbling. He looked at me happily.

"Everything is composed," he said.

The boy who had twisted the propeller waved his arms to attract Paco's attention.

"*Todo está okey,*" he said.

"*Sí,*" Paco said.

He pushed the throttle forward, the airplane shook itself and moved off, and the fat little wheels left rim-deep furrows in the damp sand. We taxied three hundred yards downwind and then, without slowing, pivoted in a small storm of noise and went tearing back the way we had come, pounding and clattering over the shallow washes and mounded piles of wrack. Paco moved his stick forward and the tail came up; then he pulled it back and the pounding stopped and we felt our way off the sand. Ten feet up he kicked a light right rudder and we streaked out over the waves in a shallow turn. We circled back over the aluminum roof of the little hangar and I could see the boy and a customs man and a soldier's gold teeth flashing. They were all waving. They were happy because we had got into the air with no trouble.

"*Okey*," said Paco. "*Rumbo Tortuguero.*"

"But take your time," I said. "Let's fly a quarter of a mile offshore, or maybe less. If you see a turtle, circle him. How low can we fly?"

"It is better not to splash salt water on the engine," Paco said.

He was good. He was the kind of pilot who would probably always get along. He reminded me of the barnstormers who used to come to our town in Texas when I was a boy. It wasn't so much his getting away with banking three yards above the breakers or taking the corroded little Aeronca twelve thousand feet over Irazú. It was the way the visor of his cap stood straight up, and the complete confidence in his smooth Indian's face, and his knowing every nut and bearing in the little old plane and how to keep them warranting his confidence. He had guts; but just guts won't keep a plane in the air. Paco had been a mechanic at the big airline shops in San José before he came to the coast, and he quit because he wanted to fly what he worked on, even if it was slow and small and ancient.

We were three hundred feet over the water and heading west, just offshore, when I saw a turtle floating. I touched Paco on the shoulder and motioned. He banked and looked where I was pointing.

"*Sí. Tortuga. Carey,*" he said.

"I think it is a green turtle," I said.

Paco turned and lost altitude and leveled off at maybe seventy-five feet.

"The *flota* is late—the big crowd of greens," he said. "The *careyes* (hawksbills) are coming out and the *canales* (trunkbacks), but everybody is talking about how the green fleet is late."

We passed over the turtle again and I had a good look at it. It was floating high and the water was clear. It was a green all right.

"I was mistaken," Paco said. "It is a green. It is one that lives here, I suppose. A few live here all the time, they say. When the fleet comes in, you see dozens. Hundreds."

"Where does the fleet come from?" I asked, as I have asked five hundred people on Caribbean shores.

"*¿Quién sabe?*" Paco started another turn. "Maybe Yucatán—they say."

We made another circle and came out over the turtle just right, but this time it was not one turtle but three. Besides the broad, bobtailed female we had been watching, there were two males—smaller, with narrow, torpedo-shaped shells and thick tails a foot long. One of them was splashing and slapping about the female and stretching his neck over her shell. The other floated quietly twenty feet away.

This amatory triangle caught my interest at once, because I had noticed the same thing many times among fresh-water turtles, which also mate floating in the water. In Florida I live on the edge of a pond, and each fall when the cooters breed I have been struck by the frequency with which a courting party comprises a female and two competing males. In our pond a good half of the turtle heads you see at any given time in October will be grouped in sets of three. Once the female has made her choice and copulation begins, the extra male goes away.

For whatever reason, I only very rarely count groups of four heads or more. I was impressed when, on the occasion of my first good view of the *Liebespiel* of sea turtles, these huge greens, courting on the swells off a tropical shore, turned up in the same familiar triangle.

"That's enough of these," I said to Paco. "*Sigue adelante*. Go on."

We straightened out on our neglected course, keeping close in to the first rise of the rollers. We saw fifteen turtles, all of which were hawksbills and greens. There were three sets of three and one mated pair. The rest were single individuals. We tried flying farther out, but saw nothing. We came in to the beach and found that we could easily spot the nesting trails in the sand, the perspective even showing clearly where the nest lay, at the apex of the V-shaped crawl mark. The trip was a success as far as I was concerned. I poked Paco.

"The charter flight is over. Now I am a passenger," I said.

"*Vaya, pues*," Paco said.

The results of this short trip were important to me in two ways. In the first place, we had seen definite evidence that American green turtles and hawksbills, like those in the Indian Ocean, mate at the same time the eggs are laid. Besides this I had proved to myself that sea turtles floating in clear water could be easily identified from a light plane flying at safe altitudes, and that nesting trails on the beach could be readily seen. This meant that small planes could be used to make turtle censuses and surveys of breeding grounds as they are used in studying waterfowl migrations. This was a good thing to know.

Paco moved the throttle up a notch and we climbed for a while. He scanned the long slant of beach ahead and suddenly pointed.

"Tortuguero is there," he said. I could see nothing but a slight jut to the shore and said so.

"The river runs along just back of the beach and comes out behind that point," Paco said.

We kept climbing, and suddenly I could see the thin break in the forest top where the river slanted in toward the sea and then ran beside it for a long way. There was just a narrow strip of land between the river and the breakers.

"And the village?" I said, looking off toward the point.

"*Mas acá.*" Paco motioned groundward toward a long, ragged patch on the peninsula a couple of miles our side of the point. "See? There."

The break in the landscape slowly resolved itself into a stand of coco palms that filled most of the space between the river and the beach for a mile or more. There were several dozen thatched roofs scattered about in the palm grove.

"Where do you land?" I asked.

"There." Paco pointed again. "At the point. On the beach."

We were near enough now to make out some detail. None of it was comforting. There had been a great deal of jetsam on the beach all along. As we neared the river mouth the litter increased, and down toward the point there was what seemed to be an almost continuous string of poles and broken booms and maverick saw-logs. I craned my neck to see more sand somewhere among the timbers, but to save me I couldn't trace a plane-wide corridor through the tumbled clutter for more than a hundred yards in any direction.

"You are not going down on that woodpile are you?" I said.

"Sure," Paco said. "That is the airport."

"But where is the strip? You need a thousand feet, don't you? What good is an airport with no runway?"

"Look at that piece just this side of the point," Paco said. "Look at it this way."

He hunched his left shoulder forward and stretched his arm, bending it at elbow and wrist in a gentle double curve. It didn't look like a landing strip to me. He touched his triceps with a finger of his right hand, leaving the controls untended.

"Go in up there," he said. "In the bushes by the point—see? You see how it lies?"

"*Jesús, María y José,*" I said, reverently.

"No, it's all right. Not too crooked. Just some bushes and sticks—no trees or logs."

"Have you ever done it before?" I asked.

"*Qué va!* I bring the guaro. When the launch is not running. I never lost a passenger yet. I lost the guaro a few times, but I never lost a passenger in my life. You can have confidence."

I looked down at a scattering of whitecaps on the sea. "How about the wind?" I said. "It is coming in straight across the—what you call landing strip."

"*No importa,*" Charlie said. "It is not very strong. Do not preoccupy yourself. You *mash* the airplane on."

I didn't recall the maneuver. But then, I had just two hours and twelve minutes solo flying in my logbook, while Paco had hundreds. Of hours, that is—I doubt if he ever had a logbook. I tried not to preoccupy myself.

We were over the mouth of the river by then and Paco suddenly banked and turned downwind and then fell into a gut-jerking dive toward the landward end of the alleged landing strip. I still could see no clear course among the debris, but we kept going. I thrust my preoccupation from me, but it came right back. We were just above the ground and leveling off to hit it when Paco and the engine exploded together.

"*¡A la gran puta!*" Paco grated out, on the instant gunning the engine and hauling the patient little plane back in a reckless climb.

Out of a bottom corner of my eye I saw the skittering shapes of twenty dogs spreading in full panic from under our rising wheels. "*¡Qué pasa, carajo!*—What's that?" I said. There was no spirit back of the question. I was too scared to care.

Paco had already relaxed. "The Siquirres dogs," he said. "The bastards! They were digging a turtle nest. They were behind the *monte* and I didn't see them." He began to chuckle over the episode.

"Well, what the hell is a Siquirres dog?" I asked testily, still too weak to want to know, really.

"It is a dog from Siquirres," Paco said.

"All right. Very funny. But what are they doing here—so many of them? Siquirres is a long way through the woods. Thirty miles, isn't it?"

"They are eating turtle eggs. They know about the turtle eggs and come over in gangs. They are all over the place in June."

We made a circle out over the water and came in and tried again. This time we slid in and stalled cleanly between two logs; the wheels and tail hit the beach together, and we raced out the straight first leg of the aisle and then lost speed reassuringly down an easy double curve that somehow lay hidden among the timbers. We never hit a thing. Just before we stopped and I started breathing, we doubled back and taxied slowly up the beach toward a manaca palm roof set on four poles stuck in the sand.

An immense black man of great age stood under the shelter. There seems to me to be a strain of West African Negro

that produces a high proportion of almost perfectly pre-
served septuagenarians—dynamic, thigh-slapping women
and vast, silver-bearded patriarchs to go with them and
keep them content and do pretty much the same day's
work they did at twenty-five. The man under the shelter
was one of these. He was a Carib, but it takes more than
the blood of salt-water Indians to dim the strong West
African blood.

Paco reached over and untwisted the wire holding my
door shut.

"*A-jah, Jorge,*" he said.

"*Buenos días, Paco.*" The old man rumbled it out from
away down in his midsection. He reached in to shake
Paco's hand, but all the time he was looking behind us,
his neck stretching and his eyes rolling anxiously.

"What are you looking for, *hombre?*" Paco said, knowing very well.

Just then George saw the top of the milk can with the
chain and padlock holding the lid on. He eased up all at
once and gave a great gusty sigh, like a loggerhead taking
air over too deep bottom.

"*Ahhh,*" he said. "*¡Qué buey-no! El guaaa-ro.*" He fon-
dled the vowels with loving resonance and made them last
and grow. "*El guaro*—the comfort of man!"

Paco stepped out of the airplane.

"This is a señor that is looking for turtles," he said. "Can
you take him to the village?"

"*Claro,*" George said. Then, looking at me closely: "You
are able to speak English, sah?"

"Yes, some," I said. "I'm from Florida. How far is Tortuguero?"

"Abaowt shree mile on the ri-beah. Not so far. I hob a
doree just the-ah, sah. Just give me a hond-up with this
guaro and we can go."

Paco had walked over to the shelter and was looking at a sisal bag hanging from a post "You have some turtle eggs?" he called to George.

"*Bastante,*" George said. "*Allá en la bolsa.* Take the bag." It was wonderful to hear what he did with the Spanish vowels.

Paco reached into the bag and took out a handful of eggs and started eating them. George turned back to the can of rum in the plane. He unfastened the lashings and tilted the hundred-pound can out of the cockpit, and before I could touch it he had swung it to his shoulder and stood holding it steady with one hand. With the other hand he took my camera bag and started to gather in my bedroll and a string of pineapples I had set on the ground.

"I'll get the rest," I said. "Can you make it with all that?"

George thought this was funny. He rumbled with humor and then said with a nice touch of sarcasm; "I think so, sah."

I went over and shook hands with Paco and asked if he could pick me up sometime after a week or so. He said I could have confidence, and we shook hands and I walked away after the old man. It was an eighth of a mile down a narrow trail to George's shack of manaca palm thatch, where bees were humming in an old mango tree and two dogs slept in the shade. Behind the house the river ran dark and quiet, and at a landing under a huge ceiba two dugouts were grounded—one good one and the other rotting and full of water and leaves and tadpoles. George put my bedroll in the middle of the good canoe and told me to sit on it. He stowed the guaro in the shallow bow and tied it down, and then took his place in the stern. He pushed us off among dipping limbs and lianas into the wheeling eddies of the channel edge.

We crossed the current to the quiet shore inside a long

bend, slipping through the glossy, black water with only the rhythmic push and suck of the old man's paddle blade to mar the silence of the gliding. We were near the river mouth and at first the shores were low plains of grass and ragged mangroves, but as we moved upstream the manaca and huiscoyol palms came in, and then real fringe forest with big trees rising or leaning at the water's edge and hung with liana ropes or swathed in the killing green velvet of vine drapery. At first slowly, then with a rush, the feel of a Caribbean river came back to me. It was little more than a half-hour trip from the landing to the village, but it took me back to all the tropical rivers I had known and to chains of long days in other dugouts driven endlessly up the current by black men with gleaming backs that never tired.

It showed that even the smallest things are not really gone from your memory—the smell of the river-bottom forest; the idle little gangs of needlefish stopping any time to jump over floating sticks for mindless fun, and the bursts of silver fire when the young tarpon roll in midstream; the snowy whiteness of Ghiesbreght's hawk; and the surprise at the sameness of water birds everywhere: the glowing rose of spoonbills all around the Caribbean, anhingas here no different to the eye from those at home, bitterns and cormorants and half a dozen kinds of herons and whole suites of pad-plodding rails and gallinules all so like their counterparts in Florida that telling them apart calls for calipers and a ruler.

I remembered the crash and start when a big iguana took the water from high up in a tree where he had been browsing; and how the voice of the great yellow-naped parrot of the lowland rivers is just the squeak of the little mountain parakeets made suitably big and raucous; and how this kind of thinking always leads into old streams of musing on the use of voice in classifying animals—and before this got anywhere at all a least green kingfisher smaller than a sparrow burst from a bush at our bow and crossed the river, raging in a comically minuscule dialect of the homely rattle of our northern belted kingfisher.

George was not a talkative man, and I was glad. He stuck to his effortless paddling and I to coming back to the tropics. The sun was high and fiery and the water gleamed like obsidian, but there was a low, steady breeze, and George was adept at keeping the cayuca in the narrow river-edge shade. Once I missed a stroke in his paddling rhythm. When I looked back I saw him peering at a low place on the bank where a tunnel-like opening came down to the water through dense huiscoyol. He pointed and I suddenly remembered how tapir godowns look on riverbanks.

"Moun-ten cow," George said. "We don' see them so often low on the ri-beah."

Another time he rested his paddle on the gunwale and called to me softly. "Look theah, sah."

He took hold of a streamer of vine that fell from a leaning limb. There was a handsome crested lizard on the limb. It was a basilisk, a full-grown male, perhaps fourteen inches long and bright-eyed, alert, and green as lettuce.

"The Sponish people call this Jesucristo. Jesus Christ, they call it. You know why, sah?"

I know why all right, but I said: "Why?" and George looked pleased.

"Because this onny-mul walk on the wa-teah. Now you watch him closely."

He jerked the vine and the basilisk jumped to another limb and stared at George with its beady eyes, and that was all. George was sad. The lizard had let him down.

I reached into my bag and took out a slingshot, a handsome one made of two cross-mortised sticks of polished hardwood, one of mora and one of rosewood. My wife bought that slingshot for me from a boy in Honduras, and I carry it everywhere I go where pistol permits are hard to come by. I shoot lizards with it, with number-ten shot. It is not so good for collecting as a smooth-bore twenty-two pistol, but it is almost as good. George had never seen a white man of my age who carried a slingshot—of that I am sure. How was it, then, that he let no fleeting ripple of surprise stir the wrinkled jet of his face? This was what I thought of, more than the basilisk. But then I saw the gap to shore growing, and I quickly scooped up some wet sand caked beside a rib of the boat, molded it into the pouch of the catapult, and let it fly at the basilisk. It splatted over and about him, and all his fine courage left and he dropped like a rock into the black river. He went under, but instantly was up again; and he came up running on the water. His thin front feet were held out in front, his tail curved up behind, and his back feet punched the yielding surface like the firing pin of a machine gun—so fast that the little plunking they made was almost a buzz, too fast to let the lizard sink. Almost before we realized he was running he had reached the shore, where he scrambled up the bank and crashed off through the litter like a squirrel caught away from his tree.

George was gratified. "You see, sah? You see why this onny-mul get the name of Jesus Christ?"

"Lord, yes," I said.

After a while we passed a wattle hut set about with naked children, and then there were several more huts. After that we saw the raw new weatherboarding of the buildings the Atlantic Trading Company was putting up, and our trip was over.

Less than an hour later I was on the river again, but this

time under very different circumstances. The manager of
the logging and banana depot, Don Yoyo Quiroz, had met
me at the dock and had graciously agreed to take me in;
and even before we looked up lodgings for me, he suggested that I go with him to a loading station up the river.
We went in a square-tailed cayuca pushed by a powerful
outboard motor.

I have an overweening loathing for extraneous noise in
the wilderness, and especially for the intrusion of outboard
motors there. Heaven knows I have been served by out-
boards and have no right to revile them on the score of
their functioning. They are a marvelously flexible and effi-
cient device. But that has nothing to do with the fact that
in the woods they are an outrage, a symbol of human
transgression, and a portent of the passing of the wilderness. Their racket and incongruous speed, the bow-waves
crashing up into the primal quiet of the vega forest, the
hideous shock to the sequestered creatures of the shore—
all these combine to keep me edgy and self-conscious and
take all savor from such journeying. The getting there fast
is good, I have to say, but the going is fiendish and ob-
trusive.

We went eight or nine miles up the river—far enough to
get into the beginnings of the tall timber. I was surprised
when Yoyo told me that Costa Rica is a poor mahogany
coast. For some unknown reason there is a gap in the
abundance of the tree and no really good mahogany country between Nicaragua and Colombia. But here on the
Tortuguero there is plenty of *cedro macho,* a good timber
for house construction, and of *laurel,* and a little distance
back from the river plenty of *cedro real,* or Spanish cedar,
in some ways the best of all the tropical timbers. Our trip
upriver took us a little less than a half-hour. We saw
nothing but the trees and water and one big muscovy

drake that let himself be overtaken when we rushed in under the low limb on which he was promenading. It goes without saying that we heard nothing but the motor.

Finally we roared around a bend and drew up alongside a small motorship tied to a platform set on piling among towering trees on a flat, wet shore. A little tributary entered beside the platform, and it was down this that the long freight cayucas came, piled high with green stems of bananas from small farms back in the good land above the flood-plain, some six or eight miles upstream. This was an "independent" banana operation and I was curious to see it under way.

A dozen Mosquito men and boys were tossing the forty-pound stems into the last spaces of the hold. The fruit was bound for Tampa, and up here it was at least six days away from its destination—even given a good crossing of the Tortuguero bar, which is never to be counted on. I recalled the febrile but ordered scrambling to synchronize fruit cuts and loadings and sailings at Puerto Cortés and Golfito; the babying of each separate stem and the cooled holds that carry a hundred thousand ninety-pound stems at cruising speeds of up to eighteen knots to beautifully timed distribution schedules in New Orleans and Mobile. I wondered how the independent companies made their money.

I asked the manager. Don Yoyo is one of the Quirozes from the Meseta, back in the high, cool interior where most of the Latin Costa Ricans live and the coffee grows, and the girls are prettier than anywhere else in America. Like others in the family, Yoyo is able and intelligent, of fair, blue-eyed Spanish stock—a stock that is not depressed by the discomforts and deprivations of tropical camps.

"How do you compete with the *Bananera?*" I asked. The *Bananera* is the United Fruit Company in Costa Rica.

"We don't compete with anybody. We just make a little profit on every stem of fruit we unload in Tampa," he said.

To me it seemed a strange thing to say. I don't understand it yet, but I lay this to my poor grasp of economics.

Back at Tortuguero, Yoyo found a place where he said I could sleep. It was the second floor of a tall, chimney-shaped shack, a kind of airy attic up under a thatched roof, open all around and reached by a nearly vertical stairway from the shuttered darkness of a lower room filled with the clutter of a banana and lumber camp abuilding. Beside the house there was a deep boarded hole in the ground—a kind of combination cistern and well—and around the premises there was a ten-foot palisade of *cedro macho* slabs that gave the place a somewhat alarming air of impregnability. It was a queer structure, and I asked Yoyo about it.

He said the fence was there to keep out the Mosquito Indians on Saturday nights, and the house was tall to get above the fence and catch the breeze off the ocean. He asked me if I needed anything else, and I said I was just about to need something to eat. He told me how to find a house where there was a woman who was a good cook and said he would tell her to expect me. Before we left I looked out of the open seaward side of my eyrie. I could see the ocean out to the horizon, and the surf, and a man standing knee-deep in it fishing with a handline; and almost under me I could see down into the midst of a cluster of Mosquito huts and behind one of them a tiny male child in only a short shirt staggering about the clean-swept yard after a game rooster.

I moved my things up to my quarters and then we climbed down and walked over to the commissary. I left Yoyo there to do some chores and went to find supper, even though it was still midafternoon. I wandered among the scattered huts of the town, stopping now and then to inquire about the woman Yoyo said would feed me. The people were mostly Mosquitos and creoles, as the descendants of the old Jamaican immigrants call themselves, but there were some Caribs from the village of Orinoco on Pearl Lagoon or even from as far away as Tela and Belize. I saw only three families of mestizos.

The village straggled on a long way down the narrow palm grove between the river and the sea, and it was only after I had almost reached the end that people began to do something besides grin or look vague or depressed when asked where the woman who fed people lived. I never was able to settle upon a satisfactory way to ask the question. Considering the character of the settlement, asking for the restaurant or the boarding-house or the *pensión* sounded queer and affected; so I stuck to Yoyo's phrasing and kept asking for the woman who fed people. Finally I spotted the broad brown face of a cheerful Nicaraguan mestiza peering out of her smoke-filled kitchen, and I saluted her in Spanish.

"Is there a señora hereabouts who will sell me a meal?" I asked.

She pointed to the last house in the ragged line, the fourth from hers, a low sprawling house of unpainted board walls and palm thatch. It was twice the size of any of the neighboring huts and was surrounded by a maze of hencoops and pigsties. Part of the house was built flush with the ground and part was on two-foot piers. Under the raised section the tallest hog I ever saw was scratching her rump against the underpinnings.

"*Ahí se vende comida*—meals are sold there," the woman said.

I thanked her with some feeling, because frustration and hunger make me sick. I walked down to the eating-house and beat on the frame of an open doorway. A refined-looking mulatto woman appeared, neat and without apprehension, and asked what could be done for me, in soft, singsong accents not Jamaican or Mosquito or mainland creole. I asked about supper, and a fleeting look of alarm showed that Yoyo's message of introduction had not yet arrived, but it was nothing serious. She thought briefly.

"Well," she said, "will you eat turtel? I have some fresh green turtel. Or some fish?"

"What kind of fish?" I asked.

"Dolphin."

"How do you cook it?"

"I can brile it for you. Any way."

I said I would have both fish and turtle. I asked about tortillas, and she said a bit disdainfully that she could get some. She blew up the coals in the stove and started to work among her pots. I inquired about lemons or limes. There were none; but we meditated a bit and she thought of a little pot of tamarind paste and brought it out, and found a big tumbler for me. I had some rum in an aluminum canteen, and I sloshed a slug of this into the glass and beat up a dollop of tamarind in it and then filled the glass with cool tan water from the clay filter. I tasted the drink and it was good, and I asked the *dueña* if she wanted one. She said she never drank anything strong. There was no overtone of piety—she went on to say she just liked drinks such as tea and coconut water and tamarind ade better.

She said her name was Sibella, and I asked about her accent. She said she was from San Andrés and asked why I talked so queer, and I told her. She said she always had wanted to go to the United States.

She asked if I wanted breadfruit, or yuca, and I said breadfruit any day, baked or fried or boiled, or any way she liked. She said that two days before she had cooked half a tepescuinte—a striped rodent as big as a cocker spaniel—but it was gone; and I said the turtle and dolphin would be fine. The moment we had agreed I should be fed, she had gone outside and from the crotch of a dilly tree had taken down a covered basket of turtle meat and yellow ovarian eggs. She went to the side of the house where a calipee—the under shell of green turtle that gives turtle soup its soul and body—was hanging on a nail; and without taking it down she carved out some strips of the thin drying jelly from between the plastral bones.

She returned to the kitchen and set the strips of calipee to boiling in one iron kettle and some of the marble-size yellow eggs in another. She cut a pound or so of the meat into cubes and chips and mixed it with a teacupful of the green fat that you scrape from the inside of the top shell— the fat that gives to this turtle its name "green." Then she found a big lilylike plant that she called an onion, but which I think was a leek; and she cut the whole thing up, green part as well as white, and mixed it with the turtle meat, dusting in some allspice for lack of *pimienta brava,* and dumping the whole mass into a skillet of hot coconut oil. While this popped and spat she slipped the membranes from the shell-less eggs, and then poured the water off the calipee and added the eggs and a little oil and a pair of mashed cloves of garlic. The meat was by now seared and browning; and draining the loose oil from it, she put it into the pot with the eggs and calipee, added a cup of water and some salt, and put a lid on. Then she went away to get the tortillas.

For a long time I sat at a table writing notes and trying to ignore the wonderful aroma of the turtle. Every so often the giant sow, by now trying to get some sleep in the sand under the floor, groaned or whined to herself or rose halfway to rub her hide against a post. I went out once to look at her again, and even lying stiff on her side she still seemed the tallest pig I ever saw, though not by any means the heaviest. I made another rum-and-tamarind and carried it out to the beach to wait awhile. It was getting late, the wind was up, and the coco leaves were rattling. It looked a long way out into the dimming north to Florida.

An adolescent Mosquito couple was courting in the lee of a log, and this reminded me how you almost never see Hondurans even holding hands in public—anyway, none but the very highest castes. Of course, calling Tortuguero beach public is stretching a point, but the difference in the people is there all the same. I went on to wonder if the reticence of the mountain Hondurans had anything to do with the alleged loss of interest of the Mayans in sex, which one anthropologist holds responsible for the race's dying out. From this standpoint the future of the Mosquito race is sound as a dollar.

The couple behind the log paid me no attention after a first mildly curious look, but when I finished my *tamarindo* I walked back to Sibella's. She had returned, and the whole place was smelling grand. I went in and calmed myself by rolling up the new tortillas and dipping the ends into a scallop shell of salt and biting them off. Sibella thought this was foolish. Corn does poorly on the coast and few of the coastal people like tortillas, or if they secretly like them, they look down on them as inferior victuals—as peon fodder.

"I like a nice slice of light bread," Sibella said prissily. "Or johnnycake."

"I don't," I said.

Supper was ready all at once and I fell upon it in a way that made Sibella stare. It was my first meal of a long day. The turtle and dolphin were both so good that it was hard

Left: leatherback (also called trunkback), two months old, Tortuguero, Costa Rica. *Below*: Sibella in her kitchen door, Tortuguero, Costa Rica.

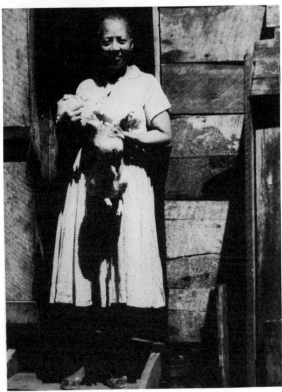

Above: leatherback (trunkback) on Tortuguero Beach, Costa Rica. (Photo by David Carr) *Left*: Mrs. Ybarra (Juana Lopez) with skins of ocelot and jaguar. She killed them in her henhouse, the former with a stick, the latter with a 22-caliber rifle. She wanted to sell them at the Tortuguero turtle camp but was only chided for killing endangered spotted cats.

to decide which to favor, but the turtle finally won out and I ate it all before my hunger waned.

I was sitting moodily contemplating the things I had been unable to eat when suddenly the air was rent by a hideous shriek from the sow beneath the floor. She was directly under my feet, and she had a powerful voice and was clearly under great stress. The first ear-splitting cry trailed off in a series of whining squeals as Sibella ran out and looked under the house. It was too dark to see, and she hurried back, grabbed a sheaf of palm leaves from a box, lighted them at the fire, and dashed out again. I followed and found her on hands and knees peering into the flickering gloom beneath the house. Suddenly she gasped.

"Lahd-me-gawd. Please to get me another leaf."

"What is it?" I asked.

"It's a turtel," Sibella said. "A big oxbull. She has the old sow crowded in a corner. She walked on the sow, I suppose."

I fetched another torch from the kitchen and then crawled part way under the floor and saw that it was as Sibella said. There was a huge hawksbill—the biggest I ever saw alive—and it lay blinking and pulsing its hyoid bone in simple-minded cogitation. It was still blocking egress to the sow, crouched indignant and groaning in an angle of lattice under a far corner of the floor. The turtle was of course not aware that it was blocking anybody. Its thoughts, if any, had to do with the fallibility of neuro-hormone chains and nesting cues, and with the hazards of instinctive living generally.

"Does this happen often?" I asked. It was not just a sea turtle crawling on a hog sleeping under a house. It was this happening beneath the chair of a turtle man come a thousand miles to look at sea turtles.

"No. We most of the time keep the sow in the sty there," Sibella said.

"I just mean the turtle under the house," I said.

"Not this house. Other people's houses, with no clutter like the pens and fences round about here."

I told her I would like to tag the turtle and let it go, and she surprised me by not objecting. There was no one to butcher it for her anyway, she said. I crawled under the house, tied a rope around one of the turtle's flippers, and dragged her out and fastened a Monel metal tag to her shell. Then I back-trailed her to the sea. She had come out of the surf a hundred yards up the beach and had gone directly to the yard of a beachside hut there. The foot-smoothed soil and loom of unfamiliar shapes must have befuddled her and quelled her drive to lay, because she had angled back away from the beach and crossed the premises of two more houses before finally reaching Sibella's. The whole trek took her a distance of at least two hundred and fifty yards, and even then it was only the old sow who interrupted it. It was a bad thing to happen to a turtle who had every right to believe her glands would take her to soft deep sand that a toeless foot could dig, just there where the sea oats rose, only a little way up the low slope from the wash of the last shielding wave.

I walked back to the house and took the turtle by a foot and skidded her down to the beach on her smooth back shell. When I flipped her over at the water's edge, she slowly stretched her neck and started her stupid lost peering again, and I prompted her with my foot. She flopped forward once and then felt the suck of an inch of back-wash under her shell and the world suddenly made sense again. She hurried off seaward and scrambled into the safe turmoil of the breakers.

I went up and told Sibella I would come for breakfast

early in the morning and then wandered off into the dark-
ening village toward my sleeping-tower. A dozen times I
missed the desultory trail that served as a street, and each
time I drew up calling for help from people whose premises I had invaded. The houses were being closed against
the night by now, but the light of lamps or cooking fires
trickled from cracks in the walls, and smoke curled from
under all the eaves. It was exciting to yell at a house and
then wait to see what language would come out in reply.
Sometimes there would be no answer at all—only low, suspicious muttering among timid or conscious-stricken occupants—and then I moved on quickly.

At last I blundered into a section of the village that I
recognized. I found the stockade and the hole in it and
gratefully climbed into the utter darkness of my high
room. I found a light and sat on the edge of my cot to
grieve over the thought of going back downstairs to the
cistern for a bucket of water.

Then I heard voices outside. I looked out of the open
front of the room and saw a clump of black men in a sal-
low wash of lantern light. They were standing around the
can of guaro that had come in on the plane with me.
George was there, sitting on a box and smoking his pipe,
and in his soft booming voice telling two boys what to do.
They had threaded a short pole through a handle of the
milk can and were preparing to carry it away.

"Hey there, George," I yelled. "What are you doing
with the comfort? I thought you were going to put it away
till tomorrow."

George looked up and rumbled and his teeth showed
white in the lantern light.

"We mek haste to lock'm up Cap'm."

He got to his feet and the two boys hoisted the pole to
their shoulders. George picked up the lantern, then looked

back toward me and said: "If you want to see the comfort working, sah, you stop by tomorrow in the evening, when these Mosquito boy get paid."

The boys carrying the can laughed shrilly, and yelps of confirmation came from several places out in the dark. I thought of the old Sambos these people came from and their abiding love for drink. The Big Drunks of as late as a generation ago were mishla parties. For days in advance of these, circles of girls chewed manioc to change the starch to sugar and spat it into canoes to ferment. The parties were a sort of ceremonial debauch, with the whole village dipping into the canoe till all were unconscious. This distilled guaro that displaced the indigenous mishla was rotgut stuff, all raw spirit and tannin and fusel oil, and it hit them hard from the first half liter, but compared with mishla it was effete, hygienic pap. I wondered idly if the boys down there had ever heard of their ancestral beverage. I called to George again:

"I guess that stuff is better than mishla, huh, George?" I said.

All around out in the dark, people howled or hooted and commented pro or con.

"Right you are, sah," George called back. "Much stronger, and not anywhere near so nosty."

Then he slapped the can and said: "Well, get on, now," and the three of them moved away in their ring of dim light, the can swinging heavily on the pole and George rumbling down inside, in Spanish, as if the fat vowels felt good there:

"*El guaaa-ro. El alivo de los hom-bres*—the comfort of mankind!"

The Black Beach

It was on the black beach that I met Mrs. Ybarra. It was the long, lonesome, log-strewn stretch from Tortuguero to Parismina. You don't see many people on that beach. Perhaps the chances against our meeting reinforced the impression Mrs. Ybarra made on me and caused her to seem more noteworthy than she really was. That you must judge when you have learned the circumstances.

I was looking for nests of trunkback turtles. I had walked five miles and had found no sign—no fresh trail that was not clearly that of hawksbill or green turtle. Even the greens were scarce. There was just a sprinkling of early layers in the van of the big nesting migration—the "fleet," as the people on the beach call it—which was already long overdue. It was nearing noon of a flaming cloudless day and the land breeze had killed the trade wind.

Two miles back I had met the Siquirres dogs—the seasonally feral packs of curs that Paco had pointed out from the plane two days before. Each May or June the dogs gather on the beach from Siquirres and the other towns along the railroad far inland, called by some unknown cue to cross as much as thirty miles of jungle, marsh, and mangrove swamp and meet the fleet, and batten on turtle eggs for the season. There were eight dogs in the pack I met,

and they were hungry and irritable. They ran yapping before me for a while, as if they thought I was somehow to
blame for the lateness of the fleet, and then they dashed
off over the low dunes and disappeared among the coco
plums. Besides the dogs and a scurrying sand crab now
and then, I had seen no living thing on land.

Seaward there was little more—no boat to watch, no
cruising fin; no whitecaps, even, nor any bar or promontory to break the sweeping surf line. Once in a thousand
steps there came the thin, lost cry of a tern, hidden out
among the heat waves.

Once, for a little while, a black patch showed on the
burnished, blue-white swells just beyond the breakers
where a shoal of anchovies had come up from wherever
they had been to flip and play and circle at the surface. I
stopped to see what hungry things would gather from the
sea and the air, as they always gather about such schools.
Almost at once the jacks came—big, flat, gleaming five-
pounders that slashed and ripped at the edges of the an-
chovy cloud, knocking chunks of it into the air in showers
of chrome splinters; and sometimes throwing themselves
out, too, in short parabolas, head-over-tail, stiff and sheep-
ish-looking. I thought what I could do among the jacks
with a bass rod and a Johnson spoon.

The crying tern saw the shoal and came in to circle and
wail above it, never changing the sad key of its song. A
gray pelican sailed up silently from behind me, rose and
dropped head-first into the fish cloud and then emerged to
float with the scattering school and solemnly appraise the
catch in his sack, while the longshore drift carried him and
the anchovies slowly southward. Suddenly, in one split
second, the million fish sounded in mindless unison. At
once the tern caught a ballooning thermal with one thin

wing and soared off into the glare; and the pelican was left floating alone.

I shuffled on through the fine hot sand. It was light, powdery dust of pumice and black glass that let you sink ankle-deep. It was so hot it burned my shanks above my shoe tops. The beach was piled with stranded timber—immense, silver trunks of cedar and *laurel* and *cedro macho* from the Costa Rican rivers and mahogany from Panama or Nicaragua, stolen from the loggers by decades of June floods and then thrown back again onto the black beach by the wild seas that batter this open coast. No tropical beach is fun to walk on at cloudless, windless midday. This one, with its endless monstrous jetsam to send you weaving from the deep, hot dunes down into the brawling surf and back again, made following the narrow strip above high-water mark, where turtle trails are laid, a trying job. My ardor for trunkback nests was failing under the sun and I was on the point of crawling beneath a propped log to sleep out the midday calm when I saw what I had come after.

It was a short, broad-limbed V, deeply engraved in the beach above the tide zone. The open end of the wedge had been truncated by the lap of the last, highest wave, and the apex merged with a broad plowed and scuffed patch in the soft blown sand just seaward of the dune front. The limbs of the V—the trails to and from the disturbed patch—were nearly as wide as the wheel trail of a tractor, and indeed the whole system of marks seemed to show that a heavy, wheeled vehicle had come up from the sea, had sunk deep in the sand drift, and after a great deal of backing and filling and churning had returned to the water.

It was the nest of a trunkback. It was the first I had ever

seen but there was no mistaking it. It was the first ever recorded for Central America, but its significance to me far transcended that statistic. To me it was the long-sought land-sign of a sea creature I had looked for since child-hood—a monster of the deep ocean guided ashore one time in each year by the primal reptile drive to dig a hole in earth and drop in it the seeds of trunkbacks for tomorrow, and cover the hole with toeless flat feet, and pound back down to the sea never looking behind. It was the work of a water reptile pelagic as a whale or a plesiosaur and at home in the oceans of the world—the last vestige of land-craft left to a bloodline seabound for a hundred million years, and left then but to one sex for one hour on one night in the year.

You will gather that I am curiously, perhaps almost psy-chotically, susceptible to the color of the trunkback. For a while, then, what with my thoughts and the sun and the quaking air, I just stood and looked at the nest.

After a while the trance of lightheaded exultation ran out and I put down my camera bag and canteen and set about appraising the site where the turtle had worked. There was a great deal of it. A female trunkback often weighs a thousand pounds or more and is full of a fanati-cal kind of gland-given zeal that would almost pass for ingenuity. Everything she does is calculated, in a purely mechanistic sense of course, to keep her eggs from being dug up again, by either herpetologist or coatimundi. She can't hide the fact that she was out on the beach, so she confounds the egg-hunter with a plethora of clues. In this case the area of flung sand in which I had to prospect for the egg chamber was at least fifteen feet in diameter and roughly circular in outline. Since it offered no evidence, at least to my eye, by which the field for search might be narrowed down, I had to cover every square foot of it; and since the clutch of eggs might lie waist-deep beneath the sand, the job ahead was imposing.

I took up my egg stick. After making a few random test holes here and there, I began moving systematically back and forth across the site, punching as deeply as I could drive the stick. When I had completed a regular and closely spaced gridwork of holes and had found nothing, I began to realize that the slim section of cane that I had found effective enough in prospecting for the nests of hawksbills and green turtles was too feeble for the work at hand. To get down through the hard sand that lay below the surface drift I needed a pole with backbone—something I could plant and swing my weight on.

I began looking about the beach for something suitable. This was an open shore and a heavy sea washed it, and there was no dearth of driftwood, as I have said. I tested one silvery stick after another, but all were either crooked as a snake or punky and spineless from salt water and sun. I found a section of timber bamboo that was sound, but you don't split stuff like that with a pocketknife, which was the only tool I carried. Halfheartedly I trimmed and sharpened a leaf stem of coco palm, and this collapsed at the first thrust.

I wanted the nest badly, and with the mounting realization that I probably would not get it my frustration grew apace. I cursed my lack of foresight in not bringing a machete. I grabbed up a sphere of drifted pumice stone and tried to put an edge on my knife blade with it, but the rounded face of the stone collapsed like sugar candy and only polished the metal. In a peevish fit I threw the stone at the face of a *laurel* log and it went to pieces there.

Suddenly, a slight, blue feist dog burst from behind the

log and started shrieking at me, lifting its feet in indignation and looking backwards at intervals as if for support
from a source hidden from me by the rise of the log.

Then, for an instant, I saw a face above the six-foot loom
of the trunk, and then the face was gone. I ran around the
end of the log and saw a woman on horseback retreating
at a dead run in the direction from which she had come.
I could hear the splatting of the horse's feet in the wave
wash and I could see in the slant of the rider's back that
she was not party to the flight but was trying to stop and
turn the horse. It was the horse who was alarmed at the
sudden, unprecedented sight and stink of gringo behind a
log on the black beach—not Mrs. Ybarra.

Mrs. Ybarra no doubt took an unenthusiastic view of me
too. But she was a woman inured to the shocks of life on
this beach. She was not the sort to turn back because of a
stranger there, no matter how unaccounted for. She gradually dominated the horse and brought it to a grudging halt
a hundred yards down the beach and turned it. I could see
that it was an ash-colored *criollo* stallion—one of the tough,
runty, and cruelly selected remnant of the old Spanish
horse that somehow survived the odds against horseflesh
on this tropical shore and that now, salt-cured, parasite-
proof, and vampire-tolerant, and economical with its tis-
sue-water as a camel, will single-foot all night in sand fet-
lock deep. The horse of the Mosquitia is almost a breed
apart. Æsthetically it compares unfavorably with a true
horse, but it is right for its milieu.

The example under Mrs. Ybarra had the odd, ratlike face
and ewe-necked silhouette they all have. He came back
toward me under pressure, against his judgment, his eyes
rolling. He came because the will of his rider was stronger
than his will.

As she approached, Mrs. Ybarra steered her mount

down beach to pass well seaward of me, gripping the reins firmly and drumming at the horse's tight belly with her heels. She gave me a quick look.

"*Adios*," she said.

Adios said that way means you are going on by. In a matrix of circumstance such as this it becomes a bivalent greeting, a salutation with connotation that a parting will follow immediately. It is a hello-goodby, and a word that, as far as I know, has no counterpart in English or North American. Spanish can be shaded delicately. It is nowhere near so simple as my textbooks and teachers made out.

There was of course no reason at all why Mrs. Ybarra should not go on by. But at the moment she spoke I saw the pearly gleam of new turtle eggs in two arroba baskets swinging from her saddle; and this made it unthinkable that she should ride on and leave me with my dilemma.

So I said: "*Buenas tardes*," and the shift in salutation changed our relationship at once and made it a point of courtesy for her to rein up, a bit warily, and see what my intentions were.

She was not the sort of woman you would expect to see on this beach, even supposing you were expecting women of any sort. She was a short, turnip-shaped woman with a thin-lipped Madonna's face and a mass of snuff-colored hair piled under a man's old felt hat tied on with a scarf. She had spindly Spanish legs and a big bosom bound in by a bodice of muslin. She wore a brown cotton smock, and a skirt of the same stuff was cleverly tucked under and around her legs, because she rode astride and not side-saddle like the women in Honduras. Her racial origin and place in life were not evident from her appearance. Her skin was very dark, but she had nothing to do with the dark people of Tortuguero, who run mostly to Mosquito and Black Carib interbreeds with a sprinkling of black

creoles from Bluefields and San Andrés. She looked like no
Costa Rican I ever saw. Except for her almost black skin
and reddish hair, and for the shameless way she straddled
the high wooden packsaddle, she more closely approached
the kind of women you see in the mountains of Matagalpa
or of southern Honduras, where the century of hardship
the old revolutions brought bred thin-faced women with
more than their share of character. She had much in common with them and much in common with her horse. She
was weatherbeaten, but she had the quiet confidence that
goes with a full stomach.

"*Buenas tardes*," she said, stopping her horse. "The
widow of Ybarra from Panal, this side of Parismina."

I told her my name. I said I was studying the ways of
turtles. I motioned toward the trunkback nest.

"Do you know what kind of turtle did that?" I said.

"Why not? *Es de canal*—a trunkback."

"That's what I thought," I said. "How do you know?"

"Only a trunkback tears up the beach like that. All this
beach is torn up by trunkbacks. It's hard to ride except
near the water."

I looked up and down the beach and for the first time
noticed that the sand in front of the dunes had an oddly
uneven topography that was not part of the wind-piled
dune system, and not like any beach I had ever seen before.

"Some of that is where animals dig for eggs when the
fleet of green turtles comes, but mostly it's trunkbacks that
pile the sand like that. Like this nest here . . . But why
don't you go on a way? I saw several carey nests in the
light sand yonder, and some of green turtles—various. I
dug two." She patted the side of one of the egg baskets.

"I don't want hawksbill eggs," I said, "or green turtle either. I'm looking for trunkback eggs."

"They're not as good as carey eggs. They have a little taste."

"I don't want to eat them," I said. "I want to measure them."

She looked at me deprecatingly. "They're this big. *Así de grande.*" She cupped her hand to show me how big.

"I mean exactly. And I want to take pictures of them."

"They are very deep. A yard—yard and a half. The animals can't find them. Even the tigers. Even the Siquirres dogs that dig out all the rest don't try to dig trunkback eggs."

"I don't care how long it takes," I said. "I would dig all afternoon if I knew there was a nest there. Maybe this one scratched and went back. Loggerheads do that."

She studied the tumbled sand for a moment. Then she wagged her finger from side to side in front of her face in the gesture of negation that all Latins use.

"*Puso—*" she said. "*Ahí puso.*"

"But how do you find the nest?" I asked. "I've punched all around here and couldn't find a soft place anywhere."

Again she wagged her finger at me. "You didn't punch deep enough. There is no soft place in a *canal* nest. You just have to find it. Please, what time is it? Midday?"

I brushed the sweat-soaked sand from the face of my watch.

"A quarter after. Are you in a hurry?"

"Today the Spaniard pays the Mosquitos. I am going to collect a debt and I want to get there before they are all drunk. I saw the airplane Thursday, and they will all be drunk by dark."

I thought of the milk can of rum I had flown with and saw that she was probably right. The Spaniard she was talking about was Don Pedro, Yoyo's *mayordomo* at the Atlantic Trading Company at Tortuguero.

"How much is the debt?" I said.

"There are two of them. They add up to eight colones."

"All right, look. I'll pay you ten if you will help me find the turtle nest."

She looked at the sand in front of horse again, and then up at the sun. She sighed and swung a leg over the tall saddle frame and stepped to the ground.

"We will try it." She said it with no great enthusiasm.

She led the horse into the sprinkled shade of a ragged old mangineel, the only real tree anywhere on the foreshore, and tied the reins to a branch.

"That is a poison tree," I said.

"It doesn't molest horses."

"But how about your hands? You have to hold the reins."

"Don't worry. It doesn't molest me either. Only the juice, or the smoke when it burns."

"I wouldn't tie a horse to that tree for anything," I said.

"It's all right. You are a stranger here and haven't found yourself."

She drew a wasted sliver of a machete from a rawhide scabbard tied to the saddle. She walked back to the turtle nest and called to the feist and it came bouncing down from the beach grass, eager to serve her with all its talents. She leaned and scratched suggestively at the sand to interest the dog in the place.

"*Huevos*," she said.

I winced, because this word said by itself like that usually means something quite different; but the dog understood and began to dig in a crab hole six feet from the turtle nest.

"Don't be an imbecile," Mrs. Ybarra said. "Here—dig here!"

The dog dropped his ears, hurt by the tone of the words; then he moved over and started digging in the turtle nest.

"With green turtles and *careyes* Filin never deceives himself. With trunkbacks he doesn't serve. Let him dig here awhile. I have to go back there." She waved a hand toward the low scrub a hundred yards inland.

"*Bueno.*" I thought she was excusing herself from me and prepared to stay and give what encouragement I could to the dog.

"No—I have to cut a stick. You come too. You can climb better."

We pushed through the sea grapes and sea oats and coco plums, and behind the dunes we came to a coppice of tightly spaced saplings. We stopped and Mrs. Ybarra peered about in the dense thicket until she found what she wanted.

"*Aquel.*" She pointed into the dim interior of the thicket. "If you climb that *palito* and trim it, we can get it out."

I shinnied up the slim, smooth stem and trimmed off all the branches I could reach. Then I slid down and cut the trunk through at the ground and dragged it out into the clear. Mrs. Ybarra cut a five-foot section from the stem, skinned the bark from it, and tapered one end to a point.

"*Ya.*" She said. "Maybe with this."

When we got back, the feist had lost interest in the turtle nest and was digging out another sand-crab hole.

"He doesn't serve," Mrs. Ybarra said.

She planted the tip of the stick in the center of the nest and pushed. The point grated to a stop in the dense sand two feet down. She tried again a foot away, with the same result. She punched a dozen holes and from each the stick emerged only dusted with the fine sand. She stopped and studied the site again on hands and knees, plucking at each twig or bit of debris that protruded above the plowed surface. After a while she found a newly broken end of beach morning-glory stem, and when she pulled on this a good three feet of green vine came out of the sand.

"Maybe here," she said. "The *canal* buried the vine."

She took up the stick and probed carefully all around where the vine had been. Still the rod broke through no nest roof and came out smeared with no yolk. Finally she stopped and shook her head, and sweat silently.

"It is *fregada*, this question of the *canal* nests," she said.

She wiped her eyes with the backs of her forearms. Her hair was falling out from under her hat, and the sweat-stuck sand had frosted the dark shine of her face. I thought I could see misgiving in her expression. I thought she must be leaning toward my view that this was a trial nest without eggs, such as loggerheads make.

"I don't believe there's anything here," I said.

"Don't deceive yourself. *Aquí puso*—she laid here. It is sure. Always it is like this. The *canal* is—ooo—very big. Her leg is like this—" She measured against her own thigh. "She reaches to a great depth, and she is heavy and she packs the sand back with her belly, harder than it was before. And the worst is, she plows so much ground it is hard to locate the nest. If you do find the eggs they are too big to eat with comfort. It is not worth the trouble. But maybe if we both pushed on the stick— The place should be exactly there."

I have seen a water-witch point out the spot for a well with the judicious precision with which Mrs. Ybarra aimed the tip of her stick. She sighted as if she were aiming a rifle at the head of a snake.

"Exactly there," she repeated.

She stuck the point in the sand and we both leaned on the shaft. It broke with a snap and split back to our hands.

"It broke," Mrs. Ybarra said. "The wood was tender. Look, do you want to try any more? I think it will be easier if you go out at night and find the *canal* when she is laying and before she has covered. Any time when the moon is over the sea, not over the land. In the black sand pieces they come out every night—one, two, three—to lay."

I said I thought she was right. I dug in my pocket and from under the sand there brought out some Costa Rican bills. I counted ten colones and held them out to her, saying that I was grateful for her help and was sorry she had got so hot and sandy.

"Ah, no," she said. "I can't accept that. I said I would find the eggs. You owe me nothing. I'll reach the village in plenty of time."

"No, look—I stopped you. I'm going to put the money in your saddlebag."

I turned and walked toward the mangineel tree behind the screen of tall sea oats. My first sight of Mrs. Ybarra's horse was his feet waving and kicking in the air, all four of them. I ran toward him in sudden panic, burst through the grass, and saw him on his back writhing and jerking and bending his short, stiff backbone in impossible, convulsive arcs. The limb to which he had been tied was broken and the reins had tangled about the bit shafts. His contortions had pushed the saddle around onto his belly and broken loose most of the bundles, which were scattered about in the sand. The two baskets of turtle eggs had been dumped on the ground, and the horse was rolling in them.

"Come, quick, look at your horse," I yelled. "Quick! What is the matter with him?"

She came running.

"Oh, my sainted mother, is he scratching! Yes, my God, he is scratching! He always scratches when he is hot, and

I forgot to watch—and look at my *carga!* *A la—!* Get up! You! *Flojo!* Stand up!"

She seized a piece of driftwood and began pounding the horse on his unprotected underside. He stopped rolling and in awkward haste floundered to his feet and stood with flaring nostrils, ears back, and eyes rolling at his mistress, stung and puzzled at her attitude.

He was a frightful thing to see. The bridle was bunched at his chin. The saddle and the empty egg baskets and some bundles that had not broken their moorings hung beneath him, and a disheveled game rooster dangled from a cinch ring between his forelegs. His back and sides were heavily smeared with a thick, uneven mixture of egg yolks and whites and black sand, in which, here and there about his surface, leaves and rotting mangineel apples and empty turtle-egg shells were stuck. He looked as if a two-year-old child had made a frosting for him. He shook himself violently, but looked no better for it.

A feeling of despondency spread over me. This poor woman—what misery I had brought her! How utterly my stubbornness had wrecked her hopes and her day! I turned to her, in my shame ready to crawl, or to force on her every last colon I could claw out of my pockets.

She was laughing.

She was pointing at the horse with one hand and beating helplessly at the air with the other, and shaking with silent mirth. I looked at her narrowly, to make sure her joy was real and not a symptom of deep nervous shock. Suddenly she found her voice.

"What a barbarity!" she shrieked. "What a brutal animal! Oh, my sainted mother, what animal more brutal!"

She was so clearly delighted that I looked back at the horse with new eyes, and this time he looked funny to me too and I started to laugh. We both laughed for a long time.

After a while I said: "I am sorry. The blame is all mine. What can we do?"

"No," she said, "it doesn't matter. I only have to bathe the horse."

She began to untangle the bridle, stopping at intervals to bend over and shake and screech with laughter. I helped her unfasten the cinches and disengage the confu‹ sion of saddle and *carga*. She took the machete and cut some clumps of grass, which she doubled and bunched and bound to make a brush. She shed her shoes and smock and skirt and strode off to the surf clad only in a sacklike nether garment, leading the horse by the bridle.

I hurriedly made a crude copy of her grass brush; then I rolled up my trousers and followed her into the water.

Within fifteen minutes the little horse was clean, or nearly so. His blue barb skin showed through matted wet hair and only a few patches of coagulated yolk clung to him here and there. Mrs. Ybarra led him back to the tree and rubbed his back with handfuls of dry grass and spread on it the burlap saddle blanket. She tidied up the saddle a bit and I heaved it on the horse and fastened the cinches while she rearranged the *carga*. The game-cock was dead, but seemed remarkably intact for having been under a horse. Mrs. Ybarra chopped part way through his neck with the machete and hung the body low on the saddle to bleed on the ground. Then she slipped on her skirt and dropped her shoes in one of the baskets. She brushed at the sand on her arms and put on her smock, then swung herself into the saddle.

Once again I held out the thin sheaf of bills.

"*Vea*," I said cajolingly. "It was my fault that you lost the eggs and the cock died."

"*¡Qué va!* The cock was to kill, and there will be eggs enough. There is no lack of carey eggs and the fleet will not be long coming. Will you be going back now?"

I told her I was going on. I must have seemed depressed at the prospect, because she said:

"All right, there's a *cocal* [a coco fringe] no more than there—just a little way. You can get a *pipa* there [a drinking coconut], and there is shade. Then if you go on six miles there is another *cocal,* and my house is there. If you go that far, it is almost certain that I can show you a *canal* tonight, laying on the high tide."

I thanked her and said I couldn't go that far. Without her noticing, I slipped the money into the basket where her shoes were.

"I'm going to dig another *canal* nest," I said. "I don't believe this one laid."

"Ay-eeee," she yelped. "You will kill yourself for nothing. She laid. This one laid. Right there. No *canal* nest will be easier to dig than this one."

"O.K.," I said. "But I'm not going to dig here any more. I'll be seeing you." ·

She gave me a look of what I think was pity, then set her mount in motion with her bare heels, guided him into the surf-wash, and squeezed him into the mincing single-foot he would hold all the way to Tortuguero. Then she turned and waved.

"*Adios, pues,*" she said.

The little feist saw her leaving and ran to take the lead. A first sudden breath of the afternoon breeze wiped the gleam from the water and turned it black. The hoof-splash of the horse faded in the distance, and when it was gone the only sounds were the roll of the waves and the fitful piping of the tern as it slipped and tilted on the swelling trade wind.

The Paradox Frog

To the Caribs it was Iere—the place where the hummingbirds were. It is also the land of the asphalt lake and where steelband music started. It is the last of the islands going south, and the happiest of all, and there is sweet country in it that there will not be time to tell about. But to me that misty dawn, heading eastward toward Toco on the windward road, Trinidad was most of all the home of the paradox frog.

I was glad of the way the world was, that morning, and it was not just the tropical day beginning or the thought of the batalí or the long turtle beaches ahead. There was going to be sand to walk all right, but that was not what buoyed me. The special part of the start of that day was the thought of the paradox frog.

It was just a notion of course, a sort of half-professional caprice, and not the real reason for my being there at all. It was the sea turtles that had brought me to Trinidad, and the good beaches and the places the turtle fishermen lived set my course and determined my stops. But that morning, rolling down to Toco, the mist in the manifold seemed to supercharge the little Austin 40, and the air had a fine faraway smell, and the lazy waves of early morning climbed the gray rocks quietly, and I was feeling good; and a good part of it was the prospect of seeing and of hearing the song of the legendary Pseudis, the paradox frog.

I have always liked frogs. I liked them before I ever took up zoology as a profession; and nothing I have had to learn about them since has marred the attachment. I like the looks of frogs, and their outlook, and especially the way they get together in wet places on warm nights and sing about sex. The music frogs make at night is a pleasant thing, full of optimism and inner meaning. It is more symbolic than the singing of birds. There is more virtuosity in the song of the mockingbird; but they say the mockingbird sings to establish his living territory, to announce to other male birds his claim to a parcel of property. The song is sweet all right, but the motive is mundane.

Now, the frog on the other hand sings for the sake of the female frog, to lure and guide her. The male sits in the pond edge and croaks or whistles or buzzes or roars, according to his kind, when something mystic outside and inside tells him it is time for new frogs, and his calling draws the females there, and this way frogs are provided for the new year. The singing of the hermit thrush is a sweet blustering. The song of a frog is a shout for the flowing on of the life stream.

This is the philosophic background of my whim to hear Pseudis. More specifically I was interested because I collect frog songs in my head as some people save stamps in a book. More sentimentally, I was interested because Pseudis is a queer frog that caused a great deal of excitement among oldtime zoologists and was cited as proof of all sorts of lurid notions, including the idea that frogs gave rise to fish instead of coming from fish as today we are sure they did.

As everybody knows, one of the typical parts of being a

frog is going back to the water to lay eggs. The eggs hatch into tadpoles and, with luck, the tadpoles become frogs again and leave the water and grow until they are a good deal bigger than the tadpoles they came from. This is one of the main features of being an amphibian. There are all kinds of exceptions of course, but the majority of frogs do it this way.

The paradox frog departs from this plan in two ways. In the first place the grown frog stays on in the water and lives out his life among his own aquatic larvæ. And what is even more peculiar, the fully grown frog is much smaller than the huge, high-tailed, potbellied tadpole that he was as an infant. The emerging froglet shrinks at metamorphosis and never gets back anything like his larval size. The adult frog has a body little more than two inches long, tapered and sharp-headed for swimming and with small arms and powerful hind legs with the toes webbed clear out to the tips. Besides this it has a long, opposable thumb like no related species anywhere in the New World, and it uses this to help cram food into its mouth or in grasping twigs or pads to support itself at the surface or hold to the bottom.

In a superficial way the mature paradox frog looks a lot like Xenopus, the completely aquatic clawed frog of Africa, the species now often known as "pregnancy frog" because of its wide use in human pregnancy tests. The tadpole of Pseudis looks like the famous Mexican axolotl, the salamander that spends its life as a breeding larva, a sexually mature infant, respiring by gills and never emerging into the arid land that surrounds its natal ponds except occasionally in tamales in the Toluca market. To look at a Pseudis tadpole you might think you had one of these sexually impatient larvæ, but you would be wrong. Like the axolotl, the Pseudis tadpole probably has something wrong with its pituitary gland, or with its thyroid, or with both; but despite its immense size it has never been known to reach sexual maturity before exchanging its gills for lungs and its high-finned tail for muscular swimming legs.

It was this big tadpole of the small paradox frog's that persuaded early naturalists that the frog was the one that hatched from the egg, and the tadpole the mature animal. Some went even farther and, deluded by the fishlike shape and high fan fin of the tadpole, and by the long, coiled vegetarian's gut that showed through the belly wall and suggested the belly sucker of a clingfish, decided that the stage into which the frog transformed was actually a fish. It was this supposed eccentricity that suggested the species name *paradoxus,* and when later the error was corrected, the false interpretation was memorialized in the generic name *Pseudis.*

In 1880 Samuel Garman at the Museum of Comparative Zoology at Harvard wrote a paper briefly reviewing the folly of his predecessors and calming the last restlessness about Pseudis by stating plainly that there was nothing queer about the frog except that it had oversized tadpoles. Since that time a long line of naturalists has seen and admired Pseudis, but strangely little seems to have been written about its life history. I made an effort to dig up something, for instance, on its breeding habits with no success at all. I found nothing on what it ate or on where and how the eggs were laid and fertilized, and, most disappointing of all, there was nothing on its song. Not even a statement or implication as to whether it had a song.

Frogs sing because they are only about half completed as land animals, and most of them have to go back to the water to lay and fertilize their eggs, and the song is the thing that calls the gang in for the frog-making bee. But Pseudis *lives* in the water—the males and the females too, and you'd think they could get together whenever the notion struck them, with no need to sing or shout or make a community project of it.

But the song of the frog is very likely the oldest voice among vertebrates—frog ancestors were probably singing long before our line got its warm blood—and frogs cling to their song stubbornly. There are a few mute species, a few, for instance, that live in roaring torrents where a song would never be heard if they had one, but on the whole the way they live makes a voice a useful thing to frogs and they hold on to it. Even the completely aquatic clawed frog has a sort of voice, and though its females need no summons to return to the ancestral mating place the clawed frog sings on none the less, in a quaint, self-conscious way. As I said, Pseudis lives much like the clawed frog, and though I had never asked anyone who knew, I was pretty sure it would have a voice too, and I wanted to hear it sing. So that morning on the Toco road, though I was heading for the southeastern shore and what I could learn about sea turtles there, it was St. Ann's in Mayaro that I kept looking at on the map, because it was there I would find the paradox frog.

First of all I would have to find the manager of St. Ann's, Bernard de Verteuil. Bernard was the grandson of the de Verteuil who wrote the big book on Trinidad, and he not only was a good naturalist himself—everyone told me—but had the rare sort of sympathetic heart that kept him restless as long as every vagrant, whim-ridden character who turned up had not found what he was after. No matter what it was you wanted to do—catch an anaconda, shoot an agouti, take pictures of a scarlet-ibis rookery— Mr. de Verteuil was the one to see. Everyone told me he was specially tolerant of herpetologists with a desire to know the paradox frog. That was why I was bound to be at St. Ann's before dark, and why this east-coast turtle census was filled with special zest.

From Matelot to Grand Riviere the windward shore is one promontory after another, with sand beach only in short arcs at the cove-heads. I stopped and looked at all of these little beaches, not with much hope of finding turtle sign, but just because it makes me uneasy to pass up any beach; and because it was good to walk on the slim, clean crescents in the quiet morning with the dark woods rising beside you and the short, rock-herded remnants of the ground swell gleaming slantwise down the narrow cove and bursting in low, quick crashes at your feet. I was mostly pleasuring myself, as I say, but at San Souci I did find a couple of old trails, too big for hawksbills, too narrow and shallow for the usual trunkback, but right for either green or loggerhead. One of the nests was lost under a welter of tracks of men and burros, and the other had been dug out and the eggs taken away. Cove-head beaches are nearly always poor turtling ground, but there is a sequestered charm about them that makes it hard to pass them by.

When I came to Shark River I stopped the car at a wide place in the road shoulder on the Matelot side of the high bridge—just where I had stopped the night before when I saw the odd eye shining. I got out and looked at the place with the new feel of daylight. The ravine was even deeper than it seemed by flashlight rays, and the river, still rumbling with last night's rain, looked even farther down.

It was as a heavy shower was ending that I had come that way the night before. Even inside the car I had heard the sound of the water before I saw the bridge, and then the upper works took shape and in the drawn-out rays of the headlights an eye showed like a little hot coal out somewhere between the rails. It was a red eye, with too much sparkle for a frog and too little for a crocodile or cayman or moth. There was too much body to it for a spider, too little heat for a goatsucker, too little yellow or green for a mammal of any kind. All this is how it seemed to me by the lights of the car.

I stopped as quickly as I dared, backed onto the shoulder, and slipped on the headpiece of my flashlight. Shutting off the headlights, I leaned out and shot the long, tight beam of my five-cell hunting light at the eye. It looked just as it had before; it was no eye I could place or match in my memory. I sat and studied it and cogitated, and as I watched I realized that it was moving. It moved ever so slowly, but even fifty yards away as I was, there could be no doubt that it was, steadily and with evident purpose, crossing the bridge. Not crossing it in the usual sense, as I was about to do, from end to end, but from one side to the other, from rail to rail. To me this seemed a strange way to cross a bridge, out there in lonely space on the tall trestle, a world of roaring darkness above the rain-mad river.

But perverse as its behavior was, the thing that hit me hardest about the eye, grieved me, really, was my inability to identify it. Shining the eyes of wild things is one of my hobbies, and naming them from their eye-shine one of my accomplishments. You may regard it as a minor accomplishment, and indeed I have never claimed that it added much to my professional or cultural stature, but all the same I feel pretty bad when I can't spot the owner of a shined eye—at least assign it to its major taxonomic category.

So the puzzling eye out there on the bridge was a kind of challenge, and I sat and thought hard about it for quite a while, but I could make nothing of it. The eye fitted nowhere in my imagination or experience. Part of the trouble was the distance—it was too great for me to get an impression of the height of the glow above the roadbed. There was no way to judge whether whatever it belonged to was an inch tall or a yard. But even if I had known this I should never have guessed the answer. I simply lacked the background. The creature the eye turned out to belong to was too far out of character and setting. There was no precedent for what it was doing, and no logic in it either.

I gave up the game in disgust and, holding the flashlight steady to keep the glow alive, walked out on the bridge to learn what had so confounded me. It was not until I was nearly close enough to reach out and touch the eye that I saw it belonged to a shrimp.

You see how unreasonable it was? It wasn't fair. I had seen plenty of shrimp eyes, hundreds of them, all kinds, but all properly submerged. Their eyes shine up at you that way, but it is a mild, muted shining, and the medium is what you expect of a shrimp. I had even caught shrimps quite like this one—prawns I suppose they really are—but always decorously covered by clear creek water. Never up on a teetery trestle over a torrent fresh from the mountain and fighting for the sea. Never walking with eight-legged poise across a bridge, at right angles to the traffic stream. There was no traffic really, but if it should have come it would have been at right angles. I squeezed the last drop of extenuation from the circumstances and it helped some, but I was still hurt.

I should have caught the shrimp of course; I can see that now. I should have put it with the frogs I had in a bag tied to my belt. If I had done that I could tell you exactly what kind of shrimp it was, the genus surely and maybe the species. But I never laid a finger on the animal, and the best I can say is that it was one of the fat, cylindrical, shortlegged, and utterly succulent fresh-water prawns that live in clear streams all around the Caribbean. They are among my favorite victuals, actually, and I should have found out long ago what shrimp men call them. I have speared and dipnetted them in streams in Honduras, Nicaragua, and Panama and caught what I took for the same thing in Jamaica, and ordered them in Havana at La Zaragozana, six on a platter in a bold design, red-boiled and seductively half-shucked, laid out on a bed of watercress sloshed with Russian dressing. Scrape away most of the Russian dressing and dribble on lime, grind on new black pepper till the red fades, provide yourself with a meter of Cuban bread and a liter of lager, and, man, the thought fairly runs away with me. . . .

That much I can tell you. It is not like having the specimen in hand, but it was that general kind of shrimp. The Cubans call them *langostinos;* the texture of their meat is like lobster; they don't occur in Florida, and they are a good excuse for making a Caribbean tour.

As I looked at that one out there on the bridge that night, I thought neither of its specific name nor how good it was to eat. I only wondered how it got there, forty feet up smooth beams above the furious river, and where it was going. And though it was clear I could never know where it came from or how it came to be where it was, I could surely wait and watch and see where it went.

I leaned against the rail and turned out my light and waited in the dark. In a couple of minutes I switched on the light for a second—for long enough to see the shrimp still walking straight ahead, fast for a shrimp and true on its course toward the far side of the bridge, which was now only a foot away. Again I waited with the light out, and the next time I turned it on, the shrimp had reached the edge of the bridge and was perched motionless at the very brink of the drop, consulting his tropisms, or gathering his courage, or whatever it was. To be sure of seeing the outcome I sneaked quickly across the road, but before I reached the shrimp its plan had formed, and with a few short, reflexive jerks of its walking legs it launched its small body into the black abyss. I stepped to the rail and turned the light beam down into the far rush of the water; but there was no sign there to show where the white flood had closed over its vagrant child and no clue to tell me why such things should be. Sunk in meditation, I walked back to the car, turned it around with scrupulous care, and went home to bed.

The next morning, on the way to Toco, it was with some slight, undefined hope that I stopped at the bridge—a vague feeling that the light of day might somehow show cause or logic in the actions of the shrimp, or at least reveal how it might have climbed to the bed of the bridge. But I walked from one end of the span to the other, examining the abutments and piers and underpinnings, and saw nothing that relieved the mystery. I rested my elbows on the rail and looked down into the tumbling stream and thought and figured till more figuring seemed useless. Then I walked back to the car and drove off toward Grand Riviere, more petulant than you might suppose over the monstrous atypicality of a creature with no backbone.

It was just before I reached Toco that I found the trunkback nest. I stopped the car when I saw white beach through a grove of trees. I got out and waded across a stream between the road and the shore, pushed through a strip of low scrub, and almost at once saw the fresh, deep-cut tracks of a nesting turtle. The two tracks came together forty feet up from the mid-tide waves, just at the edge of the morning-glories. I needed no steel tape to see that the track was too wide for any reasonable loggerhead or green, and the lay and unequal lengths of the ingoing and outgoing trails showed that it had been made on the high ebb of the current tide.

There was no good record of trunkback nesting in Trinidad. In fact it is surprising how few really definite, reliable published accounts there are of any sea turtle nesting anywhere in the Caribbean. There was little reason to doubt that trunkbacks came to Trinidad shores, but when you can't find such data in print, they don't do you much good. When I was gathering information for a book on turtles a few years ago, a careful search turned up only two documented cases of trunkbacks nesting in American waters—one an old record for Jamaica and the other Ross Allen's recent observations on Flagler Beach in Florida. As I say, I would have bet trunkbacks laid on Trinidad beaches, but that was not enough. Now I knew.

You saw in the chapter on the Black Beach that trunkback nests are not easy to dig out even when you know where they are. Well, this time I was lucky. Also, this time I had a five-foot length of old automobile brake rod with a T-shaped bend in one end to make pushing it into the sand easy. This is the best divining rod for turtles that you can have.

I studied the rumpled patch where the two trails came together. In spite of her huge size, the turtle had scuffed only a small area in concealing the site of the egg pit—a place no more than five or six feet across. I selected a spot at random, planted the tip of the rod, and pushed. The steel sank with grating reluctance for a couple of feet, then broke free and slid nearly two feet farther; and when I drew it out, the last ten inches were thickly coated with sand. The sand stuck there because the steel was sticky with the insides of turtle eggs.

I laid down the rod and picked up a hand trowel and started digging. It was just over three feet down to the topmost egg, but it seemed a good deal farther and took a long time to get there. I worked slowly because I wanted to dissect out the nest by the feel of the sand and try to get some measurements of the cavity just as the turtle had dug it; but there turned out to be too little difference between the walls of the pit and the filling, and I had to give up that project. I finally got down to the eggs and took out fifty, lining them all up in their order of size and measuring them, then selecting a few to take away. The eggs were more like tennis balls than like golf balls or loggerhead eggs. The average diameter of the fifty was just over two inches—well within the size range for the eggs of the Pacific trunkback and for those Ross Allen got in Florida. The size alone was enough to show that it was indeed a trunkback that laid them, but another feature of the clutch made this even more sure. While the great majority of the eggs were, as I said, two-inch fistfuls, there were on the top of the heap a few tiny, shelled globes, the smallest of which were no bigger than marbles. Most of these had no yolks—only white enclosed in a shell. It was as if the turtle had finished up the batch with some white left over, and instead of discarding it had made up a few pointless, yolkless eggs for the children, as cooks sometimes do with biscuits, and had laid them along with the rest. This extreme range from fingertip size to the diameter of a Mexican five peso piece has been noticed before by people who have found the nests of the trunkback of the Pacific and Indian oceans.

By the time I had finished measuring and admiring the eggs—performing my "act of immoderate veneration," as Frances Young calls such specialized seizures—the haze had burned off and there was light enough to take a picture of the eggs and the position of the nest on the beach. After that I put the eggs back in the hole and covered them up, picked up my things, and waded the creek back to the car.

In Toco I stopped and talked with a man named Hulder who had been suggested as a source of turtle lore. He seemed to know a great deal, in a practical sort of way. He knew the batalí and confirmed what other fishermen had told me about it, including the fact that it never came up on the beaches to lay. Like all the other turtle people I had talked to, in both Trinidad and Tobago, he called the trunkback "Orinook turtle," and, like the rest, the reason he gave was the belief that trunkbacks come to the islands from the mouths of the Orinoco.

I asked him why he thought this. The trunkback is a powerful swimmer, ranging the seas of the warmer parts of the world, and is the last of all sea turtles that I would consider calling by the name of a fresh-water river, even a redoubtable river like the Orinoco. I told Mr. Hulder this, and he said that was one way of looking at it, but the Trinidad trunkbacks came from the Orinoco all the same. In May and June the rainy season begins on the mainland east of the Andes, and the river rises and floods its banks and flushes out fallen trees and mats of trash and floating island and rafts of hyacinths. The flood from the many Orinoco mouths is so strong it shoulders aside the ocean current flowing westward from Africa and washes Trinidad and strands all sorts of jetsam there. Much of the river water goes westward into the Gulf of Paria, and the southern coast gets most of the continental debris, but some is carried up between Trinidad and Tobago and stranded on the east coast of the island. It is at this time— May and June—that the trunkbacks show up, and the con- clusion is that the Orinoco current brings them. This is why the trunkback is known in Trinidad as the Orinook turtle.

I don't know how much bearing the Orinoco flood really has on the arrival of trunkbacks in the island. It is possible, I suppose, that at certain times they may be abundant around the delta of the river and may even be spread about from there by the seasonal currents of fresh water. But I don't really believe there are any more trunkbacks about the Orinoco mouths than anywhere else. It seems more reasonable to attribute the synchronous arrival of turtles and current to the fact that the trunkback nesting season happens to coincide with the rainy season in northeastern South America.

In Costa Rica the trunkbacks begin their nesting in May—earlier than any other turtle—and being to taper off in late June. I believe that their hauling out in May and June on the shore of Trinidad and Tobago, when the fresh water is moving by, is just a coincidence made to seem like cause and effect by the fact that South American animals actually do come over with the Orinoco flood-rafts. The big side-necked turtle, Podocnemis—a freshwater turtle inhabiting South American rivers—does strand on the beaches of Trinidad from time to time. It seems likely that the idea that the big, strange-looking trunkback comes from the mainland somehow grew out of the occasional strandings of the big, strange-looking Podocnemis, which really does come from there.

It is certainly little wonder that the animals and plants of Trinidad are almost wholly South American. Even if the present fauna and flora do not date from the time the island was cut off from the mainland you have only to look at the mainland waifs that come to Trinidad in June to see that colonization by Venezuelan life has been going on pretty continuously ever since that time. Not only is the overwater distance short—only a few miles at the narrowest part of the Serpent's Mouth, as the channel is called—but the wet-season current is fast and steady and the hazards of immersion in sea water are lessened by the lower salinities of the river water. There must be a continuous stream of small live things ferried across inside logs or on mats of trash. Besides the side-necked turtle, I heard reports of the stranding of lizards and snakes of several kinds, and one fisherman told me he found in one big mass of driftwood a mangrove dog and a wet, hungry little monkey.

Most of these involuntary migrants probably die in the surf or in the shore scrub, or live their lives out without finding a mate to help exploit their foothold; but through the ages the chances for successful colonization must be great. For whatever reason, Trinidad is biologically a piece cut out of Venezuela. Even so, I doubt if the trunkbacks come from there.

I hid some of my skepticism from Mr. Hulder, and we parted on good terms, after he had promised to send the next batalí he got to the fisheries office in Port of Spain, to be shipped to me in Florida. I took the Toco Main Road back the way I had come three days before, passing Morne Cabrite, crossing the Tompire River, and stopping briefly in Matura to look for a turtle man I could not find.

Approaching Sangre Grande from the northeast, the road runs for several miles through a fine mora forest, a kind of woods almost peculiar to Trinidad, and the second largest of several such tracts in the island. If you like forests on any basis whatever, these tracts of mora are one of the best things to see in Trinidad.

As you probably know, one of the striking features of the usual broad-leafed evergreen forest of the tropics—the rain forest—is the great number of different kinds of trees in it. In each acre of mature rain forest there may be several dozen different kinds of big trees, and it is rarely possible to look about and get the impression that any one kind is predominating in the fight for space and light. In fact the whole idea of "dominance" in the sense in which beech and maple or oak and hickory "dominate" in forests of the eastern United States, or magnolia, laurel oak, blue beech, and hop hornbeam in a northern Florida hammock, turns out to be applicable in the mixed woods of the lowland tropics only in a tenuous, statistical way. Why there should be so many kinds of trees in the rain forest, all apparently doing the same things in the same place and way—all competing among themselves for what seems to be the same set of emoluments—has not been satisfactorily explained, at least not to me; but it is typical of the broad-leafed evergreen forest all over the tropical world.

It is typical, but not invariable. Once in a while the mixed forest gives way to a type that, though similar in appearance, and growing in identical terrain, may be built almost wholly of one kind of tree. In some of these so-called "single-dominant" forests one species may make up eighty to ninety per cent of the large trees, and may predominate in all the lower levels of the forest as well, right down to a head-high thicket of its own saplings or a continuous carpet of its seedlings. Such a woods is the marvelous mora forest of Trinidad.

The tree in this case is *Mora excelsa*, a species common as an occasional member of the rain-forest community of northern South America, especially in the Guianas, but rarely found in pure stands of any size except in Trinidad. When you enter an undisturbed piece of Trinidad mora woods, on a trail made with tact and discretion, there is the same look and feel to the interior as in the mixed forest of the mainland. There are differences in the architecture that a plant ecologist would notice, but they are subtle and do not greatly modify the atmosphere of the place. All the life-form groups are there, all the different ways of making a vegetable living. There are green plants that feed themselves and know the only real independence there is in this world, and there are the saprophytes and parasites that feed as second-handedly as any animal; there are the species that stand on their own feet, the trees and shrubs and herbs, and the kinds that depend on other plants to provide them with a high place in which to fight for their light ration—the perching epiphytes, and the vines, lianas, and creepers that have no bones in their legs, the stranglers that start like vines, asking only support, and then slowly steal around the bodies of their hosts and finally crush and smother them and take over even their ghostly silhouettes when they are dead and rotted away.

You see there, too, the sorting out of the various elements of the forest into levels, which elsewhere you have come to look for as a special mark of the rain forest. This stratification is, if anything, even more marked here than in the broad-leafed forests of the mainland. The tree-crowns group at three levels, the lower two raggedly, the topmost evenly. Unlike the mixed rain forest of the Trinidad lowlands, in which the top canopy is broken, and scattered giants stand far above the general level, it is the upper level of the mora forest that closes the community in. The roof is a layer of crowns that fit together like broken tiles. Seen from above, they make a vast plateau of foliage one hundred and fifty feet high, an undulating sea of leaves, green when mature, tan when the growth-flush is on. On the flight from Port of Spain to Tobago you pass over several places in which mora stands side by side with mixed forest, and you see how sharply the smoothly billowing mora top contrasts with the broken roof of the other.

In the interior of this tight-roofed place the ceiling closes in some eighty feet above your head and there is perpetual gloom. In this unending twilight you see the main factor that keeps out other kinds of trees and maintains the pure stand—the exclusive society—of mora.

Mora produces an abundance of big, heavy, beanlike fruits with an unusually high rate of germination. The seedlings take hold and grow rapidly in the darkest recesses of the understory and produce a corps of saplings that stand around ready to spring into any break that may appear in the ranks of their elders. According to Trinidad foresters, the seeds of none of the other lowland forest trees of the island are able to sprout, grow, and compete in the twilight of the mora woods. The community is thus a closed one, jealously replacing all casualties with its own kind and keeping its freehold inviolate till some change in climate or topography disrupts the initial fitness of the site, or until man moves in with ax and fire.

You may have galloped ahead and begun to wonder why all lowland Trinidad is not covered with mora. Ecologists who have studied the nature of the relationship between mora and mixed forest in the island say that this relationship is just what you would expect—a slow, steady retreat of the many-form type before the killing shade at the advancing mora edge. Why then, you reasonably ask, are there any other kinds of woods left? Is it that mora is a brand-new institution, a recently evolved, aggressive plant just now by chance beginning to take over?

That is pretty close to the answer. Mora is not brand-new, but it is a new arrival in Trinidad, speaking in the grand terms of geological time. Until a short while ago, in late Pleistocene, maybe 75,000 to 100,000 years back—before crustal movements had cut it off as an island—Trinidad was part of an old South American borderland on which the grassy Venezuelan plains they call llanos extended clear up to the foothills of the northern range of mountains. When the connection with the mainland was broken, Trinidad was probably almost completely covered with llanos. But there soon came a climatic change that favored the development of forests, and the first forest type to come into the island and replace the grasslands was a slightly more open version of the widespread mixed evergreen forest of the mainland. Mora took longer. It is peculiarly slow in getting about. Its seeds are cumbersome—no wind can blow them far and no bird carries them about. They grow where they fall, and this is mostly under the parent tree. Barring hurricanes, then, or transportation by the Indians, who grate flour from the seeds, no mora can hope to send its offspring farther afield than beneath the twigs of its most widespread branches, and the species will characteristically travel only a few feet in each generation. It has been calculated that, migrating this way, mora has spent sixty thousand years moving from the edge of Trinidad nearest the mainland, where the first seeds probably came in as beach drift, to the farthest point it has reached. Perhaps, then, the reason lowland Trinidad is not one big mora forest is that there has just been too little time since a forest climate replaced the old savanna climate of the Pleistocene.

I wandered about in the mora forest for a long time feeling the dim cool, looking at familiar shapes and devices in the strange flora, wondering how much difference the rain-forest animals see between a single-dominant and mixed-dominant woods. In spite of the similar structure the two must be quite different as places in which to live and find something to eat. So far there is not much in the journals about this. I hope there will be, before the woods are all cut down.

In the town of Sangre Grande I wondered briefly what dreadful thing had happened to make the Spaniards call the place Big Blood; and after some shouting at people on street corners I finally found the Eastern Main Road going south and turned into it. As I was striking out in the new direction I heard a shrill whistle and, looking back, saw a uniformed policeman waving his arms at me. I stopped, uneasy, as a policeman always makes me, and backed toward this one. He approached with an imposing lack of haste, stopped at the side of the car, and looked at me with little or no expression in his face. He was a big one, the color of oil-finished walnut.

"What is the difficulty which you are having?" he said.

"Well, none—now," I said apologetically. "I was looking for the Eastern Main Road. There weren't any signs."

"Quite right," the officer said. "Most people wishing the Eastern Main Road know which it is." He made a sweeping gesture down the road the way the car was headed. "This is the Eastern Main Road," he said.

"I was pretty sure this was it. I was going that way," I managed to point out.

The officer stepped back and with a short salute dismissed me. "Well, now you can proceed with confidence," he said.

I thanked him and drove off, with the relief you feel when you have made a clean disengagement from a cop. I kept going southeast for a long time, through places with a high proportion of East Indian in the population, passing through Upper Manzanilla and five miles beyond striking the coast again just below Manzanilla Bay, opposite Brigand Hill, at the upper end of the cocal.

The cocal is a twelve-mile strip of coconut grove that grew up by chance a hundred and fifty years ago when a ship loaded with coconuts was wrecked offshore. The cocal extends along the straight, low coast from Manzanilla to Point Radix, occupying most of the narrow band of dry ground between the great Nariva Swamp on one side and the Atlantic or Caribbean, or whatever you call it, on the other. The road ran along among the palms just above the beach. The water looked dark and I judged it was discolored from the Orinoco current, since clumps and rafts of debris and yellowed water hyacinths were drifting offshore or tumbling in with the breakers. The beach and ocean were nearly always in view through the coco grove, and in spite of the dark water it was a pleasant view, and a pleasant place to be.

I had gone only a short way when I noticed ten or twelve people standing out on the beach, all staring toward the sand just above the wash of the breakers. There was something about the assemblage—not much more than an aura, really—that made me slow down and look at it closely. As I watched, a man in the group drew back an arm and threw something at the spot they were all looking at, then ran up into the edge of the grove, scratched together an armful of husks and sticks, and ran back to join the others, who were still staring at the ground.

I shall not try to make you believe that this set of circumstances—this fragment of action out there on the open seabeach—meant *snake* to me. But it meant something. It must have, or I should never have stopped. And maybe it did mean snake. When you have keyed your senses to searching for snakes through as long a time as I have, you acquire an eye for them that seems to the unversed to border on the occult. You not only learn to tell a snake on

the road from a perfectly snake-like piece of cast tire
bead, but with no conscious effort you snatch details of
color, pattern, and form and make split-second identifica-
tions of species, when a layman is still insisting it was a
twist of orange peel you passed, or a dead cat. This is one
of the refinements of a specialized calling. Unless you have
looked for snakes on the road, dead snakes or live ones,
nighttimes or by day, at slow speeds in fair weather or fast
in the rain, for years and years—well, there are reflexes
in this world that you never dreamed of.

One of the snap appraisals the constant snake-hunter
makes is that which spots the snake-killing congress. There
is something diagnostic about the attitudes of human beings encountering a snake which a person like me, sensible
to every fleeting clue that might aid his perennial quest,
can recognize as far as he can see it—the fixed, downward
stare, the half-aggressive, half-recoiling postures, the
quick, sidelong searching of the ground for a stick or suitable missile, the upraised arm, the clutching of young and
the beating away of dogs, the grave, unhappy mien of the
most responsible male, and if you are near enough for details, the faces full of the old primate dudgeon that legless,
long, and undulating creatures should live on the pleasant
earth. I have collected many a fine specimen because I
could tell the stance and aspect of a man about to kill a
snake a quarter of a mile away.

It's nothing, really. The capacity some show for naming
makes and models of cars passing head-on is more mys-
tical.

So, it was the suggestive look of that bunch of Trini-
dadians out on the beach that made me slow the car, pull
off the road, and get out and go over to see what they were
looking at. As I emerged from among the palms, I met a
young man running up after more stuff to throw. I asked

Left: *Basiliscus plumifrons,* a very fancy arboreal lizard, Tortuguero, Costa Rica. *Below*: *Agalychnis callidryas,* the most ornate treefrog of the Caribbean coast, in a private moment.

Above: leatherback (trunkback) nesting at Matina, Costa Rica. *Below*: young hawksbill, Los Roques, Venezuela. (Photo by Larry Ogren)

him what the excitement was about. He said it was a snake.

Even alerted by intuition as I had been, I was surprised that a snake should be on the beach. I asked what kind of a snake it was. The man said it was a kind that came up with the trash from the mainland. They came mostly in the south, he said, but every year a few came up here too, and they were deadly poisonous and ruined the bathing.

Confident now that my joining the group would be a pardonable intrusion—a crisis over a snake makes all men brothers—I hurried down and pushed through the half-circle of watchers and saw a small, fat snake struggling to hide itself in a pile of wave-thrown hyacinths, while a man with a flexible stem of bamboo kept trying to rake it out into the clear to be pounded with coco shells. I had time to decide it must be a Hydrops, a kind of completely harmless watersnake that is common along the adjacent lowlands of South America. But there was no time to move in and grab it before a frenzied little dog broke loose from its mistress—a well-proportioned creole girl in a small bathing-suit—streaked over to the snake and with one strike and flip of its jaws threw it fifteen feet out into the water.

I quickly took off my shoes and rolled up the legs of my trousers and stood waiting for the snake to come up or be washed back to shallow water, but neither happened. I waded out and felt around on the bottom, as near as I could judge where the snake had sunk, and the dog paddled out and tried to help. The snake never came up, and I decided that the dog had killed it with that single lightning shake; and the water was too tea-colored from the jungle leaf-mold for anything on the bottom to show. I was pretty sure it was a Hydrops, and still think so, even though I can find no mention of Trinidad in statements of the range of this snake.

When I finally gave up the search and came out of the water, the people seemed to look at me with a certain mild suspicion, and I concluded it was my feeling for a snake with my bare feet that prejudiced them. I told them the snake was harmless, but that only confirmed my unreliability in their eyes, and I put on my shoes and went back to the car.

I drove on for perhaps two miles, passing three or four little cars parked out among the palms between the road and the sea. Beyond each car I could see people picnicking or bathing in the surf. I stopped several times to chase lizards that ran across the road, but they were all a big, fast, suspicious kind of Ameiva that kept beyond the range of my slingshot and number-ten shot. I drove on till I quit seeing cars and then began looking for a place to stop. When I had passed nobody for nearly a mile and came to a track leading out toward the beach, I turned and drove through the cocal to the seaside edge and stopped. It was a beautiful place—the endless singing palm strand and the wide, open sea and the straight strip of white sand between.

I got out of the car and found my chuck box and arranged a lunch. I had blown myself to a chunk of Stilton cheese in Port of Spain, and I had some pieces of cold boiled wahoo, which sounds dismal but smeared with chutney was good. The wahoo is a fish that fights like a fiend on a line but is thought by many to be poor eating. They are wrong—if there is any chutney around. I had bought the chutney at a bazaar held to raise funds to finish a mosque in St. Augustine. My landlady at the pension there, a Moslem woman of character and charm, was a member of the bazaar committee, and she selected the chutney for me from among at least a dozen kinds. I carried it with me in the car, and whenever the fare was under par, like cold boiled wahoo, I uncorked it and things looked up. I had a couple of long, yellow Indian mangoes, too, and a canteen of water and lime juice and Barbados rum, and a Thermos bottle of coffee. Altogether, the lunch was good, or at least a kind of lunch I like; and with a little breeze and the shade there under the coco palms and the view out over the Orinoco water toward the places beyond the horizon, it was a good stop I made.

By the time I had finished lunch it was nearly noon. I put things away, found a hat against the sun, took up my egg rod and a bag with the camera, calipers, and steel tape in it, and walked out on the beach. There was not a soul in sight either way and no sound above the waves. There was little reason to choose one direction above the other, but I decided on south because the last people I had seen were north. I strolled off southward, quickly finding my beach-walking pace and beginning to search the dry sand of the upper beach for turtle sign. I had gone perhaps a hundred yards when I heard the crash of a crushed palm frond behind me and, turning, saw a young Negro on a bicycle bumping out onto the beach from the cocal. He pedaled up to where I stood, stopped, and said politely:

"That will be two shilling, sar."

"Two what?" I said.

"Shilling. Two shilling. The parking fee, sar."

"Parking fee!" I yelled. "What kind of a parking fee? My car is up there in the cocal. There must be ten miles of cocal here. Who gets the parking fee?"

"You are parked on the bathing beach, sar. This whole piece from Manzanilla is the bathing beach and I am the guard, and the charge is two shilling."

I fished out a half crown and gave it to him and he held out a sixpence and gave me a terse ticket that said: "Parking two shillings." As I started to walk away, the boy asked what I was looking for. I told him, and he said turtles seldom laid along the cocal because the spring tides were cutting into the edge of the grove and the roots held the sand and made a vertical bank that was too steep for turtles to climb.

I am still a bit indignant about that parking fee and hate to give the boy credit for anything, but his comment on the coco strand making poor turtle rookeries was a contribution. I think he was right about the incompatibility of turtles and coconuts. It seems curious, because both are age-old inhabitants of the tropical sea littoral, but all the same I am beginning to believe that the spread of the coconut in the Caribbean (where it has increased its territory enormously in the past three hundred years, even in the past hundred years) has greatly reduced the territory available to turtles for nesting. On a geologically stable or emerging shore, cocal is no hindrance, but on an eroding beach the combination of the wall of undercut root masses and drifted coco debris must be an important deterrent to turtles. They are known to shy away from stranded piles of wrack and nut husks, and they can neither climb the root-held banks in front of eroding cocal nor make nests successfully in the root-laced sand.

The boy went on to say that it was against the law to take turtle eggs anyway; and I said I knew that perfectly well and wasn't taking eggs, only measuring them; and that, besides, I had a permit. I moved on and the guard sat down on the bank, opened a paper bag, and started eating lunch.

I had walked only twenty or thirty steps when I came to a turtle track. It looked like the track of a hawksbill. It came up from the sea and went straight to the rise of the bank and then turned southward and followed the foot of the root wall for as far as I could see, as if the turtle had been looking for a low place in the barrier. I must have followed the trail for sixty or seventy yards before I came to a track leading back into the water. When I reached this point, it meant either that I had passed the nest or that the turtle, unable to climb to dry land, had in desperation nested somewhere along the foot of the bank.

I retraced the trail. It ran along a stretch of shore on which the usual high tide reached the barrier bank and the highest spring tides must have invaded the palm grove in places. The sand was tide-smoothed right up to the base of the little bluff, and time after time the troubled turtle had left signs of her efforts to claw her way up to the dry floor of the grove above. But nowhere did a trail go inland from the top of the bank. I was about to conclude that the poor hawksbill had gone away full of her eggs and chagrin when I noticed an unusually broad patch of disturbance at a point in the trail where the bank overhung it. I poked at the spot with my egg stick. The rod went down too freely for wave-laid ground, and when I drew it up and looked at the end, there was yolk on it. The distraught turtle had laid her eggs in tide-washed sand, where the next or succeeding floods were bound to kill them. I had seen turtle nests in all sorts of places—hundreds of them in all—but only once before within reach of average high tide. That time it must have been the coming of day that disrupted the instincts of a Pacific ridley and caused her to lay on a tidal bar in the Gulf of Fonseca. This time it was the wall of coco roots that snarled the chain of tropisms and led a wild thing, whose whole life and line depended on doing everything exactly right, to do something wrong.

I dug out the eggs and measured them and took a picture of the clutch beside the nest. There were 174 eggs. All were close to an inch and a half in diameter, with none of the undersized nubbins that I found in the trunkback nest; but I was surprised to notice that a few were elliptical in shape. It is customary to say that sea-turtle eggs are round, and the majority are within a millimeter of being perfect spheres. But in this heap I spotted seven that were nearly as elongate as some duck eggs; and since that time I have kept an eye out for long turtle eggs and have found a few in every hawksbill nest I have opened and in one clutch of green-turtle eggs.

I finished making the measurements of the nest and eggs and stood there awhile, feeling satisfied that there finally was a good nesting record for the hawksbill on Trinidad, and wondering if it would be mysticism to dig a new hole for the eggs up in the tide-proof ground of the cocal, when I heard the sand squeak behind me. I turned and saw the beach guard standing there holding his bicycle.

"Lard God, sar, where did you find these egg at, sar?" he said, with surprising emotion.

"Right there," I said. "Right there in that hole beside them."

"But how were you able to know they were buried there?"

"I've got a kind of divining rod," I said, "I'm a kind of egg diviner." I was still peeved about the two shillings.

The boy looked impressed and was quiet for a while. Finally he asked me a bit timidly what I was going to do with the eggs, and I told him I was going to cover them up again.

"I have great relish for these egg, sar," he said.

I reminded him of the law he had reminded me of, and

he looked sad and could think of nothing to say. Then I pointed out that the eggs had been laid wrong and because of that might be considered forfeit, and he brightened. But then I said that the law probably made no distinction between eggs laid well and eggs laid badly, and the boy saw the melancholy logic in that. But he had suffered two shillings' worth, and I said that my responsibility to the Fisheries Office was over, once the eggs were back in the hole. I scraped the heap in, raked sand on top of them, and, picking up the egg stick and bag, walked away. A short way down the beach I looked back over my shoulder without stopping. The boy was smoothing the place around the turtle nest so you could hardly tell anything had happened there. For a moment I thought he had felt a surge of conservation-conscience, but I kept watching and saw him step up on the bank, reach down, and pull up a bunch of grass and stuff it half under the base of a palm petiole, where it would only be noticed by someone coming back later, after work, with a bag, looking for some sign of the place where the eggs were buried.

I walked on a mile or more without seeing any tracks fresh enough to follow. I was about to turn inland and walk back through the cocal to look for lizards when I heard the sound of music ahead. This meant there were people around, and the thought reminded me that I had failed to ask the ticket boy whether this section of the beach had any special local name that I should put with the data on the turtle nest. I decided to go up and find out where I was. The music came from well within the cocal, thirty or forty feet back from the beach. I tried to decide whether it was a radio or a phonograph playing. From down on the beach I could see nobody back among the palms, but as I approached I suddenly recognized the tune and then I knew it was coming from a phonograph. The Port of Spain disk jockeys stopped playing *Kitch* a long time ago.

> *Kitch* [the music went], *come go to bed,*
> *I have a small comb to scratch your head. . . .*

I walked closer and peered about among the shadows and swollen bases of the palm trees and still could see no one. I stepped up on the bank and saw the beetle-back top of a little English car parked halfway out toward the road; and between it and me there was a spread rush mat with the remains of a lunch on it. Beside the mat an old table-model Victrola was scratching out the calypso hit of half a dozen years before:

> *Kitch, don' make me cry,*
> *You know I love you, you playing shy.*

To increase my range of vision, I stood on a mound where a tree had once grown, and from there I made out two pairs of feet stuck out from behind a coco palm. I recoiled and started to move secretly away, but then I looked back and carefully studied the orientation of the feet. Reassured, I started stamping about on some dry palm leaves to make my presence known, and a Negro boy and an East Indian girl sat up and leaned into view from behind the tree. I greeted them with due humility.

They nodded and murmured something, but mostly they just sat there and stared at me. They made no move to shut off the phonograph.

> *Well, when she call me, I took the chance;*
> *I went and lie down, but—she want romance!*
> *I said: But, darling, I am misled,*
> *I thought you call me to scratch my head.*

I asked them what the place where we were was called. I said I was going back to my car and drive off south and maybe see nobody else for miles, to judge from the road map, and might never get the name of the place where I had found the turtle nest. I said I was sorry I had bothered them.

I *should* have been sorry. It was no light matter, disturbing that pair—not like walking up on Swedes or Sioux or Georgia crackers. Their preoccupation was no casual dalliance. It was the unwinding of the future. Those two were the stuff of the most fecund strain in all the exploding populations of the Caribbean, where people are spreading faster than anywhere else in the world. The Caribbean Afro-Asian is one to keep your eye on—your descendants may be a lot like him. They could be a lot worse, too; and if they get the African tolerance and humor out of the deal, the world may be saved after all. But meantime the thing that makes me nervous is, there are just getting to be too many people; and it is obviously going to get worse before anybody finds a solution. The minute you give that strong new hybrid stock medical care and a decent diet, you had better stand aside—or be ready with a brand-new and very handy contraceptive.

The boy and girl in the coco grove were, as I said, of African and Hindu background, but they were not self-conscious about it, and not aware that fate was there in the cocal with them, and that somebody has got to figure out a way to keep the world from filling up so fast. They only wished I would go away.

I left, and at once lost the thread of concern over the earth as a whole. The sun was too hot to worry under, and anyway I recalled how the Puerto Ricans stopped their suicidal breeding just because their living standard rose. This makes no sense, but it was a way to let the future look out for itself and let me look for lizards. I walked away through the palms, and the wind was falling, and the words of the jocular old ballad followed me a long way up the shore:

She say: But, Kitchy boy, you playing you want to hide?
You know the reason why I tell you come inside?
I said: Well, darlin', yes, I think I know your aim—
But why you con-tin-you to call me by that name?
Keeeech. . . .

There were plenty of lizards in the cocal. I was under-gunned with the slingshot and number-ten shot, but with patience and stealth I managed to kill a couple. These lizards I was after were, as I said, Ameivas, a genus that you can find back of nearly any beach in the Caribbean from Mexico to Colombia and from the Bahamas to Trinidad. The group is not found in the United States, but the common silk-skinned, six-lined race runner of the Southern states is a relative. They are handsome, energetic animals and I like to see them foraging in the beach drift. They have a severe expression of face, but I think they mean little by it. They are easy to tame once you catch them, but they are hard to catch. I took the two I shot back to the car and laid them out, belly-up, on a coco frond. I took out an aluminum bread pan and removed from it, and unwrapped, an injection syringe and needles. Then I poured some water into the bread pan and from a plastic bottle added enough formaldehyde to make a ten-per-cent solution of Formalin. Filling the syringe with this, I injected each lizard in the belly, head, legs, and tail. On two slips of parchment paper I wrote the date and locality and the kind of place it was where I got the specimen; I rolled the tags and stuck one in the mouth of each lizard. I poured most of the Formalin out and laid the lizards in the bread pan, prodding them into shape, arranging their legs and curving their tails to fit the container. I placed a sheet of plastic over the pan and fastened it down around the rim with a heavy rubber band, then set the pan on top of some wrapped specimens in a tin box in the car and shut the lid. After a few hours the lizards would harden and I would wind them in damp cheesecloth and put them in a Pliofilm bag. Pliofilm bags are a blessing to a herpetologist. You used to have to carry a can of preservative to put your critters in, but now, in Pliofilm, you can carry them home in your suitcase if you don't mind the reaction of the customs men.

When I had finished the embalming, I stowed things in the car and, without stopping again, drove to the end of the cocal. There I turned inland, took the ferry across the Ortoire River, and a short way beyond the little town of Pierreville found the Atlantis Beach Guest House beside a church on the beach just south of the St. Ann's Estate. I engaged a room and then walked up the beach to find Bernard de Verteuil.

I found the estate and the manager's house, with the help of some creole boys, but Mr. de Verteuil was not in. His wife, a pleasant Frenchwoman from Martinique, invited me to supper. She said she might as well because her husband was sure to the minute he learned I was interested in frogs and vermin. She said they already had two anthropologists staying with them, and that they would all be back in a little while.

I thanked Mrs. de Verteuil and said I would go and talk to some fishermen sitting about an upturned cayuca a short way up the shore. There was a fair-sized crowd there discussing the feasibility of launching the huge dugout in a heavy surf that was beginning to run. I found a knowledgeable-looking pair of Negroes and asked them about turtles. They took me up to a little house at the edge of the beach and, behind it, showed me two female green turtles lying on their backs, and said both had been taken the night before when they came up to lay. I walked with the men a short way up the beach and found the trail and nest that one of the turtles had made. The law prohibiting the molesting of nesting turtles seemed not to be worrying the men, and I said nothing about it. They corroborated what I had read in the old accounts about the former abundance of turtles in Mayaro, and said that when their grandfathers were young there was a big green turtle rookery there, but that now they came up only seldom and that it was an unusual thing to get two in one night. They thought the decline was due to the steady catching of nesting females. I asked them if they believed the spreading coco strand might be a factor, but they saw little merit in the idea. That was because they lived on a section of the beach that was not eroding, and where the root wall did not form at high-tide reach.

I thanked the two fishermen and walked back to the de Verteuil house. I knocked at the door and stood waiting a minute and then came face to face with a wild sort of coincidence in the person of John Goggin, a University of Florida archæologist whom I have known for twenty years, and who, as far as my reckoning went, should have been back in Gainesville teaching his classes. He and his wife, Rita, were working with Irving Rouse of Yale in an Indian mound a few miles north of St. Ann's. They invited me to come out and see their dig the next day, and then Mr. de Verteuil came out and took me in tow.

Bernard de Verteuil is the sort of a person, as I said earlier, who gives any expedition that touches him a transfusion of energy. No matter what your problem is, if it is a varmint you are after he is under way at once. He knows the Trinidad countryside in detail and understands the people, and they understand him. In fact, he is such an irreplaceable adjunct to any expedition to southeastern Trinidad that I wondered how he avoided being persecuted by people looking for help and advice. But he seemed as lighthearted about my turning up unannounced as if he hardly ever had a visitor—as if he did not have three at the very time. When I mentioned my desire to see a paradox frog, he was delighted. Showing people the frog ponds was a thing that stimulated him a great deal. He asked if I had caught a morocoy, and I said I had not. He was distressed at that and said it was next to impossible to go out and find one on call, but that maybe the Chinaman had one.

The morocoy is *Testudo denticulata,* a land turtle, a relative of the giant tortoises of the Galapagos Islands and the only true tortoise in the tropical part of South America. It seems to have escaped and gone wild on some of the other West Indian islands, but it is native on Trinidad. In a chronic sort of way I wanted one for the collection, but as Mr. de Verteuil said, it was not the sort of thing you just go out and find, and I had little hope of coming across one. I told Mr. de Verteuil that it was the paradox frog that weighed most heavily on my mind; but he insisted that the morocoy was getting scarce and I ought to take one home. He pointed out that I could ship it by boat and still have room in my luggage to take smaller specimens back on the airplane with me. He said the Chinaman was bound to have one or two and the only problem was making him part with them. He said we ought to go and try, anyway. We ought to go right away. That was how Mr. de Verteuil was.

We ran out and got into his Citroen and rushed off through the palms, turned south when we came to the highway, and after a short run drew up in front of a small general store beside the road. There was a woman sitting behind the counter in the store. She was a neat, personable mulatto and Mr. de Verteuil told me she was the wife of Lee Yow, the proprietor. He greeted her and asked if her husband was in. She got up and went to a door that opened into the family residence at the back of the store and called, and a voice yelled back: "Yannnh!" and the Chinese proprietor came inside. We got out and went in to talk with him. He was the most outrageous-looking Chinese I ever saw, a character from poor melodrama, a debauched Fu Manchu of a Chinaman. He was short, fat, and unwashed, with spiky hair, mouth slacked open, and belly hanging free. The only thing he wore was a pair of dirty duck trousers held up by a strand of manila rope that was mostly hidden by the overhang of his abdomen and rolls of fat at his sides. He stood, barefooted, and looked at us, scratching at the back of a shank with his bare toes, and picking his teeth reflectively with the sharpened end of a black duck-feather.

Mr. de Verteuil explained our errand, leading up to the point gradually, gracefully managing to reveal our desire for a morocoy as a sort of humorous caprice. He talked quite a while, Yow just standing there looking noncommittal, or maybe slightly suspicious. Finally Mr. de Verteuil came to the place where he dared risk Yow's decision, and he put the question straight.

Yow said: "You wanta buy molocoy?"

Mr. de Verteuil said that was right. He said he knew Yow didn't keep them for sale, but he had some visitors and would kind of like to have a morocoy for them, and he wondered if Yow would do him a favor and sell him one. Yow said he had only two and that he kept them to eat, not to sell. Mr. de Verteuil asked if we could just go back and see them and Yow looked doubtful; but Mr. de Verteuil insisted and mentioned that he had done Yow favors in the past, and Yow's wife insisted, and finally he said we could go back and look at them. He went out a door at the rear and we followed him and walked across a clean-swept yard crowded with ducks and chickens and dogs. Yow opened the door of a small outbuilding and stepped in, and we entered behind him. The floor of the building was a bare, hard-packed clay. There were mango seeds scattered about and a smell of soured fruit and a wide pan of water at one side of the room. One of the morocoys was sitting in the water and the other blinked at us from the far end of the room where it had been chewing idly at a bearded mango seed.

Yow looked at the tortoises for a moment with a rapt reverence and they stirred him so deeply he could not be silent.

"Oh, sweet!" he shrieked. "Oh, velly sweet, oh-oo-oo-oo . . ." His voice trailed off in a long moan of falsetto ecstasy.

I looked nervously toward Mr. de Verteuil, but he seemed perfectly at ease.

"How much will you take for the big one, Yow?" he said.

The thought was panic to Yow. He looked wildly around the room until his eye fell upon the small dingy form of another turtle that was almost hidden among some stones in a dark corner. His face brightened and he pointed at this recourse excitedly and said, with pitiful eagerness:

"You buy galap? Fine galap heah. Oh, fine galap."

The galap is Geomyda, a semiaquatic, tropical turtle that wanders about the woods of Trinidad and is more frequently met than the morocoy, and has nowhere near as big a liver.

"No, we've got a galap," Mr. de Verteuil said firmly.

"What we want is the morocoy. The big one. How much?"

Yow looked at the tortoise tragically. He was an unusually emotional Chinese. He seemed about to weep, but instead he started bouncing up and down on both feet, at first just jiggling, but gradually jumping harder and faster until it made his belly slap. As he jumped he kept shaking his hands in front of his face.

"Oh, lovely!" he shrilled. "This get fat a long time." He ran over and picked up the tortoise in both hands, then ran back and showed it to us. "Eat many, many fig, many mango! Oh, liver so big, like this—" He hastily lodged the tortoise under an arm and held his two hands together like a big liver. "Oo sweet, oo lovely, lovely liver. . . ."

It looked hopeless to me and it was a strain, too. I was ready to get out and take my chances of finding my own morocoy or going back without one. But Mr. de Verteuil said brusquely, as if Yow were just being a bit cagey about the deal: "All right, Yow, how much for the big one?"

Yow suddenly stopped bouncing, and with the tortoise still held out in front of him he closed his eyes so tight the fat piled up around his Mongolian folds and made canyons of them, and screwed his face about in a flexible sort of way that seemed completely unoriental. Then he said, just louder than a whisper: "Three shilling a pound."

Mr. de Verteuil began to protest, but I was sure Yow hoped we would not pay it, and I quickly said we would take the tortoise. Yow looked as if I had said we would foreclose a mortgage.

"You pay three shilling?" he said sharply.

I said I would indeed, and without a word Yow carried the tortoise out of the shed, across the yard, and into the store, where he placed it, back-down, on the scales and started shuffling the weights about. It weighed fourteen pounds and when Yow read the amount his excitement came back on him, and he began to jump and shake his hands again like an untidy, corpulent child agitated beyond finding words adequate.

"Is gain two pounds and quarta!" he shrieked. "One month stay here, eat velly many flutes! Oh, fat—have eggs in too! Oh, lovely!"

He was obviously on the verge of repenting the folly of parting with the prize, and I hastened to find the price of the morocoy and give it to him. Then we quickly said goodby to Mrs. Yow and carried the morocoy out to the car and drove off, leaving Yow standing there looking after us with a half-stunned look on his mobile face, as if we were making off with his first-born.

We drove back past the St. Ann's turnoff to the St. Joseph's Estate, where the paradox-frog ponds are located. We stopped and talked with the manager, who said it would not be misconstrued if we showed up after dark and played a light about his pastures. Then Mr. de Verteuil pointed out the best pond, and since the frogs were hard to see and impossible to catch by daylight, we went back to St. Ann's for supper.

After supper Mr. de Verteuil was called away somewhere on business, and about nine o'clock I returned to St. Joseph's alone. It had rained a little but had cleared off, and the moon was up. I left the car by the manager's house and walked down a lane and through a hedgerow and across a dew-spread pasture in what I thought to be the direction of the frog pond. For what seemed a long time I heard no sound ahead and began to grow uneasy over the thought that Pseudis might be a sporadic, unpredictable singer like some frogs, perversely silent for days or weeks at a time in the heart of what ought to be the singing season. But then I caught some raveling ends of noise that might be frog-song—nothing intelligible, but enough to give me a bearing. I walked faster, and lesser notes fell in and the source localized, and as I neared the pond, a full chorus flooded up and over the brush at the margin and rolled out past me like unseen fog.

I gradually sorted out the parts and voices and decided that three species of frogs were singing. The call I first managed to unweave was a timid, monotonous chant, a low *kuk-kuk-kuk* that carried no hint of range or direction. Unable to pin it down, I was about to give it up and go on to one of the other songs when a string of the soft *kuks* fell into focus where a bush rose just beside me, and I looked closely at the twigs and suddenly saw the source.

It was a green tree-frog with a body as long as your finger and little broader, and huge hands and finger pads, and legs so slender you wondered how they worked. He had gold eyes with vertical pupils that narrowed down to slits in the light beam. The instant the light swung his way the *kuk-kuk* stopped; but I cut out the light and the song began again, and when I quickly switched the light back on, I caught him singing.

After that it was easier to trace down the *kuk*-song, and I located two more of the slim green frogs, both calling in the same lackadaisical way from twigs over the water. Most frogs measure their love in decibels and sing with all the volume their rations of wind will allow, and I knew of no precedent for the spiritless song of the *kuk* frog. Considering what he was singing about, it was a strangely wan and casual ditty of a song, like something you might distractedly hum under your breath, thinking of something else.

The slim frog was an Agalychnis, one of a number of species that lay their eggs in little nests of leaves glued together, in trees or bushes hanging low over water. But in

spite of this innovation the eggs have to be fertilized
when they are laid in it, and there will be no point in the
clever leaf nursery if either sex is away when the time
comes. It is the male who thinks of this first, as with other
frogs, and it is his singing that reminds the female of the
time and tells her the place, and keeps things straight that
way. I would have liked to wait on there for a while to see
if anything came of the bush frog's listless, lustless bid
for love, but out in the pond the chorus was swelling, and
the voice I had come to hear was still lost in the mingling
dins.

Once the Agalychnis was weeded out, there were two
calls left, all mixed and overlapping at the edges, but dis-
tinctly two. As I listened with this in mind, one of them
suddenly took a shape that I knew from somewhere else.
It was a quick, cricketlike eruption of a song, coming from
hundreds—maybe thousands—of throats at once and ranging in timbre from a noisy buzz to an almost musical trill.
It seemed to rise mostly from patches of tall grass in shallow water and even before I tracked down one of the
singers I knew it would be a tiny tan Hyla like one I had
known in Honduras and Panama. The other section of the
bedlam, the main base and body of the chorus, was the
voice of the paradox frog.

It was not melodious, this song I had so stubbornly
wanted to hear. It was strident and mechanical—a harsh
snore and a coarse rattle: *rrrrrr-rrrrrr*, ripped out sporadically or at ragged intervals. If you know your United
States frogs, it was in tone and texture somewhere between
the call of a leopard frog and that of a squirrel Hyla. The
frogs sang floating in the deep parts of the pond, floating
high and horizontal, some holding to twigs or pad rims,
some drifting free in the open places. I waded about,
waist-deep in the dark water, sneaking up and snatching

one after another. They were intent on their singing, and while lanes of quiet opened in front of me wherever I walked, the preoccupied males held well without diving, and even with the strong moon watering down the rays of my flashlight I easily caught six of them. Then I shut off the light and stood there with my odd fulfillment, listening as the Pseudis chorus closed in around me. I stood like a shitepoke roost in the thin dark—a Full Professor in the prime of life—with my navel in the pond and five children back home going through their shoes; hearing the rare song and stowing it away, wondering why a water frog with his females there floating beside him under the moon should sing on in the dark, through the ages.

The Little Hyla sang to toll his mate from the thickets, and the frog in the bush to show what twigs could lodge a leaf nest. Was it just because he had a voice that Pseudis sang? Because it was fun to sing? Or did singing mean something different to a paradox frog? For a long time I stood there among the pads with the frogs shouting all around, but I never could say what the shouting was for. There was no flaw in my contentment, though, when I finally sloshed out to shore and pushed through the rimming tangle, and all the way across the pasture dripped pond water in the dew.

The Mouths of the Bull

A JOOK IS A dreary place in the morning. Even if you have slept well the night before, most jooks seem threadbare by forenoon light, and I had hardly slept at all. I sat at a table and felt the cool of a bottle of beer and looked out over the rail. I looked out beyond the Mouths of the Bull to the open sea, where six little boats, six tiny specks in the distance, floated in the monochrome mixture of sky and sea.

I felt pretty low. I have no objection to jooks at night; but in the morning, on a tropical shore, when I wanted to be out and under way, this place seemed sordid in spite of the beer and the shade and the view of the sea. It was more frustration than anything really wrong with the jook, but I was getting a penned-up feeling.

My trouble was due to fundamental causes. It all went back, I suppose you would say, to the inclination of the axis of the earth. The earth was squarely in between the positions of equinox at the time—just halfway around in its orbit. The irksome part of this was, it made the north pole tilt toward the sun at a crazy angle, and the sun's rays hit the ground squarely somewhere away up north of Panama where I was and the days up there got long and hot. It was the time of the northern summer, the time of least contrast between the tropics and the temperate zone. It was the time of the summer solstice, and it was playing hell with my plans.

I was in a place called Bocas del Toro, and I had to go to Chiriquí Beach, forty miles back along the coast toward Colón. I was in a hurry. There was just a week to go and come in, and the only way I had found to get there was in a sailing cayuca. The cayucas made the trip on irregular schedule. They usually waited for the wind, for one thing, and that is where the solstice had me hogtied.

You see how it was—the long days up north warmed the air over the land and caused it to rise; and this changed the pressure relations over the northern lands and southern seas and shifted the air masses all over the place, even down as far as latitude 10° north where I sat—even beyond. The air masses make the weather, and the weather at Bocas went to pieces.

The pressure belt they call the doldrums grew restless and snaked about the big belly of the world and shoved up and shouldered the trade winds northward. This left the Isthmus at the mercy of local convection and of other things you couldn't count on. Some days the heating of the shore by day and the cooling by night gave you a fitful daily seabreeze-landbreeze cycle, with lines of thunderstorms where the wet doldrum air soared at the land-edge. Some days the trade wind came back down and held strong for a while; and all the dugouts sailed madly for where they had to go before it should leave again. Some days, even some weeks, there was no wind at all, and the sea looked lacquered under the motionless air, and the sun was close and fierce through the thin haze. This last was the way it was the morning I turned up sitting in the jook at Bocas.

It may seem to you that I have gone to odd lengths to explain my position. The thing is, I want to get all the facts before you. I was traveling on a grant from the American Philosophical Society, and to a sponsor like that my sitting in a jook with a beer at midmorning would sound like pretty irresponsible behavior. I want to make it clear that I was at the mercy of elemental forces. I was a pawn in the hands of capricious air masses—weak perhaps, but not overtly dissolute.

Besides this, I owe you something on that word *jook*. I realize that my spelling is not preferred, but I have convictions about this. We got the word from Southeastern Negroes. According to students of West African dialects it is a good Wolof term, originally a verb, meaning to misconduct oneself. It survived at several points in coastal Georgia and northern Florida and long ago got into the vocabularies of all but the most rightminded of us cracker folk. You may also recall that the word began its spread into the national language when Florida had a legislative hassle over the licensing of its jooks. The fuss attracted the attention of the national press, and when it was all over, the spelling that stuck, over most of the country and in Webster, was *juke*, which can only rhyme with *duke*, and which is not the way to spell what is meant at all. In Gambia and Senegal and Charleston and Fernandina the word has always had the sound of *took*, and the only way to get that is with the double *o*.

Of course, as Tom Pyles says, usage is the one thing that makes words right. The people start saying them and then later on you listen closely and write them down. But the millions of Americans, and now even Englishmen, who talk about *jyuke*-boxes got their pronunciation from *reading* the word, and not only is this reversing the normal process of word evolution, but what they read was a defective transliteration to start with. As a native of the Coastal Plain I have a proprietary feeling about the word. I've been saying it right ever since I learned about the sin there is in the world, and I refuse to be led by any tone-deaf journalist into mistreating it.

So what I was sitting in, the roofed deck on piling out over the bay at Bocas, was a jook. The specks I was watching—the motes out in the mingled sky and sea, that might have been still mellowbugs or hovering gulls or even just something wrong with my eyes—were turtle cayucas, slim, chopped-out logs of ceiba or cedar, paddling for the open sea to stalk and strike the green turtles feeding and cooting on the offshore flats. There was a place in one of them where I might have been. I had spoken for the vacant seat and had it promised, but the other chance had come, the possible way to get to Chiriquí with Mr. Shepherd in the sailboat, and I had stayed behind to take my chances on the wind. Now it looked like another day of flat calm, when nobody would sail anywhere, and the turtle boats were beyond recalling, out where the sea looked like part of the sky, and I was left stranded in the jook.

I suppose it was a good thing, really. The canoes would be out all day long, rising and falling on the long ground swell, the air stagnant with calm, the sun coppery behind the thin heat vapor. Except for long-spaced spurts of action when turtles were struck, there would be nothing to do but ease your seat and trim the log and look at the shining back of the iron-man in front of you, or out to where the horizon was hidden in the haze. I had been out like that before, and I knew that, depressing as the jook was, on such a day I was better off there than on the flats.

I sat hunched over with my elbows on the oilcloth and idly listened to the conversation of two men at a table across the deck. They were the only other people in the place, except the bartender. They had been talking, over a succession of pints of rum, since the evening before. Through all the noise of the night—the blare and pounding of the orchestra and the moaning of the piccolo; the shrieks and tittering of the girls; the coming and going, and the haranguing and sporadic shouting of the men; the buzzing-in under the floor of outboard-driven cayucas from the nearby islands, seeking spirits for suburban parties—steady and true through it all, the droning dialogue went on. The men were cacao-planters who owned farms back on the lagoon—old friends unexpectedly met, I gathered, on a rare trip to market. They were celebrating the meeting and a good price for their beans with a talking jag. Now in the mounting light their eyes were swollen and their heads dropped between their shoulder blades like buzzards', but they talked on and on. They talked in English and this was a good thing for me, because Bocas English is so elusive you can drop the thread of its meaning whenever you get tired of it. Lord knows, the Bocas creole Spanish would not excite the envy of a Madrileño or a Bogotano, but it is an idiom you can understand with no special effort if you know the mother tongue to start with.

Bocas English is just about the most weird I have heard anywhere. The creoles there are mostly bilingual. Each day most of them have to do some talking in both English and Spanish, but it is English that they cherish and cling to as their traditional language. They are so stubborn about this that the Panamanian government is growing alarmed and has begun a campaign to popularize Spanish on the coast, but so far this has had little success.

As in Nicaragua, the most bizarre speech is that of the younger folk. Not the children—they are easy to understand, partly because they use less slang, partly, perhaps, because their talk is kept in check by schoolteachers. The very old people, too, speak clearly and with a decided English accent, and while their phrasing is often quaint, there is no great difficulty following them.

The young creoles are the wild-talking ones—the noisy numerous people between, say, fourteen and forty. I wish I could contrive for you a valid sample of how they talk, but I don't know how to do it. I might manage to show its odd phonics and the weird slanting and offset shading of the meanings of words, but that would hardly begin to show what the dialect is really like. The striking feature is the unique cadence—the way the syllables are set apart and intoned. This is what makes the spoken stream so completely unfamiliar.

Listening carefully to a group of post-adolescent boys, for instance, shouting at each other as they do—each trying to keep the floor by virtue of superior volume and continuity of utterance—if you don't know at the start what language they are talking you will probably be a long time making up your mind. With close attention you eventually pick up a vaguely familiar sound that may or may not be a word, and later on another; and by snatching at these stray sounds you gradually build an impression that English is the language in progress. But you still don't know what the boys are yelling about. *Understanding* Bocas talk is a matter of training and practice.

Sitting there in the jook, I tested these observations on the cacao men, who appeared to be about thirty-five years old. They were talking plenty loud enough for me to hear every sound; but sure enough, it was easy not to get the sense of what they said. The point settled, I turned back to looking for things to see.

The jook was open to the bay on three sides. The bay was the harbor of Bocas del Toro, the little town on one of the passes that connect Almirante Bay and Chiriquí Lagoon with the Caribbean. The passes are the *bocas* and the *toro* is a big rock out in front of the town that old sailors said looked like a bull. The *Bocas del Toro*, then, are the Chiriquí passes, guarded by the stone bull, and the town is known by the same name. The place was important to the buccaneers as a source of turtles and manatee for provisioning their ships, and in recent years it has served as a minor port for the Almirante Division of the United Fruit Company, though the ship channel into the mainland farms does not go by Bocas.

Straight out behind the jook, out beyond the bull, was the open Caribbean, where the specks of turtle boats were inching away from the land and getting smaller as they climbed the shimmering sea up into the shimmering sky. To the left, well back inside the bay, a little palm-set island broke the clean blue-green water, and against the near side of the island an old Negro in a tiny pitpan was fishing. He was a black Carib, the bartender said, come down from Belize so long ago he had almost forgotten. He was fishing four ways at once, to be sure of something. He had a line out on the bottom baited with conch, for snappers and grouper. This is what he tended most constantly. Coiled on the bottom in front of him he had a short, stiff throwline baited with something shiny, and this he cast into any vagrant patch of sardines that moved by, with the hope of tolling out a jack or kingfish. Slantwise across the gunwales were two long poles, one gig-tipped for spearing fish about the rising heads and one with a progging fork for crawfish. These he unlimbered when he raised his anchor to change his fishing place, and each time he moved he searched the bottom all the way through the glass of a water bucket.

On the far side of the little island there was a beach of clean white sand, and off it concentric arcs of white combers slowly flared and faded. Back of the beach there stood a little casino of concrete and thatch. This served as a bathhouse for any guests of the Miramar who had the energy to paddle out for a swim. Surfbathing, then, was another of the facilities of the oddly complex establishment in which I was staying.

The jook I sat in was part of what a sign out front called, with almost perverse understatement, it turned out, Hotel Miramar. The part of this that you approached from the center of town was a general store, a small rural version of a Colón Bombay Store. Seaward of the store, under the same long roof and merging with it, was the hotel part, where six high-ceilinged, small-windowed rooms were set along a narrow corridor that ran from the store in front clear back to the jook in the rear. On back past the rooms, the hallway was flanked by a pair of vast, sunken water closets, to each of which water was run from somewhere several times a week. Between times, when the pipes were dry, a round-faced Indian boy came twice a day with a bucket of water and flushed the toilets, and carried away the boxes of paper beside them.

Behind and adjoining the bathrooms was a dark area labeled *Restaurant and Bar*. You walked through this, between a row of booths along one wall and a long bar along the other and you soon came out into the light and air of the overwater part, with its own little bar and with chairs and tables. This is the part I am calling a jook. A sign on it called it a *Marine Bar*, but it was pretty close to what we call in Florida a jook. You could get beer and rum there, and there was room for dancing; and there was a "piccolo," a jook organ, which played well in the two or three hours before dawn when most of the lights of the town were out and when the current was strong; and a small local band came in when the piccolo was quiet.

Since many patrons of the place arrived by water, the back platform stepped down to a dock, where boats from the islands, or from other sections of the waterfront, were forever bumping in or leaving.

None of the signs said so, but the Miramar was also a house of convenience. Not a place with fancy ladies in residence, understand, but one that simply smoothed the way for sex. Sex was not provided there, but if you brought it along, the Miramar would help you make the most of it. When I turned up looking for a room to sleep in all night—maybe three nights—the thought was so novel it threw the whole place into confusion. The *dueño* was away, and while the woman he had left in charge was perfectly capable of running the place so long as things went smoothly, she was not equipped to cope with bizarre or unusual situations, and my proposal to pass the whole night in one of the rooms seemed to demoralize her.

I can see why, too. That first night I stayed there I was out until two o'clock in the morning, paddling about the bayshore and walking the near beaches. I returned to the hotel prepared to face the noise from the party back in the jook—you could hear that all over the bay—but a thing that took me by surprise was the traffic in the hallway. I don't know how many times the five rooms were engaged that night, though I could easily have kept count if I had wanted to. People filed back and forth in the hall like ants on a twig, only more noisy. The ones not able to find a room vacant stood around outside the doors stamping and grumbling. Once they got a room, they never seemed to rest well in it.

I didn't rest well either. The partitions between the rooms stopped two feet below the ceiling. This helped ventilate the place, but it also let you keep track of just about everything that went on anywhere in the establish-

ment. For a while I tried wrapping a towel around my
head and over my ears, but it was a halfhearted move and
quite futile. I got up and turned on the light—a small,
dusky bulb that hung down just even with my chin on a
wire from the middle of the ceiling. The glow it gave was
enough to show where the curl of hot filament was, but
not enough to help me find my flashlight. I groped about
the room and finally found the light, snapped it on, and
put on my clothes.

I opened the door and stepped out, and a couple was
standing there looking expectant. I said good-evening and
then pointedly turned the key in the lock and rattled it,
though the night latch had already locked the door. The
couple wilted and looked sad and I felt pretty mean.

I walked back to the jook. It was packed with people,
mostly creoles, but with mestizos scattered here and there
among the dark clumps. There were two or three East
Indians and at least one Chinese, an extroverted youth
who seemed very popular. There was a small nondescript
orchestra—guitar, trumpet, and verdigreed tenor saxo-
phone, a boy with a bongo, and a melancholy fellow with
a pair of claves. The wind section was ordinary, but the
guitar was played well and the boy with the bongo had
a certain genius. The main trouble was that they tried to
play Agustín Lara instead of Afro-Bocas stuff. It wasn't
bad, though. It is hard for any kind of a Negro band to be
really uninteresting.

I pushed through the dancing, necking, declaiming
crowd and got a beer at the bar. Since there was no place
at a table or anywhere around the railing, I went down the
ladder to the dock but immediately stumbled over a
couple in the gloom and climbed back upstairs. I stood
around awhile listening to the music and watching the
bongista, but after a while the general din got too bad

and I headed back for my room. Pushing past the restive queues in the hall, I unlocked my door and, ignoring the envious mumbling, went in. By the light of my headlight I shoved the head of the cot up against the wall and then ripped some pieces off a handkerchief and stuffed them into my ears. With the headpiece of the light strapped to my head, I propped my back against the wall and started reading A History of the Bishops of Panama, which the local priest had lent me that afternoon.

I felt no special concern over the background of the Faith in the Isthmus. I was looking for stray references that might shed light on the size and distribution of turtle populations in Panama in the old days. There was not much about turtles in the History of the Bishops, but I did find a short piece on the history of Bocas, in which Bishop José Teleoforo Pare grew amusingly sour over the predominance of Protestantism among the Bocas creoles of seventy years ago. He recited the untulgy antics of the local Methodists and Baptists with such evident zest that I copied a passage in my notebook:

> There is a church here [the Bishop said] built by the Methodists, and another in Old Bank, both small and made of wood. A minister called Bovron lived here for twenty-seven years and died last year almost demented. After his death there came a woman accompanied by a man, who by some unknown art transmitted to the Methodists, and especially to the women, a disease of convulsion which used to cause them to lose their reason. They called that "revival" and they even reached the point of removing the benches from the church, and spending the night with the doors closed, men and women together, praying, singing and uttering loud shouts caused by the spells. The promoters of these commotions and illness . . . eventually disappeared when a minister came from Colón and forbade them; but to purge themselves of those sins he told them it was necessary to be baptized by

immersion because baptism by infusion was not valid, and almost all the Methodists were led by him to a point where he built a wharf, and thus, standing in the water, he immersed them in the sea. An old man, almost an octogenarian, died eight days later as a result of such a sacrilegious baptism. Today the Methodists are Baptists and have seized the old chapel. . . .

After this was off his chest the things the Bishop said failed to keep me awake. I went to sleep with the headlight strapped to my head and burning, and the next morning my batteries were dead.

It was eight o'clock when I awoke, and new noises had started coming in from the street and waterfront. I dressed and walked down to a little three-table café in a Chinese general store and had breakfast. I sat around a while afterwards trying to see if the proprietor knew why nearly all Chinese turn to storekeeping in the Caribbean, while back where I came from they ran restaurants and laundries. He only shook his head and looked cunning, as if I had asked about one of the mysteries of the Orient. Then, because it was already getting hot outside, I walked back to the hotel to wait for Mr. Shepherd in the shade of the jook.

Mr. Shepherd was a middle-aged creole who ran a sailing cayuca up and down the lagoon. He lived near Chiriquí Beach and had agreed to take me there, when I had been unable to find any faster way to make the trip. He said we would sail if the wind should come back, and if it stayed calm he would have some boys to paddle.

People I had talked to in Colón had told me that Chiriquí Beach was a good place for sea turtles. They were all talking from hearsay and were pretty vague about it, but they told me enough to make me think I ought to go there and find out about the place. It was the year after I first visited the Turtle Bogue rookery in Costa Rica and I was anxious to see whether the Chiriquí nesting assemblage was comparable to that at Tortuguero. The place, as I said, was at least forty miles from Bocas, and with no wind it was hard to see how we would ever make it in Mr. Shepherd's big dugout. But he seemed confident, and I had agreed to let him pick me up at the hotel dock in the middle of the morning. That is how I came to be there waiting, nursing the beer, gazing out over the rail, to the casual eye squandering in idle living the funds of the American Philosophical Society.

After a while the old fisherman, the Carib in the log boat over by the little island, began to doze at anchor over his still fishing, and my eyes wandered away and moved around to the right, where the town of Bocas was strewn along the crescent of the bay front. Of all the Caribbean waterfronts I had seen, Bocas was the most untidy, the most fantastically disheveled. If you made a faithful delineation of seaside Bocas, people would call it an abstraction. The buildings along the shore were a welter of shapes and sizes and degrees of decay, with tin roofs that collided at random in a bewilderment of tilted planes, some of them new zinc or aluminum, but most just odd old pieces laid on as needed and then, wherever rust spread, daubed with paint of any color on hand at the time.

It was only a short way from the bay to the bay-front streets, and the structures in between had edged out into the water. All the privies stood behind the houses on teetery heron legs, staggering about the shallows just outside mean low-water line, tied to the houses they served by narrow catwalks of poles or scantling. Sharing with them the back-yard water were little docks and pole walks, net racks and cayuca sheds, pole-supported pens, cages, and coops, palisaded crawls, and various pile-propped excrescences of the buildings themselves.

Some sixty yards down the shore from where I sat, the big roofed wharf of the town market shouldered aside the press of private works and blocked my view for a short segment of the curving shore. Just under me, joining the premises of the Miramar, there was an intricate structure of poles, boards, and palm thatch, which a little study showed was a clever amalgamation of pigpen, privy, and turtle crawl.

There were six green turtles in the crawl. They had all been harpooned the day before, but had evidently forgotten it, because the males kept up an almost continuous chivying of the single female penned with them. I was interested in this. In all my prying into their private ways I had never seen the mating procedure of the Atlantic green turtle, and it has never been described in scientific literature. This crawl next door stood, as I say, only a few feet from where I sat, and since the angle down to it was steep, everything that went on was in view. I had watched the turtles awhile the afternoon before, but the female had been unwilling, and the chasing and strife had kept the pen so churned up that I could see the creatures only when at the surface. Now, after passing a quiet night, the males had renewed their importunings, and first one and then another tried to embrace the hard, slippery shell of the still coy female.

I had a notebook on the table, and whenever the turtles seemed to be doing something worth while I made notes. I had explained what I was doing to the bartender, a blue-black, bushy-haired, outgoing young man, and he had concluded from this that I was a physician; and as customers arrived, and could not help noticing me staring fixedly into the neighboring back yard and making notes on it in my book, the bartender told them about me. People next door going back to feed the pig or visit the *servicio* soon grew accustomed to my surveillance, and sometimes even waved a friendly greeting before letting the burlap privy curtain fall behind them. Once when I returned to my table after a short absence I heard chatter and giggling coming from the backhouse. I wondered idly what the source was, but continued recording the antics of the turtles, from time to time rising and standing on the chair to see if some outburst of fighting in the pen might show in a photograph. The half-suppressed tumult in the privy kept up, and after a while the bartender jumped down from his seat on the bar, came over to the rail, and yelled: "What de mateah in deah, God oll mighty?"

The sack door was pulled aside three inches and the whites of a number of eyes showed anxiously in the gloom within.

"Go on, get ott deah now," the bartender said. "Watt wrong wit you?"

A hand emerged from between the sack and the door casing, a timid finger pointed my way, and a voice piped: "What dem doin'?"

The bartender snorted. "Watt you keah watt de docteah doin'? Watchin' de tettle coot—ain showin' you no notice. Get out deah now, you finish you bizness."

The burlap swung aside and three little girls ran like rats across the pole walk, squeaking softly till they reached the sanctuary of the kitchen and then, hidden, shrieking with relieved delight.

After a while a big black man in a cayuca paddled and pushed up to the turtle crawl, opened a gate in the side, and with a loop of heavy rope started trying to lasso one of the turtles. I asked if he wanted to catch a particular one, and he said just any of the males, because they were the ones that kept the pen in commotion and lost weight and worried the females till they were worn out and sometimes died. Finally the loop closed on a foreflipper and the man dragged a turtle out, beached it and turned it over, and picked up a big knife to cut its throat. I had no interest in the slaughter and turned to look at other things.

I looked down into the water. It was transparent as the air over it. The litter of junk on the bottom—the bottles and garbage, the unidentifiable and unprintable dejecta there—made me wonder how a poor little town like Bocas could spew forth such a volume of waste. Most tidewater towns hide their offal under turbid water, but here in Bocas nothing jettisoned was lost; it only lay and spread, and every day the water renewed itself through the mouths of the bull and kept so crystal clean and unabused that you could see the feelers of shrimps on the bottom and the eyes of anchovies swirling in the sparkling wash around the piling. Most places the pelagic mackerel-kind shy away from dirty little port towns, but here kingfish came in almost under the docks. I am not unusually fussy about dirt or disarray, as you must have concluded, and I know that waterfronts are bound to be untidy places where you hook all manner of dismal miscellany off the bottom. But the thing is, where most towns meet bay or estuary, the water is not much to start with and, as I say, hides with its own burden of fine corruption the macroscopic mess it covers. In Bocas it wasn't the garbage itself that offended, so much as seeing it through the beautiful water, and seeing the little unsuspecting reef fishes that you had known only in pristine seas over coral groping there in the garbage like lost jewels.

Grieving over the sullied sea, I heard a quick crunch of barnacles and the bump of a docking boat. I leaned over and looked down at the dock, and Mr. Shepherd was there in his long dugout. He threw a line around a cleat and asked me what time it was. I told him ten thirty and he asked if I was ready to go. I looked at the open boat and up at the sun and out at the glassy sea. I said I guessed so; but my heart was not in it. I pointed to the lack of wind, and Mr. Shepherd said he had three boys to help with the paddling. He said there were settlements all along the way where we could stop and eat or get out of any bad weather that might come up. With any help at all from the wind, we should get to Chiriquí by noon the next day, he said. If we had to paddle the whole way it would take us till sometime after dark.

I asked him to wait a few minutes while I got my gear. He climbed out of the boat and up the ladder, and as I walked off to my room I heard him yelling over to the paddle hands on the market wharf to let them know we would soon be leaving. Back in the room, I threw the things I thought I would need into a canvas duffel bag, and then took my suitcase across the street and left it with the woman in charge of the hotel. I carried the duffel bag out to the dock and lowered it into the cayuca, where Mr. Shepherd stowed it under a worn tarpaulin. He was drinking a bottle of ice water the bartender had given him.

"Dis de las cool wateah we hob fo long time," he said.

I knew that very well. Mr. Shepherd finished the bottle and set it on the dock. I handed it up to the bartender and then lifted the loop of the bow line off of the cleat and stepped into the boat. Mr. Shepherd pushed us out, away from the dock, and turned the bow up the shore. The bartender leaned over the rail smoking a cigarette, looking sad for us and saying over and over: "Cam, hot day, very dam cam hot day."

We slid out beyond the broken rank of backhouses and headed for the market wharf, where three well-grown boys, one of them Mr. Shepherd's nephew, were waiting to come aboard. As we drew up to take them on, I saw a long motor cayuca in a slip beside the market. It was full of hawksbill turtles, stacked on their backs, their flippers tied with grass across their bellies.

"Where is that boat from?" I asked.

"Chiriquí Beach," Mr. Shepherd said.

"Where we are going?"

"Dot sem plee-us, yes sah."

"But look, those are *careyes*—oxbulls. Do oxbulls lay up there too?"

The boys and some men working in the market laughed and hooted.

"Eeeeeeee!" one of them keened.

"Don' any other kine, scarcely," Mr. Shepherd said, politely.

"Wait a minute now, man. I came here for green turtles. They told me in Colón it was green turtles that nested there. Is the Chiriquí rookery oxbulls?"

"Only oxbull, sah."

"Are you sure?"

"Quite shuah, sah. If you wish we osk the mon that breng this tettle."

"We better ask him," I said.

Word passed along the dock and through the market that we wanted to talk with the man who had brought the load of hawksbills. After a couple of minutes a boy came running to say that the man had gone across to Provision Island and would not be back till noon. I was sitting there in the canoe wondering what to believe and what to do when a slim, gray-haired mulatto with a kind face strolled into the back of the market, eyed me politely, and asked somebody what my trouble was. When he learned, he came over and told me his name was Peterson, and said

Mr. Shepherd was quite right, the Chiriquí rookery was hawksbills, pure hawksbills and nothing more.

This was a serious thing to hear, against all my preconceptions and with bearing on the course of my existence for some days to come. Limited as my time in the tropics was, I could not afford to waste a week on the Chiriquí trip for the sake of hawksbills. There is nothing wrong with hawksbills, and there are a lot of gaps in what we know about their life history, and I have a great deal of curiosity about them, but, this trip, I was after information on green turtles. Somehow I had to get the straight of the Chiriquí stories before I went there.

Mr. Peterson was the most reliable-looking man I had seen in Bocas, and I set about getting acquainted with him. He was a Colombian by birth, a native of San Andrés, from where people have been coming to Bocas to escape the Colombian taxes for more than a hundred years. He told me that the turtle fishermen of San Andrés, and of the neighboring island of Old Providence have always specialized in catching hawksbills. He said they catch them not just for the sake of the tortoise shell but because people in the islands like to eat them and even prefer them to greens.

Many places you find hawksbills looked upon as just short of inedible—in a few places as actually poisonous. Until I talked to Mr. Peterson I had heard of only one place in American waters where they were preferred to green turtles, and that was the island of Cayman Brac, where there is a tradition of hawksbill-hunting as old and ingrained as that of the Grand Caymanians for greens. On Cayman Brac they would rather eat hawksbill than green turtle any day, and their stew of young chicken hawksbill is famous. The truth of this moot matter of hawksbill edibility seems to be that there is some basis for each of the divergent views. Being a largely carnivorous but indiscriminate feeder, the hawksbill takes what falls to its lot in a victualing way, and like some of the domestic animals that people eat, its flavor varies with its current feeding regimen. The alleged poisonous qualities, which have actually resulted in a few fatal cases of poisoning, are probably due to a dietary foible that leads hawksbills in restricted areas, or at certain seasons, or on sporadic occasions, to eat poisonous invertebrates or plants. This appears to be the case with respect to a number of species of tropical fishes—especially those of the family that includes the balloon fish and the parrot fishes. In the United States the common box turtle has poisoned people who ate it, and here the best explanation seems to be that box turtles sometimes eat the death-cup toadstool, *Amanita phalloides,* and though themselves immune to its poison, they retain the harmful compounds in their tissues. It is quite likely this sort of thing that accounts for the pan-Caribbean bickering over whether a man is a fool to eat a hawksbill. I have eaten them several times and was not poisoned. I thought they were good, though possibly not so good as a green turtle. Very few things are as good to eat as green turtle.

When Mr. Peterson saw that a forty-mile sailboat trip hung on what kind of turtles made up the Chiriquí rookery, he offered to walk with me out to the edge of town where there was a man who knew more about turtles than anyone else in Bocas. I gladly accepted the offer, and Mr. Shepherd agreed to wait at the wharf till we returned. As we walked, Mr. Peterson continued to talk about turtles, and I began to believe that he knew what he was talking about. He said that Chiriquí Beach was more than just a place where occasional hawksbills came to lay—it was probably the best hawksbill rookery beach in all the Caribbean. He was qualified to hold the opinion because he had navigated the Caribbean from end to end a great many times and spoke with authentic familiarity of remote little places that I happened to know. Moreover, he said that Tortuguero, or Turtle Bogue, as he called it, was the biggest of all green-turtle rookeries—and I knew that this was essentially true. He told me that the contract for turtling on Chiriquí Beach was held by a man named Robinson, who continued to buy it each year in spite of what plastics have done to the tortoise-shell market. He asked if I really thought plastic replaced *carey*, and was pleased to find that I thought that good tortoise shell has a combination of qualities, æsthetic and mechanical, that no imitation has approached. He thought so too.

He said that the Chiriquí Robinson sent most of his turtles to the market in Colón, another place where people eat hawksbills, and one where the outlet for the meat helps make stripping and shipping the shell a barely profitable undertaking. He said that in the old days prime *carey* brought as much as fifteen dollars a pound in Bocas, and that a rise to two dollars in the current price would make Robinson a rich man because he was holding a warehouseful of shell.

When the houses of the town had begun to thin out, we came to a tiny store set back from the road. It was the last building of the town. We turned and Mr. Peterson knocked on the doorframe. A ponderous black man rose from a room behind the shop, shuffled in, and greeted us. Mr. Peterson told him our errand and the man said we had come to the right place to talk about hawksbills and learn whether stories about them were right or wrong. He said a lot of lies had been told about turtles.

He was a hawksbill man all right. He was contractor for the north beaches, from Bocas to Sixaola. When the price was good he had always had twelve or fifteen men on the beach full time in the season. Now the market was humbugged and he was sick, and though he still had the contract, he took only what shell the people on the beach could get in their spare time; and since the share of the *velador*—the man who catches the turtles—was half, the amount they brought small, and the price only a dollar a pound, there was nothing in it for anybody. He took us into the little sitting-room and opened a locked door to a connecting shed. It was full of tortoise shell—stacked tight to the ceiling with it. Like the Chiriquí Robinson he was hoarding *carey* and waiting for the rising market he was sure would come when people realized how poor the plastic imitations were.

When I asked him about green turtles at Chiriquí, he said green turtles nest all along the Panamanian coast, but the only turtles that congregated in a rookery at Chiriquí were hawksbills. The big green-turtle nesting ground, he said, was Turtle Bogue.

Mr. Peterson smiled and looked as if he had not needed the confirmation, but was pleased to get it. I thanked the hawksbill man and he gave me the best piece of shell he could find in the front tier in his storeroom, and we left.

The Chiriquí trip was off, and my feelings were mixed. It was a disappointment that the rumored green-turtle rookery did not exist; but the added stature of the Bogue beach perhaps narrowed down my field of action and simplified the migratory picture. Maybe it did. It might be simpler to trace the migratory routes leading to one big rendezvous than to plot the maze of trails to a number of smaller goals. I still don't know. But however the course of the reconnaissance stood to be affected by the change in plan, my person stood to profit. Curious as I was to see Chiriquí Beach I was not sorry to be freed of

Above: green turtles in crawl, Miskito Cays, Nicaragua. (Photo by Anne Meylan) *Below*: Archie Carr with hawksbill and green turtle (and dog). (Photo by Stephen Carr)

Above: green turtle, Tortuguero, Costa Rica. *Below*: prehensile-tailed porcupine, Tortuguero. This one turned up on the porch of the turtle station one evening.

the prospect of a forty-mile trip in a sailing dugout in a dead calm.

When we got back to the market, I paid Mr. Shepherd what I had promised him for the trip and he seemed content. He decided at once to stay over till the next day and drink more ice water at the bar. He offered to paddle my belongings back to the Miramar and return them to the room I had left, and I thanked him. I stayed behind to talk with Mr. Peterson a little longer.

We ambled about the dock watching people butcher turtles. The only parts of a turtle they threw away were the top shell, after the cartilaginous edge—what they call the chine—had been sliced off; the bones of the lower shell from around which the calipee, the cartilaginous part of the plastron, had been taken; and the large intestine. All the rest—meat, flippers, head, tripe, chitlins, liver, lights and all—was sorted into buckets to be sold. Some places turtles are dressed as fussily as hens, but here they had the wits to know that the whole beast is edible, like a hog. Some of the rustic people on the islands around Bocas still stew turtles whole in their shells as people do in many places. They remove the plastron and large intestine and use the top shell as a sort of kettle in which to cook its own contents. If it is a big turtle the neighbors may be invited, and they add plantains, yams, and breadfruit to the stew, soup up their appetites with guaro, and call the resulting fiesta a *carapash* (with which compare *calipash* and *carapace*), after the container of the main dish.

Except for the boatload of Chiriquí hawksbills in the slip, the turtles in the market were all greens, most of which had been taken with the iron on the flats off the mouth of the bay. They were all males and at first I wondered at that, but then I realized why it was. This was the mating season, and, as I say, these were harpooned turtles. I recalled how the *Liebesspiel* of the greens I saw from Paco's plane usually involved extra males; and an old saying of the turtle men came back to me too—one that says that in cooting time you strike the female and you get two turtles, maybe three. In fact, I remembered a long string of tales of the ardor and dedication of Chelonia in rut, but most of these would not be seemly in print.

I can say this, though. I can say that the single-minded drive of the male sea turtle in season is an imposing thing. You strike an attended female, and her swain may try to follow her into your boat. If the craft is a hysterical dugout to start with, this development can seem grave. Foiled in such an attempt, the loving turtle, aslosh with hormones, crackling with short circuits in his vagus control, may thrash about your boat in a wild, trial-and-error quest for an embraceable substitute. He flaps, scrapes, and bites at the planking, he chews your paddle blade or hugs your oars till they snap off. Throw out a board or a buoy and he assaults it frantically. Fall over yourself and you're out of luck.

In many places where greens are taken with nets, the males are lured into entanglement by crude decoys called "mounting boards." Some turtlers take pride in making their turtle decoys beautifully realistic, or exciting abstractions, but this is not necessary. It is a good means of self-expression for the turtle man, but it is wasted on the turtle. In Tobago they just float a turtle-size board near the net, with a short chunk of log rising slantwise from it to increase the range of visibility. They say the males sometimes break these to bits.

Male green turtles, about which I am talking, usually weigh no more than two or three hundred pounds. From all I hear, trunkbacks behave in the same way, and trunkbacks may weigh over a thousand pounds—sometimes almost two thousand. When you think how it would be to receive the passionate attentions of a male trunkback, it is frightening.

A short while ago my friend Felix O. Assam, a field man for the Trinidad Fisheries Office, met with a trunkback in such a mood and wrote me a letter about it. While I think he got off pretty lightly, his account is certainly worth quoting:

"Late one afternoon we were about half a mile up the river from the mouth in a dugout canoe. We were returning from an oyster cutting expedition, whereupon we felt a great thud on the bottom of the boat. Without guessing, we both knew that something live had come into contact with us. That particular area is noted for Manatee (Sea Cow) and at once we thought it to be that and became settled. A few yards further on the animal surfaced near the stern end and in the moment of anxiety that ensued we tried to move away quickly and the paddle (only one in the tiny craft) came into contact with a front fin and was taken away from the paddler's hand. Before it could be reached the beast was making maneuvers to come aboard. It was flood tide and the water had little pace, but the paddle could not be reached and we were pushed in all directions by the animal's approaches. The huge leather-back, presumably a male, must have wandered up the river in search for a mate. We were nevertheless most uncomfortable with the presence and annoyance of our unwelcome visitor and it was not until we had molested him with every bit of oyster-laden mangrove that was in the boat that he left us some twenty-five minutes later. We eventually managed to regain our paddle."

I have heard of other instances of these creatures just suddenly bursting up and trying to get into small boats whose occupants were not even thinking about turtles. In most cases the person telling you the story believes, pardonably, that he has been the object of an unprovoked attack by a hungry or ferocious predator, or by some demon gone berserk; but I agree with Assam that in most such cases the turtle is probably just in love.

Whatever the motive of the turtle, it must be an awful thing to be boarded by one. It is bad to be boarded by anything uninvited, or even approached in a suggestive way, especially if the thing comes up informally out of the depths and is ponderous and aggressive, and blows a lot or snorts.

I am not especially skittish about boats. I suppose I have no more fear of wind and waves than the average. But my confidence lasts only so long as I am not being boarded. Any undue attention from one of the large denizens of the sea and my morale declines sharply. I think I was marked this way as a child. My aunt had an old book with a distressing illustration showing a giant squid half aboard a schooner in mid-ocean, some of its tentacles snaking about after the harassed deck watch, others trying to unstep the foremast. I am sure this picture left its scar.

Also, I remember the time my wife and I were fishing Stew Springer's shark lines off Lemon Bay in Florida while Stew was away somewhere for a couple of days. We were three or four miles out in the Gulf, off Stump Pass, and were hauling in a ten-foot cow shark with a block and tackle. Suddenly something exploded from the twilight under the boat and cut our shark in two, clean as a bacon slicer cuts, just back of the pectoral fins, where a shark is thickest. The burst of water drenched us, and the jolt knocked the launch sideways, and while for an instant the aggressor was hardly six feet from our noses, it was all so quick we never even saw what had happened to us. It must have been another shark—but, lord, what kind, and how big?

Mr. Peterson and I stood around on the dock talking

about this general kind of thing for quite a while, and became the center of a sizable group of fishermen, all willing to contribute something on the theme. When the subject had at last been suitably explored, Mr. Peterson said he had better be leaving. We shook hands and I thanked him for saving me the trip to Chiriquí. When he had gone I decided my presence was not required for re-establishment of relations with the Miramar, since no one ever used the rooms there in the daytime, and went to look up lunch.

I walked down a short street bordered on either side with masses of little rain-lilies. There were three colors of them, yellow, pink, and white—good clear colors with no sign of intergrading. These lilies grew all over town and often took the place of grass in yards and on road shoul-ders. In some places one color predominated, in other places another; but every patch had at least a few of each of the three colors. They were volunteer plants that no-body bothered to cultivate, and nobody even knew where they had come from to start with. Several people had told me there was another color that showed up infre-quently—a light blue—and I had done some desultory searching for it with no success.

The dense stands of lilies made me think of an acid flatwoods in north Florida in April, and how T. Barbour used to time his visits to Gainesville to the atamasco-lily bloom, and used to get my wife and me to drive him out to look at the good patches every day he was here, and sometimes twice a day. And those lilies were only white. I wondered what T. B. would have thought of the tricolor lily fields of Bocas. Or maybe he saw them—he went al-most everywhere.

I did a little more prying around after the blue lily, got off my course, and wound up at the *casa de bomberos*—

the firehouse—and spent a while there talking to the chief and admiring the brass and red paint on the forty-year-old fire truck. It was so lovingly polished, and so terribly old, and the chief was so confidently proud showing it to me, that with the high sun on my head and the hunger inside I began to feel pretty maudlin and as though I needed lunch. I said goodby and moved on to find the restaurant. I took a side street along which wooden houses with railed verandas stood flush with the pavement and reminded me of Puerto Limón and Bluefields. I soon came to a wider street with Chinese shops along it, and a short way down this I could see the sign saying Murphy's Restaurant, and the plaza two blocks beyond.

I had located Murphy's the day before. It was a good place to eat, once it recovered from the fact that you were a North American. My first meal there was Spam, fried potatoes, and canned green peas, which most Caribbean people feel is a creditable approach to what a gringo is used to. I soon came to an understanding with Mr. Murphy. He was a lively man of middle age and Caymanian extraction, married to a Bocas woman who was a pillar in the local school system. He seemed relieved and stimulated that I wanted Bocas victuals. To show how serious I was, I went out and found a dozen fine crawfish and took them to him. He had a big kerosene refrigerator and a good cook, and with the sea outside there was no call for him to serve me dull provender, and I told him so. The second meal was on a higher plane than the first. And now, unexpected at midday, my arrival caused no consternation at all.

"We got turtle," Mr. Murphy said.

"Shuck me a crawfish too," I said.

The cook back of the swinging doors cackled at this hint of sympathy for her line of work, and Mr. Murphy opened the refrigerator and lifted out a red rock lobster and handed it back into the kitchen. I went out to stave off my pangs with a beer.

When I returned, the crawfish was on the table and I finished the beer with it. After that a ten-year-old Indian waitress, who looked to me exactly like a Japanese, brought out roast turtle, which despite the prosaic sound was an unusual dish, a pot roast of a pectoral cut from a big male green turtle. It was like good venison, but not so dry. Mr. Murphy told me with relish that it had been marinated in wine and cooked with Spanish onions and a few of the local marble-size tomatoes that grow on high vines. He said the recipe came from San Andrés. It was my first experience with baked turtle, and the excellence of it surprised me. With it there came out black beans and rice, baked plantains, sliced *azucaron* pineapple, and coffee.

I sat around with the coffee for a while, trying to get the little waitress to talk, but after some futile sallies the cook yelled that I would have to talk the local dialect, Cricamola, to her. This was out of the question, so I paid my bill and walked out into the wilting sunlight toward the plaza.

The Bocas plaza is called Parque Bolívar. It is a small replica of Parque Vargas, where I communed with the sloths in Limón. Like Vargas, one half was deeply shaded by big trees and the other was a formal, Moorish-looking garden with flowers laid out in geometric beds and borders flanked with palms. The cool twilight at the shaded end drew me, but I walked over to the Palacio de Gobierno, which stood at one end of the square. I was after information on the *Milla Maritima*, the coastal strip of public land that in Panama and Costa Rica is leased each year for the sake of its coco and turtle harvest. The exploitation of this

Maritime Mile is one of the main factors in the depleting of the few remaining turtle rookeries, and I have gone to some effort to learn about local regulations and systems of managing it. In the Palacio I was directed to a room at the end of a long, worn hall, where I found a thin agreeable woman of mixed Chinese, Negro, and Caucasian blood. She was in charge of local details of the leasing of government lands. She offered to make me a copy of the lease for the Bocas-Sixaola beach, and I went outside while it was being typed by an Afro-Asian stenographer.

I walked into the gloom of the shaded end of the park and sat down on a bench. It was curious how the feel of the shadowed air, surrounded by the heat and glare of the streets outside, reproduced so subtly the air of Parque Vargas. It was the same dim, grateful contrast with living in the sun-flooded streets—the same submarine look and relief to the eyes, the same cool feel on your skin and filtered freshness in your windpipe. The cool of these tropical parks is something almost tangible, and something good. Most of the spate of talking I did about Parque Vargas in another chapter could pretty well be said of Bolívar, except for the difference in size. In the sloth pasture in the Limón plaza there were, you may recall, twenty-eight trees. Here in Bolívar there were only two.

But they were two big ones, with spreading close-leafed limbs that swept out laterally and canopied a vast area, and dropped little spherical fruits on the ground. I leaned forward and picked up one of the fruits. It looked familiar, and I glanced back at the tree; and this time I noticed the glossy, lance-head leaves, the flat profile of the crown, and the fluted, buttress trunk with matted droproots fused into its substance as if melted there. It was only then that I realized that these trees were the same Indian fig, the so-called *laurel de la India,* that made the shade and sheltered and fed the lively Petes two hundred miles up the coast in Parque Vargas.

This of course was not in itself a thing to wonder about. The *laurel de la India* is one of the best of all shade trees for town planting in hot countries, and is found in parks and plazas all over the tropics. But that was not the point. The point, the thing that struck me, was that the first intimation I was under *laureles de la India* should be that tenuous sameness of the air. A most subjective character, the feel of the air, and one you never see mentioned in the botany books. Of course, it took the fruit and trunk and leaves to clinch the identification; but all the same it was odd. It was almost like looking up and seeing a lively Pete on a limb and working out the name of the tree from there.

Musing idly this way, I looked up and saw a lively Pete on a limb. That is, I thought I did. It was a dark mass, not moving. In my experience, dark masses not moving on *laurel de la India* limbs were just about always lively Petes. I stood up on the bench and shaded my eyes with both hands. Ignoring the curious looks of the other people in the park, I studied the dark mass carefully, and finally I concluded that it was moving after all. A projection from one end of the mass was making rhythmic, almost imperceptibly slow swipes at the side of the mass proper. It was beyond any reasonable doubt a sloth scratching.

You can imagine my excitement: two confluent trees surrounded by town, and a sloth population in them. I carefully scanned the lacy crown above me, but could see no other dark mass anywhere. It was, then, a sloth population of one.

Deeply stirred, I turned to a young couple on the next bench and, pointing at the sloth, asked how it came to be there.

"Lively Pete," the girl said. She was mestiza.

"Slote," said the boy, who was creole.

"Yes, but how did it get into these trees?" I insisted.

"Dem live deah," the boy said.

The girl took exception to the implication that Providence furnished the sloth. With some animation she began telling her companion and me how an old man, a creole Limonense who took care of the park, put sloths in the trees from time to time. They did no damage and he liked to see them there, because he was from Limón and the sloths reminded him of home. The girl looked quickly about the park.

"There he is," she said. She pointed to an antique stooping figure with a push broom, slowly herding *laurel* leaves at the edge of a walk. *"Aquel viejito—*the old man there," she said.

I thanked her, walked over to the caretaker, and asked him what he knew about the sloths. He said that Bocas was not a good town like Limón, but with sloths in the *laurel* trees the park was a lot like Vargas. He said he had found the latest sloth in a cecropia tree near the cemetery. He had brought it to the park three weeks before. Like others he had installed there, it seemed to thrive, and had even borne a baby a few days after its arrival. I remembered that in Limón I had never been able to get a good look at a baby sloth resting, as they do, on its mother's upturned belly. I turned and went back to the tree, and the old man followed me. I stood on the bench again and looked hard at the scratching sloth. It was not high, but the filigree of dark leaves and burning sky made it impossible to see whether there was anything on its belly. I asked the caretaker if anybody would object to my climbing the tree. He said it was against the law, but the law was mostly for children, and being a gringo and pretty old, I would not be molested.

I found hand- and foot-holds in the ladderlike binding of aerial roots and scrambled up the trunk to a big lateral limb and walked out it to a point under the hanging sloth. I got a good clear look at her. I could see her strange face and the unwholesome color of her coat and even the coarseness of the individual hairs; and I could see that there was no baby sloth anywhere about her. I swung down the tree to the ground, into the midst of a good-sized crowd. The crowd had gathered to watch me in the tree —not the sloth.

"There's no baby sloth there," I said.

The old man began peering about, searching the faces of the people around us. His gaze fell upon a clump of children, six or eight black boys and girls with books and a third-grade look, and stopped there.

"Whe de young slote?" he said.

The group burst into clamor of denial. The old man silenced them with a snort and a sharp gesture. Looking squarely at the weakest point in the front, a clean little girl with a number of hair ribbons, he said again, sternly: "Whe de young slote?"

I reinforced his accusing stare with my own, and the strain was too great; the child rolled her eyes toward a boy at one side of the uneasy covey.

"Dem tuk 'em down," she said. "Dem stone 'em."

The one accused erupted in coloratura protest and began to dance about in his excitement, pointing a finger at the others and shrieking: "Dem stone 'em too! All dis nex chillen stone 'em too!"

At that a full, shrill chorus arose, so strident it hurt my ears. The old man stood gazing at the children for a moment and then, with a shrug of resignation, turned and shuffled back to his sweeping. I walked away too, and as long as I stayed in the park I could see him shaking his head and muttering as he measured the young of Bocas against Limón children of forty years ago.

The second night I passed in Bocas was more restful than the first. No orchestra came to play at the Miramar. The cacao men had gone away, and I was too tired to be sensitive to the underpowered din of the piccolo. It had rained in the afternoon, and after a supper of broiled king-fish at Murphy's I walked out the cemetery road to listen for frogs in the flooded ditches and pastures. Several species were calling, and I managed to catch a few, but it was a sorry show compared with that of a wet summer night in Florida, where you can find mixed choruses of a dozen kinds or more singing in a single pond. I picked up a young boa, and fell into a swollen ditch trying to grab a turtle that took fright when it saw my light. After that I went back to the hotel and wrote a few notes and then went to bed and slept till morning.

The semiweekly plane was due that morning and the agent had told me I would have no trouble getting on it. The airport was only three or four hundred yards from the Miramar. It was just a long cleared strip scraped out of the scrub, with a small wooden building at one side where the radio and baggage scales were kept. A clatter-ing carryall stopped by and picked up my luggage, and would have picked me up too, but I knew I could hear the plane coming in plenty of time to get there on foot. I went back to the jook to wait in the shade and have a beer and see what new turtles were in the crawl.

When I finished the beer it was nine thirty. This was the time the plane was scheduled to leave, and though I had not heard it arrive, I said goodby to the bartender and strolled out to the airfield, taking my time and looking for lizards on the way. When I reached the little strip-side office the agent weighed my things and told me the plane was having trouble with an engine in Changuinola but should be in any time. As we talked, the radio man called: "*Ya viene*—it's coming now," and pretty soon we heard the drone of engines in the north. People began to get off the benches and fuss with their luggage. The passengers waiting for the airplane were nearly all prosperous-looking creoles and Chinese, mostly going to Colón; though some, like me, were on their way to Panama City. One girl was a schoolteacher going all the way back to her home in San Andrés. When the airplane slanted in toward the landing strip, most of the passengers picked up their things and looked expectant.

I sat down on an abandoned bench. Some ways I am cynical. A pickaninny came by with a box slung on his shoulder, and the fine smell of pineapple turnovers in it aroused me and I bought one. The plane taxied up and fanned itself around. The door in the side opened and the boarding ladder was rolled up. A few passengers stepped out, blinking in the sunlight. The Bocas agent went over and counted them, peered about inside the plane, and then studied a clip-board that he held. He frowned deeply, and when the pilot appeared at the door he started talking fast and with emotion, tapping the clip-board for emphasis and from time to time motioning toward the cluster of people waiting to board the plane. The pilot looked indignant at first and then hopeless. After a while the copilot came out and two men seized his arms and spoke to him rapidly, and after a bit he shrugged and looked hopeless too. The mechanic finished chocking the wheels and went over and joined them, and three or four of the in-transit passengers joined the discussion for a few minutes, and there was a lot of spirited talking, after which all fell silent together and shrugged and looked hopeless. After a while the agent glanced my way and left the dejected group and came over and spoke to me in Spanish.

"Pardon, señor," he said. "It is necessary to dilate a little. We have to adjust the load."

"Why?" I said unsympathetically.

"There is too much load," he said.

"Well, all right," I said. "Just so you don't adjust me."

He smiled feebly, the last time for quite a while.

"There is no need to preoccupy yourself," he said. "It will be a question of freight and local passengers. It will only waste maybe half an hour."

I was glad I was a long-haul passenger. I was going clear across the Isthmus, maybe ninety miles in all. I thanked the man, then shoved my bags under the freight counter and walked back to the Miramar, because it was hot back in the scrub and the jook was the coolest place I could think of. I ordered another beer and watched the old fisherman push himself slowly around the island and peer down at things on the bottom through his water bucket.

After a while the engines of the airplane roared up and popped and roared again, and I quickly finished the beer, said goodby to the bartender again, and walked back to the field.

The noise of the plane was a false alarm. It was only the mechanic fussing around one of the engines that was spouting an unreasonable amount of blue flame. I could see by the aspect of the little group of officials that the question of the load was still grave. As I approached, the agent came out to meet me, eying my spare frame anxiously.

"Señor," he said, "as a favor—how much do you weigh?"

I told him and he recoiled from the meager figure as if I had hit him. He passed from me to a robust creole girl and must have asked her the same question because she grinned and shook her head and he led her over to the freight scales. I could not see his face as he read her weight, but I could tell by his back how it moved him. When he had recorded the weights of seven or eight ticket-holders, he added them quickly and, when he got the sum, made a grimace of anguish and rushed out to the group of his colleagues still arguing in the shadow of the plane wing.

He showed them the total and they all flung their hands into the air and started saying: "*¡Ay, qué bárbaro!*" and then suddenly assumed expressions that meant they washed their hands of the whole affair. The Bocas passengers began to look uncomfortable, except for a corpulent East Indian salesman, who had arrived while I was away and now sat on his two vast sample cases looking aware of his rights. The officials kept casting pregnant, half-hidden glances his way, but he only looked inflexible.

I hope you have noticed by now that I am not one of those gringos who wander about the tropics looking for things to sneer at. The type exists, and ought to be discouraged. I like the tropics and Central Americans. I am usually able to see why the Caribbean people do things the way they do, and usually find their motives valid. They don't annoy me and they often stimulate me, and I enjoy most of the details and events of travel in remote and rural places. But, upon my soul, there is one aspect of Central American life that is to me incomprehensible, and that is the way the smaller internal airlines sap at your morale by open lamentations over the inadequacy of flying conditions or equipment. Where airlines of the Temperate Zone meticulously hide any slightest hint of uncertainty over their ability to cope with things, the local tropical lines keep none of their misgivings to themselves, and in fact sometimes even draw the passengers into discussions of the hazards of a projected flight. Strangely, the effect of this eccentric psychology on the passengers is not so bad as you might expect. Most of the people exposed to it are of course largely of local origin, and they must know something I have never been able to find out, because they seem to gain a certain fatalistic elation from the sessions; and though the women do a lot of appealing to the Virgin to witness their anguish, you rarely see one of them back out of even the most unpromising take-off.

For some reason the size of the load for any given flight usually takes everybody by surprise. Most often it is the pilot, who, running his eye down the list of passengers and cargo items, suddenly stiffens and turns a look of reproach on the local agent. An argument swells, and all other personnel within earshot is attracted to the scene. Nearly always there is some lady employee who turns up, is made acquainted with the situation, and then cuts loose and raises the group mood to a really high level of despair.

About this time the passengers begin stirring, some muttering to one another about how barbarous it is, others joining the official group with advice or suggestions. There are weighings and reweighings, addings on the fingers and on clip-boards, dismal reminiscences, with much histrionic business, of other overloaded flights, and direful cataloguings of the odds against the safe completion of this one. There are sighs, shoulder-raisings, and hand-spreadings of hopelessness. It is the damnedest thing you ever saw.

Through all this there usually has been one specially heavy or lately arrived or locally destined person who, like the Indian salesman at the Bocas séance, becomes the crux of the dilemma, and who is politely approached at intervals and told the merits of other flights or methods of transportation. When it is clear that this key man in the overload will remain adamant, and that nothing can be done, nothing at all, resignation spreads among the harassed officials and after a while the talking tapers off and stops. Then everybody, passengers and all, looks at the pilot.

Right there before your eyes the pilot is transformed. He puts on a new character like a clean shirt. I have seen it a dozen times, in half a dozen hot little countries. He doesn't say a word; but in a beautifully devised and timed sequence of expressions of face and body, of a subtle virtuosity achievable only by a Latin with Arab in him, he tells everybody watching that he will do it—he will take the airplane up. In spite of all the mess and confusion, the weakness of men and machines and the adversity of nature, he will make the flight; and because of his reserves of talent and experience he will pull us all through at the end.

Everybody exclaims with relief—everybody but me—and becomes awfully jocular, and the officials all grab the pilot and start wringing his hand, and the mechanics run to crank the engines. It is as if the flight had been saved by the courage of one man alone. It is an extraordinary thing, and it is practically standard pre-take-off procedure with a number of small lines that I know. And the worst part is, the more frail the facilities of the company the more open the agonizing of the personnel.

Actually the airplane at Bocas was a good one, once the mechanic had quenched the flames the manifolds were belching, and despite all the excitement the load turned out to be not really excessive. When the period of tension was over I hurried to get aboard and find a seat from

which I could look down on the beach going back to
Colón. When the loading was completed, the pilot taxied
to the end of the strip, tried his engines, and then let go
and went barging down the runway to the very end before he even tried to lift us. Not quite too late to miss the
rough, the rumbling stopped and we rose sweetly over
the scrub and skimmed out over the bay.

Then we began a long turn and the wing dipped on my
side, and all at once Bocas was framed there, the arc of
crazy waterfront and the town scattering inland behind
it. For an instant I could see it all—the market and the
jook jutting back from the long roof of the Miramar,
the little island with the fisherman anchored by it and the
concentric crescents of deepening blue where the bottom
fell away on the seaward side. Out in front of the market
wharf a narrow black dugout lay almost still in the water, with a man dipping a paddle at the stern; and in the
bow three more figures were bent over, working hard at
something. Suddenly I realized that this was Mr. Shepherd's boat, the one I almost took to Chiriquí Beach, and
this was the morning he was leaving. As the growing circle of our climb shut out the scene it came to me that
the men in the bow were trying to do something foolish—
they were trying to step the mast. But instantly they were
gone, and I was left with only the folly of what they were
doing.

But then my side of the airplane turned seaward, and
by stretching my neck I could look down the bay and
over the rock bull and out to the open sea. Beyond the
islands flanking the entrance there were patches of black
wind-ripple racing in through the mouths of the bull and
sweeping down the bay toward where Mr. Shepherd's
cayuca lay. And out where the patches came from, they
fused in a vast field of black, laced and slashed with white,

and spreading to the horizon. Where the dark water began, the six little turtle boats had raised slant-sparred sails as white and sharp as terns' wings, and they all ran shoreward together, the new speed showing in the white froth streaming in their wakes.

Suddenly I could feel the thrust and throw of those six logs come alive, and the roar of the airplane's engines lost its comfort; and the trip Mr. Shepherd would make without me seemed something forever lost.

For the trade wind was back from where it had been, come home for a day or a week to its winter range. The good, strong, constant sea breeze was suddenly back, to rout the doldrums and rattle the palms, and send the big cayucas flying and foaming over the lagoon, and down to Chiriquí.

Stuffed young hawksbills, now an important trade item, which poses a grave threat to the species.

Tiger Bogue

I AWOKE without knowing why, or even where I was. I groped for a light in the dark. I thought it must have been the wind that woke me. The high room was full of the wind—the last petulant flurries of the falling day-breeze. It rattled the thatch and the palms outside; it panted at the cracks and windows and rushed about the bare hardwood bones of the tall shack.

I found a flashlight and snapped it on. The first thing I saw was a coconut husk on the floor. Slow as my wits were, I knew the husk had not been there when I lay down. While I pondered the mystery another husk flew in at the window and thumped on the floor, and with it a voice came up from below, just louder than the wind, but insistent:

"¡Señor, es hora—it's the time. Oígame, señor!"

Then suddenly it came to me that this was Chepe's voice and I had slept all afternoon and this was the night I was going out to meet the fleet. I waved the light in the window and began pulling on my clothes.

I had been back at the Bogue—Tortuguero Beach—for a week, fooling around, walking the beach, fishing and collecting while I waited for the breeding schools of green turtles to get there. It was too early again. Only a handful of forehanded females had arrived, and the *veladores* had not yet set up their *ranchos*—their little palm-thatch shelters—for the season. But the little plane from Limón had stopped in on its weekly flight that morning, and Paco had said the fleet was on its way. He had seen a great school a few miles south and was certain it would get to Tortuguero by night, or by the next night surely. This was what I was after, and the thought of it woke me up like a cold shower.

I found no green turtles that night. From the standpoint of its main zoological aim, that night on the beach was a failure; but all the same I shall relate the events of the evening in as much and as faithful detail as my notebook and memory will allow, just to show how full an unsuccessful evening on the beach can be.

When I go back home from one of my rounds in the tropics, the question people ask most often is whether I don't get bored, away off all by myself, looking for things I half the time don't find. I don't. I get hot and wet and sleepy. I get impatient, mad, and sometimes hellishly hungry—but not bored. A situation that would bore me badly above latitude 20° north is fun down there. I have an unprofessionally naïve enthusiasm for the tropics and for the kinds of people who live there, and this breeds an uncritical acceptance of conditions that would seem annoying or dreary in other places. A few times, when I got stuck in some city or town and couldn't get out, I have grown restive; but out in the woods there's no trouble keeping your enthusiasm up. Take the night on the beach when I woke up in the wind.

I was knocking the sand out of my shoes when Chepe called to me again. I went to the window and leaned out and turned the spot on him.

"*Ya voy,*" I said, "I'm coming."

I gathered the clutter of stuff you take on a walk when

you go out to tag turtles. Impatiently I checked over the items: headlight, camera, tripod, flashgun, bulbs, film— both black and white and Kodachrome—tags, wire, drill and bits, pliers, canteen, steel tape, notebook, pencils. I added a rolled plastic raincoat and some collecting bags to the pile, stuffed the things into a couple of knapsacks, hoisted them, and swung down the rungs of the ladderlike stairway to the ground.

Chepe met me at the gate of the palisaded compound. He bore little resemblance to the short, sweating Indian with the mountain accent and two stems of bananas on his bare shoulders whom I had engaged to help me. He now wore a pair of blue serge pants, creased Lord knew how, and a long pleated shirt, some Nicaraguan tailor's interpretation of the Cuban guayabera, too big for Chepe and stiff-starched, gleaming white. He had on store-new, heavy, two-tone shoes, squeaky Managua copies of a foreign pattern in stiff, mangrove-tanned steerhide. His hair was greased down black-glass smooth. He carried his machete stuck in his belt behind, but this was not enough to reassure me. I looked at him with misgiving.

"We might go a long way," I said. "We might work hard."

"No—that's all right," Chepe said. "We'll work."

"But tell me, why the elegance? Why arrange yourself like this? We're going on the beach. I don't see why you get dressed up to walk in the black sand."

"It is that it is Saturday night," Chepe said, as if I had forgotten. "I always put on good clothes Saturday night. *Es que es costumbre.*"

When they start something *es que* you might as well give up. It means you're a foreigner after all, and some nuances of custom in a strange land must always elude you and must remain as they are. Wilson Popenoe calls it having the eskies, and dreads it; and I knew better than to argue about Chepe's clothes.

"Well, all right then, I suppose," I said. "Let's go, then."

I handed Chepe one of the bags and he looped the strap over his beautiful shirt. We walked off down a clean, deep path toward the sound of the surf, threading our way among the erratically placed huts of the Mosquito Indians and crossing a bare-swept little plaza-like clearing about which they were set. Most of the shacks were shut up tight and strangely quiet, with only an occasional mumbling voice or cry of a baby audible through the thatch walls. But one building, a wattled structure bigger than the rest and set out farther toward the sea, was clearly alive inside. Like the others it was closed, windows and doors, but bright light showed through the cracks, and inside people were talking and guitars and drums were feeling each other out.

Chepe jerked his head toward the hut and pointed with his lower lip.

"That's where the Mosquitos are. They're not really happy yet. *Mas tarde, sí*—a little later."

You could hear the skins and strings catch at something that seemed right and suddenly start driving it. The thump, boom, and rattle of the drums built a slow design and then started tearing it up, and the guitars clanked and jangled and people began to hum and pat their feet and fill the breaks with half-sung comments or snatches of falsetto harmony. Then a young contralto voice began to sing and the talking stopped and the melody drew in the others one by one till the little house sang like an organ.

The tight-shut doors and pent music and the frayed slips of light from the cracks had a familiar feel for all the wild setting. I thought back to my boyhood on the

Georgia coast where the Negroes used to shut themselves
in on Saturday nights, in tiny cracked cabins, and coax
along their shy relief with guitars and drums like these,
keeping it all to themselves in the steaming room.

I wanted to stop and sit in the shadows and listen, but
there was no real excuse for it, and Chepe was impatient to get away from the place, so I slowly followed him,
clinging to the fading magic of the music. Beyond the
dance hall the huts spread apart and strung out along a
path through the dune scrub. This was the main trail south
to Parismina, laid here among the low dunes because even
this powdery dry sand gave better footing than the floc-
culent mush at the water's edge. We followed the path
to the edge of the village and came to a clearing in the
brush, a tiny pasture, where scant, close-cropped grass
sent myriapod runners angling separately across the sand.
At the near edge of the clearing a white horse, tethered
to a stake, was clipping at the sparse herbage.

It was a one-eared horse, thin, worn, and taller than
most of the local breed. It was newly arrived in the village, surely, because I had ransacked the place the day
I came for a *bestia* to use on the beach and had found
nothing. The horse looked good to me.

"Maybe I can rent that horse," I said. "Where will the
dueño be?"

"He's getting drunk," Chepe said. "He's an old man from
Mile Twelve. A *velador*. He can't *velar* till the fifteenth
and he came up here for the *guaro*. Who knows where he
got the money?"

I made up my mind I would find the man the next day
if I had to follow him all the way to Mile Twelve. The
horse was a sad thing, but any horse is better than walking ten or twenty miles in the dark. In the deep Bogue
sand a camel is what you really need, but that thought

only breeds frustration, and I put it out of my mind. I ran my hand covetously along the galled, sharp ridge of the white horse's back and he turned and eyed me, mildly curious.

Chepe bent and took off his shoes, standing on first one foot and then the other. He tied the strings together and carried the shoes into the bushes at the edge of the clearing and hung them over a twig. He rolled up the legs of his pants and unbuttoned the starched shirt. He kicked sand with widespread toes and commented that shoes didn't serve in the sand. They were only for rocks and to look good. On Saturday night. Or in town.

We were setting out to walk perhaps ten or fifteen miles. While the sand was fine and soft, it was, after all, broken glass and pumice, and a couple of miles of it could abrade to the quick the thin hide of effete soles like mine. But Chepe had the feet of a mountain Indian, shod in natural rawhide, with stiff, stubby splayed toes, the great toe trained out to forty-five degrees by sandal straps and by riding with a toe stirrup. I wasn't worried about Chepe's feet, now that the shoes were off. I envied him.

"Do we go?" he said.

We took a dim side track that cut through waist-high grass and came out along the beach. As I felt about for the stride and pace that would last in the sand, Chepe began talking. Unburdening. I had not known what an outlander he felt himself to be here, or how actively he resented this place. He had no use for Mosquitos, or for Negroes of any kind, or for Tortuguero or Limón.

"All here is loose," he said. "There at home is different. There they *play* the guitars and don't beat them. There it is happy."

"It seemed to me the Mosquitos were getting happy. Back in the shack."

"Not like in Ocotal. Here all is loose, and in Limón it is worse. All this people lives the deceived life, and women snatch at you from doorways. In Limón it is degenerated."

"You're just with nostalgia. It isn't so bad here. I like it here. I like the Mosquitos."

"With a gringo it's different. Here there is a great scarcity of tortillas."

"That is a true thing and a sad one," I said.

"At home is nothing but tortillas. In my house two have the palm—my sister Angela and my mama, and tortillas never lack. And cheese and curds and thin-butter. Here is only flour of wheat and coco grease, and both are not healthy."

"You are with plenty of nostalgia," I said. "But you're right about the tortillas. Why don't you go home?"

"I'm going. There is more money here. I'm going home when I make some money."

Through the growing dark I noticed a scattering of curly white eggshells on the sand in front of us. I stooped and picked up one of the shells. It was still fresh and leathery. I looked about and saw no gaping hole in the sand such as an egg thief would have made digging out a nest.

"They are hatching," Chepe said, peering about for baby turtles.

It was early, but a nest of hawksbill eggs could be hatching. I knelt and poked the sand in a disturbed place and felt a loosely filled crater there. I pushed my arm down in it above the wrist and touched a small, responsive body and clutched it. It scratched and twisted loose, dived up out of the sand, and in a little storm shinnied up my arm to my shoulder and over my ear to the top of my head. I slapped at it there and it jumped into the dark grass edge and was gone before either of us could get a glimpse of it.

Chepe crooned a long, marveling obscenity. "*¿Que fue?*" he said.

"I don't know," I said. "If it was a turtle it was as active as any I ever saw. Let's try again."

I took out my flashlight, hooked the battery box to my belt, and fastened the lamp on my head. By the rays we both leaned to the digging, removing careful handfuls till Chepe felt something and pulled out his hand quickly. With still more caution we scratched away the remaining sand until finally a form took shape, and suddenly we made out a big, green, jet-eyed head jutting from an egg skin.

Chepe yelled: "Snake!" and in one sideways flip rolled four feet away. But the beady eyes blinked, and being on somewhat intimate terms with reptiles, I knew it was not a question of a snake. Then I remembered how iguanas nest in sand, wherever they find it. I took up the moist, sand-frosted infant, and it clamped its jaws on my finger and kicked off the shell from which it was hatching. Suddenly two others burst from the nest, whipped across my legs, and streaked into the bushes. I dusted off the iguana I had and held it out to Chepe.

"*¡Garrobo!*" he said. "On the pure beach!"

We sat up close to the hole and mined young iguanas for half an hour. They were wonderfully bad-tempered and quick, and several got away. One that I helped out of its egg got away. We managed to put thirty of them in a bag. They were all lettuce-green and between eight and ten inches long. In poking about the region of the nest we broke into the fresh nest of a hawksbill turtle no more than a yard away from that of the iguana.

I had never seen young iguanas hatching before. I once found an iguana nest—I wrote something about it—on a sandbar in a river in Nicaragua, where the lizard had laid squarely on top of a cayman's nest. But this nest out on the seabeach was nearly half a mile from the nearest iguana territory—the big trees of the gallery forest along the Tortuguero River! It would be hard to name two reptiles more divergent in their day-to-day life than an iguana and a hawksbill—the latter a putterer about undersea coral reefs, the former a high-climbing, leaf-eating denizen of tall trees in fringe forest. And yet the freighted females of the two see eye to eye on the proper place to hide eggs. Both are reptiles after all, and part of being a reptile is burying eggs; and the sea sand here was the nearest and best incubating medium for the arboreal lizard and for the salt-water hawksbill turtle as well.

When we had obviously reached the bottom of the nest, I took some crude measurements of the cavity for my notebook's sake, gathered some unhatched eggs to take away, and tied up the bag of lizards and hung it on the trunk of a palm while we slapped at the sand on our arms and on the seats of our pants. Then we took up the iguanas and the shoulder bags, and moved on.

It was dark by now. From time to time I switched on the light and swept the long cone across the beach ahead. Chepe suggested that you can see turtle tracks as well in the dark as with a flashlight—maybe a bit better.

"You see a streak of different dark," he said.

I knew what he meant, and there is something in it. But to an old hand with a headlight it seems wrong to walk in the dark when you know there are so many eyes to see. With a focused beam you see little lights sparkling on the dunes like strewn rhinestones or burning in the bushes like low stars. These are the eyes of wolf

spiders, prowling the open beach for sand fleas or climbing grass stems for sleeping insects, or of queer paper-
thin crack spiders plastered on the smooth stems of the
coco plums. You see moon crabs in many-legged flight,
crossing the unseen sand beneath them as if they slid
down tight wires, escaping to the sanctuary of the surf
or to the sanctuary of their holes, whichever seems best
at the moment you surprise them. You look down the
long lane of light for the flashing yellow of coon-kind eyes,
and if there is no foraging coon or coati along the brush
front, there is nearly any time the incongruous great flare
of the eyes of a brooding goatsucker, and if you see it a
dozen times you still think for a heartbeat that it's something vast and hungry. Sometimes a constellation explodes
at the limit of your range and its dimly lit stars streak
apart like wasting meteors; and then yapping in the scrub
tells you it was a party of Siquirres dogs you scared, hunting hawksbill eggs till the green-turtle fleet should arrive.
If you shoot your beam across the low bush to the real
trees of an inland coppice, you may ignite the pinpoint
eyes of a two-inch moth to a fire the size and color of the
eye-shine of a six-foot alligator. Turn your head a hundred
times seaward and you see no eye at all, but you flush
surf-feeding schools of flat little fish into top-skipping, air-
diving frenzy; and the hundredth time you may spatter
reflection from the shell of a hawksbill riding in on the
waves to lay.

We had walked for half an hour when, straight down
the beach ahead of us I picked up a reflection at once
clearly familiar and wholly wrong for this place. It was a
dim, pink moon of an eye, a planetlike glow instead of a
star's sparkle, a clean-scribed circle in outline, and beyond any doubt the eye of a frog. In the tenuous light
of the ray's end it seemed hung in space, but I took no

stock in this impression and walked forward till a log took shape under the eye. It was a weathered saw-log two feet thick, half sunk in the sand, with the upper end salt-white and the other wet-black from the slosh of the waves. The frog with the eye sat just where the wet part joined the dry.

To you this may seem a trivial thing. To me it was a marvel. The eye belonged to a Hyla—a tree-frog—a big tropical species usually found about open ponds or ditches of fresh water. Of all the air-breathing vertebrates, the amphibians, the frogs and salamanders, are the least tolerant of salt water, which, for physical reasons hard to explain in plain English, draws water out of protoplasm and makes things hard for naked, wet creatures. There is no truly marine species of amphibian known, and existing kinds nearly all shun even passing contact with the sea. Toads of course are thick-skinned and less inclined to lose water than their kin, and you sometimes see a toad out among the dunes at night, or beside a brackish estuary, but not often.

This Hyla on the log was defying all precedent, as far as I was concerned, sitting there in the spray-whip. According to the textbooks, he should have been in a sad osmotic predicament. He should have been shriveling from loss of his juice to the brine outside. Instead, he sat with the wind in his big eyes, feet tucked under his chest, throat swelling and flattening as he breathed the salt air and waited, I suppose, for some unwary sand flea or boat louse, or whatever alien victim might wander within his reach.

For all his insouciance in breaking the taboos of his kind —in hunting strange food in this half-world here at salt-poisoned land's edge—you could be sure this frog came from somewhere else. He was not born in the sea or in the sand. He was surely hatched in fresh water. He could have wandered windward from some fresh pool in the forest or swamp along the river; but that was a dreary way back from here, across dry scrub hateful to Hylas of all sorts. On a sudden hunch I swung my light into a strip of palm grove. There I made out a piece of sagging thatch in an old vine-tangled clearing. Leaving the frog and Chepe, who was seeing little good in this encounter, I walked over and looked around the clearing and found the ruins of a boarded well—one of the only faintly brackish wells that you somehow get if you dig this dry ridge of sand between the tidal river and the salt sea. The cover had rotted and fallen in and the walls were caving badly, but a glint of water showed at the bottom, and when I shined the light into it and tapped a board, I saw the scurry of tadpoles in the murk.

I knew then how the frog came to be so near the beach; but I don't know what had moved him to seek and hold a station there in the salt wind. I returned to the log and found the frog where he had been, and Chepe on the dry end smoking a cigarette. I put the frog in a bag, and we walked away southward down the long shore.

We had gone perhaps two miles by now and had seen no green-turtle sign at all. The school was not in, and it seemed unlikely that it would come that night. Concerted as its movements usually are, there is always a trickle out in front to give you warning. A steadier man of more single-track science might have gone home to rest for the next day. But the beach stretched ahead twenty miles unbroken, and the breeze still held strong enough to sweep the sand flies away. The separate dim pulsing of heat lightning far out in the southeast showed where the safely distant squalls were squandering their rain in the sea. Why go back? There was still the chance of a solitary green, and the *careyes* and trunkbacks were still coming in. It was too soon for the *veladores*, and the beach was lonesome, and nearly anything from the forest might be out after eggs. Whenever there is a beach to walk, you'll likely find me talking this way. Walking a wild beach in the tropics at night is an end in itself to me.

Still, from the standpoint of our original motive and aim, it was pretty futile; and I pointed this out to Chepe and asked if he wanted to go back. If you're bound to walk the dark shore at night just more or less for the hell of it, you want to be sure of your company, or do it alone. It was no problem to Chepe.

"It's savory out here on the beach at night," he said.

I guess no other young man from Limón to Colorado Bar would have chosen to take that walk, for no stipulated fee, on Saturday night, with the *guaro* can in and open. It took this homesick Spanish Indian from back inside to see the good in it. In a Latin Indian like Chepe homesickness is a strong disease.

I started asking Chepe about his home, about the obvious things such questions run to: family and crops and girls and wages, but all the time feeling for the essence beyond questioning—the things I was homesick for too: the smell of drifting mimosa smoke at daybreak; the windsong in the pines over the long mule trails at noon; the distant cry of a laughing hawk and the look of a little tile-roofed hut stuck on a hillside by the red gash of a milpa, or suddenly seen at a cove-head.

From the time Chepe heard I had lived in the hills and knew Ocotal he had, in a reticent sort of way, looked to me for comfort. Now that it was Saturday and his need for support heightened, I think he would have carried my bag to the end of the beach if I had walked that far.

"Here all the Saturdays it is only the parties of those crazy Mosquitos," he said.

You could see how it was Saturday nights that made the coast so bad. It being Saturday night both places, here and at home; with the props and trappings so much the same and the spirit so different. *Guaro*, girls, and guitars here, and there in Estelí—and beyond that no shade of sameness in the way things worked out.

You can figure how the leisure of Saturday afternoons loosed his thoughts to fly back over the lowlands and across the ranges to another place where the weekly *guaro* flow was starting; where washed men gathered in the cantinas or in clumps at trail crossings or under trees beside the dusty roads and drank from government bottles and watched the girls and talked about them. There were guitars there too, in the cantinas and under the trees, but how different the sound of those guitars! In Mosquito hands they seemed to Chepe more juba fiddle than guitar, with their cannibal jigs and wails wrenched from slack strings, their bare bones of melody slapped and pounded by the skin-bass and mocked by the patternless clatter of sub-times.

The wonderful Mosquito music meant nothing to Chepe —nothing good or pleasant. In fact, it almost made him weep to talk about it. Where he was from, it was Mexican guitars they played. Six strings flung honey in showers of little drops, or flared in brief Moorish fire, or moaned and murmured the wonder and sadness of being Indian. They raced with the driving *corrido* time or throbbed with the aching sweetness of a *huapango*. The guitars looked the same as here, but what they said was a world away.

The worst part of all was, the girls in the village didn't serve.

The Mosquito girls were more disheartening than the drums and the ravished guitars. The big, athletic, black-polished wenches were too overt for a Spanish Indian. They just pulled you into a bush. Latin men talk about sex more than anybody else, but being pulled into a bush takes them aback and quenches all their fire. I think I am right in saying it was the Latin in Chepe that was offended—I can't believe it was the Matagalpa Indian. Anyway, the girls Chepe was used to, you had to court and cajole. Even tuned to the week-end—mellow with Saturday-night acquiescence—the Ocotal girls stayed pleasingly coy and parried advances with just the right shade of indignation. Towers of piety to the point of yielding, they yelped throughout whatever happened to them with piteous conviction of sin. This way the fatal virility of the male was affirmed, the blame for the event was laid squarely on the shoulders of the devil, where it belonged, and the whole thing seemed more inevitable and more refined. Sex in Estelí was a ceremony. Here on the beach it was a function.

Bemused by the trend of Chepe's rambling nostalgia, I failed to see the loom of a human figure down at the water's edge till it was almost abreast of us. I touched the switch of my light and the rays lit up a young mestizo, slowly walking ankle-deep in the backwash and holding a coil of liana rope that stretched out seaward beyond the breakers. It was an unlikely thing to be doing and I could make nothing of it. Chepe made a sound of recognition.

"What's he doing, fishing?" I said.

"*Saber,*" Chepe said. He didn't know either.

I called a greeting to the man, and said that neither of us could figure out what he was doing.

"Would you do me the favor of telling me what you have on that vine?"

"*Tortuga*," he said, "or rather, *carey*. Very big hawksbill."

"What are you going to do with it?"

"I'm going to eat it."

"I mean on the end of the line," I said. "What's the good of standing in the water with a turtle on the end of a vine?"

"Is it for you something new, this manner of taking a turtle home?"

"For me it is." I looked at Chepe. "How about you?"

"Me too," he said.

"Well, then," the man said. "I can show you how to do it. It's very practical. I won't draw in the *carey* to show you, but look here."

He backed out of the water, paying out line from the coil. When he was on dry sand he stopped and stooped and put a foot on the line to hold it and with a finger he engraved a circle in the smooth sand. He put four flippers and a head on the circle and made it a turtle. He scratched a bar from the off fore flipper to the shell. "You tie that one to the shell. You rig a harness around the shell and run your line from the near side. Then you push the turtle into the water and hold the line and walk in the required direction. That's all. The turtle does the rest."

"Very pretty," Chepe said.

"A kind of paravane," I said.

"What?" the man said.

"I can't say it in Spanish. Maybe the turtle isn't one anyway. But it's a good trick. You would have trouble getting her back any other way. Where did you learn the trick?"

He tapped his head with two fingers. "Here," he said. "I invented it."

"Very pretty," Chepe said, looking proud of the man. "He's a Nicaraguan."

I was sure I had heard of that way of taking advantage of turtles somewhere before, but there was no use saying so. The man picked up the coil and walked out into the surf, taking in line as he walked.

"It's slow, this way," he said. "But one arrives."

As he vanished into the dark and racket of the surf I called to him: "Have you seen any green turtles tonight?"

"No, señor. The fleet is delayed. When the fleet comes I won't be pulling turtles home like this."

The last we saw of him was the swish and flare of phosphorescence around his shanks.

"That man is a Nicaraguan. A compatriot, only from the coast. Very intelligent," Chepe said.

For a long time after that we walked in the dark, seeing only the stars and the pulsing glow of the surf, and hearing only the swing of the waves and squeak of trodden sand. When Chepe began to talk again, his mood had shifted a little. The unaccustomed sympathy and the encounter with an ingenious countryman had taken the sting out of his nostalgia for a while, leaving pure patriotism.

"Do you know Entrerios?" he said.

"Just the edge. From the Honduras side. Far enough in to see *Viva Sandino* painted on the cliff faces."

"*Yo, sí,*" he said. "I am a knower of all that region. There it is formidable and there are not many who know it. There is where Sandino beat the gringo soldiers."

"He didn't beat the gringos. He was just hard to catch. I think that's the way it was."

"He cut off their heads," Chepe said.

Above: turtle boat and rancho, Miskito Cays, Nicaragua. The ranchos are located in open, shallow water, far away from land, to get away from mosquitoes and sandflies. *Below*: tepescuintle from Tortuguero, Costa Rica.

Above: Miskito turtle boat, Miskito Cays, Nicaragua. *Below*: *velador*'s rancho, Tortuguero, Costa Rica.

"Well, not all of them."

"Their heads or their *cojones*," Chepe said.

"I've seen Marines from there—talked to them. Their heads were on, and I'm pretty sure they were entire."

"I doubt it," Chepe said. "Sandino was *muy capaz, muy hombre*."

I caught the glimmer of glass in the matted seaweed at my feet. I thought there was a bottle there and kicked at it, but it rolled away fast, too straight for a bottle. I went over to where it stopped and picked up a six-inch glass ball, one of the maverick net floats that you find on the beaches of many lands. I handed it to Chepe.

"It's one of those," he said. "A glass ball. You know where they come from?"

It was another of the things that are left hanging in my mind. There must be some place to learn where glass floats come from. All I know is they are used by some Mediterranean people and by the Japanese. I never saw them on nets anywhere in the Caribbean. Perhaps the nearest glass-float fishermen to Tortuguero would be the Sicilians in New England and the Portuguese in the Azores. Just looking at a chart of the ocean currents I decided that the Costa Rican floats must come from the Azores. I'm probably wrong, but it sounds exciting that way, and makes finding one an event.

There is no mark on the balls to show their place of origin. They come in two shades of glass—light bottle-green and pale blue. They are pleasing objects and I like to find them, but they are uncompromisingly round and fairly heavy, and you don't carry many of them far.

"Listen," Chepe said. He was shaking the ball beside his ear. "Water. It leaks."

I recalled this mystery too. I took out the flashlight, lit it, and looked at the float. There was half a teacupful of water in it, but no crack or visible perforation anywhere.

"How did the water get in?" Chepe asked.

"*¿Quien sabe?* There must be a hole you can't see."

"I imagine," Chepe said, "that it is the force of the waves."

That was as good as I could do.

Chepe asked if it would be all right to put the ball in the bag he was carrying. He wanted to take it home as a *recuerdo*. He had wanted to take one home for a long time but never got around to it. I told him to stow it down under the other stuff where it wouldn't break anything or mash the iguanas. He shifted things about in the bag and reached deep to lodge the ball at the bottom, beneath the varied clutter. Then he said:

"Would you like a *pipa*? We are reaching where some low trees are."

A *pipa* is a jelly coconut, and I would always like one.

"*Claro,*" I said. "Where are the low trees?"

"Shine your light—*ahí no masito*—just a little way." The ridiculous way of saying it, heard after so long, cheered me as much as the prospect of a *pipa*.

I fixed the light on my head and scanned the cocal and located a break in the ranks of tall trunks.

"Right there," Chepe said.

As we started to walk toward the place there was a quick slash of light from the upper beach ahead of us. I swung my beam full on it and two eyes blazed for an instant, then winked out, then stabbed back again from halfway down to the sea.

"Some kind of animal," I said stupidly. "What kind of animal would that be?"

Chepe leaned and peered along the pencil of light to get the full reflection. The eyes flashed and faded, then reappeared in another spot and circled and swooped like dancing fireflies, then streaked down the beach into the wave-wash and held steady there for a bit.

"It's something jumping around," Chepe said. "I don't know what animal would go in the sea like that."

"*Venite*, then. Walk by me and we'll find out."

I put a hand on his shoulder to keep us together for the stalk, and we walked slowly toward the eye-shine, now zigzagging crazily in and out of the edge of the water. We went quietly and I held the light as still as I could to keep the creature with the eyes from knowing what was happening to it. But there was no need for stealth. Whatever owned the eyes was already in a sweat too great to be heightened by a light. When we were some thirty feet away and still not able to make out what we were stalking, the eyes turned square on and came looping toward us, straight down the strong ray of the light.

We stopped and let them come. The gap closed, and a body took shape. In one voice Chepe and I yelled "tepescuinte!" and dashed forward to block the flight of the animal and drive it back into the water. We moved with inspired agility, because, as Chepe began to moan under his breath, "*tepescuinte es la mejor carne que existe*—the best meat there is"—and finding it out here on the beach was a chance straight from heaven.

The tepescuinte, you may know, is Nelson's paca, a kind of twenty-pound rodent, normally a secretive, nighttime lurker in river forest or plantation border. It is a kind of caricature of a rodent, with bizarrely oversized buck teeth and overdeveloped jaw muscles that give its face a bulbous, idiotic look—a much accentuated version of the pleasingly silly look a squirrel has. It is the look so arrestingly shown in the picture of the March Hare in old editions of *Alice in Wonderland*. But this look has nothing to do with the meat of the animal, which is superb. Moreover, the paca can run and dodge like a jack rabbit, and this is what the one at hand was doing.

The beach was wide where we were. It is possible that the paca was lost and traveling at random all the time, though you will see shortly that this is unlikely. Once the nervous creature saw us, however, it quite clearly lost any plan or course that may have guided it before. It sought only to elude us, in a despairing, fluctuating sort of way, trying one new direction after another. This kept our hands off it, but did nothing to lessen the basic weakness of the paca's position—it was still blinded and spotlighted on bare sand with no cover available.

But our position was weak too. All the time our one thin thread of contact with the prize was the ray from my flashlight, and as we scrambled and skidded in the dark, the battery box kept falling off my belt and bouncing after me at the end of its wire, tripping me up and almost dragging the lamp off my head. These times we would pray softly till the box was retrieved and the quarry safely lit up once more. Then in and out of the surf we went, sprinting, circling and reversing, as the frantic tepescuinte dashed about before us, between us, between our legs, or for an anxious instant out somewhere alone in the dark, always moving and always just missed by our snatching hands and swinging feet.

If you know this animal we were after only from books or in the zoo, it may be hard for you to make sense out of our actions. This man, you may say—the gringo—is a college professor, no longer young and, moreover, a sample of our civilization on view in a strange and critical land. And this line of reasoning is valid. And let me add that Chepe had dignity of his own—a good deal more than I had. The only thing I can do is stress, again, the allure and the compulsion. I believe I can say that no new-formed Aphrodite just out on the starlit sand, foam-fresh, kitten-coy, and fawn-fleet, would have been chased with the lust with which we chased that great rat.

Even so, the odd ballet could not go on all night. I had begun to wonder vaguely how it would ever end when I caught a sideways gleam from Chepe's hand, raised high behind his shoulder. I turned and saw that he had somehow fished up the glass float from the bottom of the bag and was poised for a throw at the paca. Then in a flash I had an idea too, and I stopped my headlong chasing and stood still and held the spot of my light dead-center on the running paca.

"*¡Asi!*" Chepe hissed approval.

Now at last we had a plan. As long as I stayed where I was and the quarry kept within a hundred yards, Chepe would be able to see it. The glass ball was an unpromising missile, to be sure. I recalled the impunity with which pacas take bullet wounds; but quickly I recalled the unearthly aim and speed of rock-throwing mountain urchins such as Chepe once was, and hope flowed back. Then the arm with the float lashed out and a short gleaming arc flashed from hand to paca, and suddenly the chase was over.

I ran to the spot full of joy and wonder. The tepescuinte was lying on its back with a bubble of blood at the tip of its nose. Chepe was bending over it.

"*Pegué*—I hit him," he said, reverently.

"*Pegaste*," I said. "On the head, too."

"*¡A la puta!*" Chepe said. "On the pure head!"

He poked the paca with a finger and its leg jerked. He rose and walked back toward where he had dropped his machete during the heat of the chase. I sat down to do some systematic breathing. We had won a hard race, and with the prize in hand I was ready to go home. Or maybe just go to sleep right there.

Chepe was searching in the dark, and I snapped on the light to help him. When he had found the machete, I idly swept the spot of light along the scrub edge the way we had come. It neared the end of its range and I was about to swing it back when the scrub screen down the beach blazed yellow-green fire, distant and disembodied, but hot, high, and thrilling. The adrenaline crashed about in me again, and I jumped up, not tired any more, and steadied the rays on the spot. As the dim end of the light-cone centered, the blaze grew and held strong. There was one flaring point for a moment, then two side by side, then one again. Whatever was there was looking from Chepe to me and back again.

"*Paráte, Chepe*," I called in the lowest voice I thought would reach. I started walking slowly toward the reflection, holding the paca in one hand and keeping the light true with the other. As I drew even with Chepe I whispered for him to come up and follow me closely, and I waited for him to get there. As he approached I started walking again, my neck held so stiff it ached, my feet groping for quiet steps. Suddenly Chepe saw what it was we were after and loosed a chip of an oath.

"*León*," he whispered in my ear.

"Maybe," I said. "Or *tigre*——jaguar. Or ocelot. Maybe just a deer."

It was something good, something big this time. The eyes looked waist-high, and were very wide apart. Dogs were out on the beach, but dogs in June came in packs and ran when a light fell on them, and growled or yapped. The eyes we saw were no *pucuyo*—no goatsucker—on a waist-high limb; the full-face spread showed that. Running down the list in my mind, I suddenly realized why the poor paca had behaved so queerly, skipping about the ocean beach and dashing into the surf for no evident reason. It was to get away from those eyes. They were no deer eyes, then; and that left only the big cats: puma, ocelot, and jaguar.

I had seen the shined eyes of pumas before, and of ocelots many times, and while the blaze in the bush could have been either, it seemed too fiery for an ocelot. But with bodiless reflections from a single point in the dark the uncertain range and lack of perspective make such judgments difficult. And in all my hopeful wandering about jaguar habitat, I had never seen a jaguar. I wanted this to be a jaguar.

When we had closed the range to forty feet I could see that the eyes were burning through an open screen of sea grapes. We would have to get very close to see the body clearly, and the thought that the beast might grow uneasy at the stalk and move away put my nerves on edge. I stepped up the sneaking pace to a half run, and the light wobbled on my head. The eyes went out and I cursed, in Spanish so Chepe could benefit. I stopped and slowly scanned the brush with the beam. There was nothing there.

"He went away," Chepe said. *"Cabrón."*

In a pet of frustration I dashed up to the scrub where the eyes had been. Ducking and bobbing my head about for an opening, I found one that freed the light beam down a corridor leading a long way back among the bushes. But there was nothing back there to see.

I was dejected. I began to feel tired again. To be doing something I started to break through the sea-grape front to look for tracks in the sand. A twig whipped my face, and I jerked. I sensed a field of convulsion to the half-lit left, and when I turned, a wall of broken color blotted out what was beyond. My eyes tested the limits of the wall, and there was a jaguar standing there, ten feet away, broadside on, crouched for another jump, stiller than the trembling leaves about it, and staring straight at me.

I tried to signal to Chepe behind my back. I tried to tell him *tigre* without making a sound or a motion. But all I did was stand frozen, staring at the vast, golden cat, soaking him in, not sure what second he would go, showing myself over and over that he was indeed a jaguar and not an ocelot because the black marks on him made rosettes and not ocelli, then not being sure whether I had it right or reversed, then judging the rise of the shoulder and depth of the great chest against a sapling in the background and seeing too much brawn and spread there for any ocelot, then happily passing the spot of my light up to the great head that no ocelot ever approached for mass and power.

You may wonder at my doubts, since a jaguar may be almost the size of a Bengal tiger, and even the relatively small ones in Central America often weigh two hundred pounds or more; while an ocelot is no bigger than a setter dog. But the night and the sea-grape leaves, the black-and-gold pattern common to the two animals, and the hard spot of a hunting light at ten-foot range could easily fool you. I wanted to be sure. This was a thing I had wanted to see as badly as anything I had come for. This was my first jaguar and I wanted him to leave me easy in my mind about him.

Suddenly Chepe saw what held me so quiet.

"*¡Santa madre!*" he said. "*¡Tigre!*"

He leaned forward abruptly and grabbed the tepescuinte that hung by a leg from my hand. He tossed it out into the dark. The slight commotion and thump made the *tigre* crouch two inches lower. I thought how foolish I might have looked if the cat had decided to take back the game we had stolen.

I heard a tiny sing of steel and knew Chepe had found his machete and had just drawn it out of his belt. I hissed and wagged my finger back at him to quell the machete reflex, and then set out upon a train of reflexes of my own. I groped behind me for the bag Chepe carried and hauled it off his shoulder, never letting the light move from the tiger's head. I felt in the bag for my camera, found it, and quietly lowered the bag to the ground. From my own knapsack I took out the flash gun and felt out a bulb for it. There was no sense in what I was doing; but there was no sense in what the jaguar was doing either. With competing fingers I pressed the bulb into place in the reflector, then felt for the catch on the camera case. The light beam never wavered. I found the catch and pressed. It let go, and the case fell open with a slight click.

I saw the jaguar's head move, and then he was gone. With no other motion he left empty the place where he had stood so still. From ten feet in front of me the night took him in, whole and instantly, and left Chepe and me standing alone.

"¡Qué barbaridad!" Chepe murmured, with all the feeling the phrase can carry. After a moment he dropped to the sand and clawed in his pocket for a cigarette and lit it.

"Pretty the skin," he said. "But what a brute the animal!"

"Sí, hombre," I said, just to be answering. I was still feeling the sight of the big beast standing there in the sea grapes.

"Shame you carry no gun," Chepe said.

There was no shame in it for me. I had all I wanted. I could even see as funny my mindless moves to take a picture. After six years the *tigre* and I knew each other. I had missed the turtles, but it was all right. I had seen a jaguar.

"Hell, man, we've got a tepescuinte," I said.

Chepe sprang up and ran off the way he had thrown it. I could hear the sand shucking as he quartered the beach, feeling for the paca with his feet.

"Haven't we?" I asked.

"*A-jah*," Chepe said suddenly. "That, yes we have."

I don't remember much about the walk back. For me the trip should have ended when the tiger disappeared. There was no point in anything else happening. We stopped and drank the *pipas* we had been looking for when the paca came out. After that the seven-mile walk back to camp was just a matter of setting one foot in front of the other a great many times. There seemed no hope that the van of the turtle fleet had come in behind us, and no other event could stir a soul fresh steeped in painted jaguar. I took the light off my head and walked all the way in the dark, the first part of the trip in a kind of reverie, reconstructing the meeting with the tiger, the last as near asleep as you can be with your feet moving under you. I remember nothing about the trip, as I say; and there is nothing in the notes I wrote the next day to show that we saw or said a single thing of interest. It took us nearly three hours to get to the village and there was nothing about the walk worth telling, except the way it ended.

It was back at the pasture where we had left the white horse that I began to come to life. As we neared the place, Chepe turned out of the path to look for his shoes and I switched on the light to help him find the bush where they were hanging. When he sat down to put them on I moved the light about the opening till it fell on the horse still standing where we had left it. It looked up, after a moment, more polite than inquiring, then turned back to its grazing. I was wondering how to go about hiring the horse, bones and all, when I noticed an odd black patch on its shoulder just at the base of the thin neck. The horse had been all white before, I was sure. Steadying the light, I walked across the grass to within perhaps twenty feet, and then quickly stopped, cut off the light, and ran back to where Chepe sat tying his shoes.

"There is a vampire on the horse's neck," I said.

"*¿Sí, no?*" Chepe said, not wrought up. "Scare it away."

I never saw a picture of a vampire bleeding a victim. Pictures may have been made, but probably not often. Getting one without staging it seemed a worth-while project, and this looked like the time to do it. Everything was propitious.

I can't make out whether I'm the most inept photographer there is or just the least lucky. Take this time.

I got the camera and flash gun assembled, adjusted, and set. With Chepe holding the light on the bat, I walked back to within the twelve-foot distance for which I had set the focus. I had time to compose the shot neatly and even to refine the focus on the ground glass. The picture was in the bag, and I snapped the trigger triumphantly. The bulb failed to flash. Even punched by the twenty-two-volt capacitor designed to make bulbs flash under any conditions, the wretched bulb did nothing. Petulantly I snatched it out and threw it behind me, scratched another out of the bag, and twisted it in. Again I raised the camera, and the horse lifted its head to chew, and on the instant the bat finished its meal, flopped off and fell halfway to the ground, caught itself up with a stir of air, and veered away among the palms.

I am so used to that sort of thing that I only swore for a short while.

"*Se fué*—he went away." Chepe said. "The *jodido*."

That primed me, and I cursed a good deal more after that.

After a while I looked back at the horse. A pool of blood was spreading on its neck. I decided to test the miserable flash gun and document the fiasco by photographing the bleeding horse.

I let the blood gather for a while. The saliva of a vampire is anticoagulant, and a bite, though just a superficial scrape, bleeds amazingly. Chepe walked over to see what I was doing. He remarked that vampires were partial to white horses. I recalled that in Honduras they said the same, and that my white horse Meto used to turn up with his neck blood-smeared much more frequently than the bay and the roan he grazed with. Of course it may be simply that white horses are the easiest to see.

When the blood had spread down the neck of the unconcerned horse and started spilling to the ground, I raised the camera and tripped the shutter, and everything worked beautifully. I began to swear again, but then cut it off to keep from having to explain to Chepe what ailed me now.

As I took the camera and flash gun apart, it began to rain. It was no thundershower, but a fine drizzle, half mist, that seemed to rise and drift as fast as it fell and made the prospect of going to bed seem good. My shack was only a quarter of a mile away and we began to walk again, at a faster pace. We cut the distance down to half before the rain had begun to come in drops. Just as the drops got big enough to drum on the stiff palm leaves, we heard a sound of shouting ahead. Chepe touched my shoulder and stopped to listen.

"What's the *bulla*?" I asked.

"*Los Mosquitos.*" He shook his head. "Drunk completely. The big drunk is on."

This was my third visit to the Mosquito Coast, but I had somehow never been on hand at one of the Big Drunks. It was not by choice, because I long ago had heard that they were extraordinary events. As I told you in another chapter, they are rundown orgies with the original ceremonial point forgotten, with rum replacing the native beer, but with all the relaxation left intact. When the race was formed, some four hundred years ago, by the blending of shipwrecked Guinea slaves with the coastal Indians, both strains brought a firm tradition of ceremonial inebriation, and the custom lost nothing in the merger. It came out, in fact, fortified with hybrid vigor. These Big Drunks are not to be confused with that other Mosquito fiesta, the Maypole, which begins as a dance, and in which the central theme is not liquor at all. Women attend the Maypoles—in fact, they are the life and essence of the Maypole. The Big Drunk scares the women away. I had been told everywhere that the Big Drunk was one of the ethnic features of the coast that you ought to see—that you can't know the Mosquito Indian until you have seen the Big Drunk.

But this time, in the predawn rain, I was too tired, too full of the events of the night, to care about the Mosquitos and their party. Though the noise grew imposingly as we approached, I was determined to ignore it as a minor distraction from my main objective, which was bed. But ignoring it was not going to be easy.

Traveling at a trot, we passed the corner of a hut and abruptly were in the middle of the uproar. By the light of a dropped and smoking lantern and two dying fires of driftwood we could make out the outlines of the shambles. The whole open area was a hell of tumbling, rolling Mosquito men, all crazy drunk, all fighting and all howling. I stopped, appalled, and played my flashlight beam about the clearing. The place was strewn with conflict. There seemed no plan or integration to the struggling, but only an inchoate urge in the mob to destroy itself by bits. The men were fighting in pairs and threes, or in small, tangled, quantitatively doubtful clots, some swaying about on foot and swinging and clutching at one another, some writhing and thrashing on the ground, all screaming or bellowing threats and obscenities or piteous cries for mercy or just unformed sounds of hate or anguish or fiendish joy. I give you my word, it was the most awesome scene of violence —the most utterly bloodthirsty looking and sounding show I ever imagined. It made me repent of my long insisting that backwoods people are as easygoing as anybody else. It made me wonder if I was about to end my wanderings at the stake, or even eaten.

The only way out of the mess was straight back the way we had come, and I moved to take it. Switching off my light, I stepped backward and bumped into Chepe. I turned and looked at his face. To my surprise, he seemed just annoyed at the Indians, instead of scared stiff like me. He motioned toward the arena.

"Go ahead," he said. "The water is coming. It's going to rain hard."

I was incredulous.

"Go down that path?" I said. "You're crazy."

"Why not?" Chepe said. "It's the only one there is."

"But look—how about those *demonios* there? They're killing themselves. I wouldn't go down that path for anything. Let's go back to the beach and come in from the other side."

I pushed him in the midriff to get him started.

"What the hell," he said, pushing back. "Go on the way we're going. Those bastards do this every Saturday night. It's their custom. The *guardia* takes away their machetes and knives. They only hit and bite, and they're too drunk to get hurt. But you live by them—didn't you see last Saturday?"

"I was away last Saturday. I'll be away every Saturday if I can arrange it."

"It's nothing," Chepe sneered, moving in front of me and striding off down the trail, toward the middle of the melee.

I hurried to close with him for company, and together we half trotted out into the plaza. We stepped around or over all the maniac clumps in the way, and tried to look only straight ahead. Halfway across we were still unnoticed. We came to a struggling pair lying squarely across the trail. One man sat on the other man's chest, and they cursed each other in three languages; each was shouting that he would castrate the other and string out his tripes. As we started to go around them, the man on the bottom stopped yelling. I could almost feel him see us. He mouthed something in Mosquito and the man on top looked up and saw us too and began to yell in a high warning tone. An ominous quiet spread about the clearing.

"Let's get out of here, Chepe," I said.

"Don't worry. They won't do anything. Even this way they won't molest a gringo."

The beam of a flashlight shot across from somewhere and played over us. We kept walking, looking straight ahead. There were scattered choruses of mumbling, shouted taunts and suppressed drunken laughter here and there, but none of the Mosquitos moved. Then another spot of light hit us from nearby. It moved over us slowly, from one to the other, up and down. When it came to the paca swinging at Chepe's side it stopped.

Quick abortive curses and sounds of excitement rose about the plaza. I heard the word *ebina*, and remembered this Mosquito name for the paca, and how Mosquitos regard paca meat. We were now the center of attention, with every eye on us, and the wild men who had been destroying one another two minutes before now passed the word *ebina* from hand to hand about the clearing like a token of truce, and wherever it went flurries of chatter stirred.

Suddenly a female voice called something in Sambo English from inside a closed hut, and a huge young buck rose from the belly of a friend he had been punishing.

"*Ebina*," he called to the girl in the hut. "Dem got *ebina* heah, Sponymon got 'em. I get for you."

"Come on, Chepe," I whispered. "Don't be a fool. Run."

He still wanted to argue. He had not understood the English. But the great bare-chested black youth came lurching up the path, quite clearly after us, roaring:

"Hey deah, Sponish boy. Let'm fall thot *ebina*, understan'?" "*Dame ese conay-ho,* let me hob that what you call 'em, *guarda-tinaja*. Set 'em on the groun' now, God dam, set 'em down."

Chepe got that all right and shed his bravado, and we lit out. We dodged two sprawling parties in the way and then ran free in the rain for two hundred yards before we stopped to listen. There was yelling behind us, and it sounded bad, but it was not getting any closer.

"*Negros jodidos*," Chepe said, panting. "We are the ones who have the tepescuinte—but hell, what pubic hairs those Negroes!"

We walked the rest of the way to the compound without talking. It was raining hard now. The rain felt good, but sleep was the main thing. When we got to the gate I asked Chepe where he lived. He said he had a room in a little shack on the river. I asked what he would be doing in the morning, and he said helping the carpenter working on the bed of the motor dugout. He said he would clean the tepescuinte and bring it to me before lunch. I told him to keep half of it, and he seemed happy about that. He swung the bag off his shoulder, took out his glass float, and handed the bag to me. He said good-night and walked away toward the river.

"Be careful the Mosquitos don't catch you," I called after him.

"They don't do anything, those pubic hairs." He had got back his contempt. "They only make a noise."

I turned and opened the gate and climbed the ladder to my loft. I dumped the bags and shed my sodden clothes and stretched out wet on the cool tight canvas of the cot. It was a fine feeling—the jaguar safely seen, the paca to eat tomorrow. The turtles would come another night. The rain made a wonderful pattering on the palms and thatch, and away out beyond that, just over the far rumble of the surf, with all the menace wasted by the distance, I could barely hear the crests of sound from the mad chorus in the clearing.

Miskito turtle ranchos and boat, Miskito Cays, Nicaragua.

The Captains

I T WAS DAWN and the wind was down. Curls of mist rose and drifted, thinned and dissolved into the calm confusion of sea and air. A low ground swell gurgled at the stem of the anchored schooner, and the soft, sputtering climb of water at the anchor chain scared schools of young half-beaks and they bored up out of the unseen surface, sound-less and splashless as a handful of flung needles. The cook rested his belly and elbows on the rail and looked sleepily after the catboat sliding away in the fog, leaving behind it the only streak of difference between sky and ocean.

There were three men in the catboat, the captain in the bow and toward the stern two oarsmen sitting one before the other on either side and each pushing on a single long sweep tied to the gunwale with thatchrope lashing. The unstepped mast and furled sail lay across the seats with two fork-handled Mosquito paddles and a boat hook. The captain sat with a tall water glass between his knees, and the smoke that rose from his pipe showed strong blue against the uncertain white of the mist. Except for the captain's occasional soft-spoken directions—more like sug-gestions than orders—nobody said much; and the only other sounds were the creak of the oars and the whisper of parted water beneath the lapped planks of the hull.

The hour was early but the day was late, and the angling winds streaming into the Caribbean could spin out a hurricane any day. The nets were all set close to the ship to make it easy to call in the catboats if the glass should start to fall. Before the bulk of the schooner had dissolved behind them, the captain made out a patch of disorder ahead, a flaw in the smoking gray glass of the sea top. It was made by two corkwood floats anchored a hundred feet apart to mark the ends of a turtle net stretched over a coral head. Rings of wrinkles raced out from the floats, and between them the net line sliced in and out of the water. At one place along the line a churning tumult came and went. That was the place where a turtle was struggling in the yielding, holding strands of the tangle net.

The captain stood up in the bow, lifted the water glass, and rested it on the gunwale. As the boat slid closer, the commotion stopped and the water between the floats smoothed out. With one hand behind him, the captain signaled to the men to rest on their oars, then dropped the glass into the water and leaned forward to look at what was framed where the pane mashed the surface flat. The undersea dawn was lagging and it was dim, down there, but the captain could see the swoop of the long limbs of the net that came down together out of nothing and converged in a mess of lines and meshes swathing a form that rested lightly on a coral crag. It was a turtle, a big green. The captain studied it for a while. Then he drew in the glass, turned in his seat, and began sucking his pipe alive. He was a conservative man who never jumped at things. But the man at the after oar was impatient.

"Well, how abot it, Cop'm?" he said. "Is it him?"

"It's him," the captain said. "Had to be him all the time."

The captain set the water glass behind him and took up

the boat hook. As the boat slid over the slanting net line he grappled it up, pulled in a length, and tested it for feel.

"It's free of the head," he said. "Take him in."

The two men began taking in the line. Their weight and the pull of the net with the turtle in it tipped the narrow dory, and the captain slid to the off side to trim it. He did it reflexively, thinking only of the oddly deformed turtle and of how he had seen it there the night before; and then he thought back to the morning months before when he had caught the same old turtle and sent it away to Florida.

There was a bump and then a sharp hiss as the turtle gasped at the surface; and both men crouched and grabbed the two front fins, the thin round upper-arm part near the shell. They heaved together and the turtle slid over the side of the boat and his back smacked the bottom. He lay there craning his neck, hissing and blinking, fanning and slapping his chest with his long front paddles. The edges of all his flippers had been notched by fish bites. It was a striking set of scars. There were an extraordinary lot of the bites and they spread with odd regularity all around the thin ends and after-edges of all four fins. It was not the sort of injury you would expect to see in a turtle. It made you notice and wonder what kind of ambitious little fish had taken out the pieces. It was all the sign the captain needed to be sure this was the same three-hundred-pound male green he had caught on this same rock and sent to Key West eight months before. The scars were all he really needed, but just to clinch it he reached down and held back one of the old green's slapping flippers and rubbed the crusted belly shell, and then traced out the brand that he himself had cut there.

Captain Charlie was seventy-eight when he told me the story. The thing had happened a long time before—close to thirty years—and the dates were fuzzy in his mind, but the facts were not. There was nothing wrong with his memory, you just forgot exact dates unless something special burned them in. Anyway, it didn't matter, because once the captain decided it was thirty years ago, I worked out the schedule of the events by tracing the hurricane that loosed the scallop-fin turtle for his wonderful trip on the high Caribbean.

Once I had Captain Charlie's outline of the story and he had figured it had to be 1923 or 1924 that it happened, I got Tannehill's *Hurricanes* and some old newspaper files out of the library and had no trouble at all finding the hurricane I needed. It had to be an October hurricane—that was something else Captain Charlie was sure about—and it had to have passed near Key West. There turned out to be only one October storm that had come close enough to Key West to have brought the heavy seas that washed out the turtle crawls, the pens of the Norberg Thompson soup factory, and that was Tannehill's Number VII.

Those were the days before scientific hurricane-detection, before every tropical storm was given a fetching feminine name and, from its first petulant spinning in the far south, squired across the sea and among the cowering islands, tended and tested for temper by anxious airplanes. The hurricanes of those days were known only from the complaints of the ships and shores they hit, and for most of their lives they churned about in unheard fury, anonymous and alone. So the only name I know to give to the hurricane that let Captain Charlie's turtle go is Tannehill's Number VII, 1924.

I suppose it is just coincidence that Number VII made up and got its initial drive only a short way north of where the notch-fin turtle lived on Mosquito Bank. It would be mysticism to think anything else. There has got to be a limit to the personification of hurricanes. You have to remember they are only wind, in spite of the loving names and notoriety they get. But, all the same, it seems worth mentioning that the first anybody ever saw of Number VII was at Swan Island, a lonely place in the sea off Honduras, a place only a day's easy sail from the home ground of Captain Charlie's notch-fin turtle on the Nicaraguan bank. That gets to be a curious fact when you learn that the only noteworthy thing Number VII did in Florida was to wreck Thompson's turtle crawl and free the old turtle to swim home eight hundred miles to his den rock and home pastures at Mosquito Cay.

The storm hit western Cuba hard; by the time it had got to Florida it had lost power—or else it just missed the weather stations, because it passed on across the glades and keys and into the Atlantic and left the newspapers talking only about the rain it brought. Nobody said much about Thompson's crawl, except perhaps Thompson himself. But what happened to that crawl was a fateful thing that should have made the headlines before anything else the storm did. It was the pen washing out that sent the notch-fin green away on his incomprehensible journey.

To appreciate what that turtle accomplished you have to be sure you understand what he was up against. When the storm freed him he was in strange water eight hundred miles from home by air line, and a good deal farther by any route accessible to a sea turtle. He had come by schooner, on his back, the whole way out of touch with whatever landmarks cruising turtles might see and use. His home, then, was only a detached memory, a dim reptilian memory of somewhere beyond untracked space; a goal to be sought, you would think, by random wandering if it were sought at all. He was a shallow-water creature that had passed his life on the Nicaraguan banks, where the daily movement from den to grazing ground could be guided by bottom topography, or even by landfalls. Now, suddenly, in a rush of hurricane water, he was loose to seek the fine familiar days he had known before—if only he had the wit to recollect them and want them, and to get to where they were.

The eight-hundred-mile straight-line distance from Key West to Mosquito Cay was a detail of little interest to the turtle. That course is measured across the western end of Cuba. Any green turtle the Cubans caught walking across Pinar del Río would almost surely be made into a number of clever and savory dishes—and anyway, green turtles can't walk, to amount to anything. The feasible routes were all longer.

Suppose turtles have some occult apparatus for keeping track of their travel, even on their backs on the deck of a ship—a sort of recording gyrocompass capable of following out even a passive, involuntary trip and of "remembering" it. The course home for the notch-fin would in that case have been the course of the Annie Greenlaw in bringing him to Key West. Going back that way, he would strike out south and almost at once collide with the six-knot sweep of the Florida current, the borning Gulf Stream, nozzling in between the keys and Cuba. Here he would need to adjust for the proper westing. It is hard to imagine how he would know about this, but say he did. Once he had breasted the stream and reached Cape San Antonio at the westernmost tip of Cuba, following the Greenlaw's course he would have barged right into the Equatorial Current crowding into the Gulf through the Channel of Yucatán; here, of course, another set of extrasensory calculations would be required. Once reoriented

there and with a corrected heading, he would have clear
southeast sailing, through open sea the whole way, with
only a steady westward drift and the trackless sea and
running waves for landmarks, and down under his belly a
dim mile of water.

Of course, there were other ways to do it. Maybe he
crossed the Straits of Florida without fighting the current,
just letting it carry him along, hitting Cuba somewhere
about Cay Sal Bank, coasting the length of the island and
entering the Caribbean with the current that leaks in
through the Windward Passage. Once through the shallows off western Haiti, he could lay a southwesterly course,
and Jamaica and Pedro Bank would break the deep-water
runs with feeding-stations and resting-rocks. But that way
the trip is longer—a thousand miles at the very least and all
of it unknown to the traveler; and with who knows what
hazards and distractions along the way.

The other possibility—the least probable one, I think—is
that the notch-fin turtle followed the cluttered continental
shelf the whole way home, circumnavigating the Gulf of
Mexico, rounding Yucatán, following the Central American coast down to Cape Gracias a Dios, and then racing
happily out to his own coral tower through the warm,
familiar sea of Mosquito Bank. That way the distance
could not be less than 2,400 miles, with all the local veer-
ings and detours, and it probably would be a great deal
more. And every mile so purposeful and filled with the
lure and image of home that all the confusions and fric-
tions of the crazy shoreline were resolved and dominated,
and an average daily progress of at least ten miles was
maintained.

No matter how you look at it—no matter how he came
home—the voyage of the notch-fin turtle was the most
extraordinary outcome of the October storm of '24, of

Tannehill's Number VII; and not a word about the wrecking of Thompson's crawl in the news.

When Captain Charlie told me this story, it was exactly the kind of story I had been looking for, and I made careful notes on what he said, on even the way he said it. He started off saying:

"I was me own captain and me own owner of me own schooner. I've been going to the Bank since the time when there were thirty or forty schooners in the fleet. I can say I know turtle. I can tell you a turtle's instinct surpasses the intelligence of a man."

That's what he said. Then he told me the story. He told it simply, without any fancy feelings about it; and even looking hard for parts to doubt, there was nothing for me to take hold of. Captain Charlie was a practical man who told a story as it seemed to him and without decoration. He told it well, though, with the events all in order and with a good ear for emphasis. When he got to the end it was a marvelous story; but he had left one thing out, and I prompted him.

"What finally happened to the old turtle?" I said. I was sure he would say he let the turtle go. Most people would have let him go, I think.

Captain Charlie looked as if he had kind of expected the question—as if he was happy I had asked it.

"I sent him back to Key West with the next load," he said. "Old Thompson bought him all over again." Captain Charlie snickered with thirty-year-old satisfaction. "He never knew it, but he paid for that turtle twice. You didn't often get the best of old Thompson."

That was not the first time I had heard stories about turtles going back to their homes from remote places, but it was the first time I had ever heard one from the man who had seen the thing happen. The yarn meant a great deal to me. Getting that sort of thing straight from the source was what had brought me to the Cayman Islands to start with.

As I am going to show in the last chapter, the green turtle is in a bad way. Its populations in American waters need protection by international laws, and the laws will have to be based on an understanding of the life history of the animal. But the sad fact is, we really know too little about the ways of the green to work out means of protecting it. For instance, there is no scientific information at all on its migratory movements. Fishermen everywhere believe that green turtles migrate—make long, seasonal deep-water voyages from home ground to a nesting beach; but there is no real proof of this at all.

To protect an animal, you have got to know where it is —not just once in a while, but all the time. In the case of the green turtle, for example, you have to know whether an effective conservation program would require closed seasons and policing all around the Caribbean shores, which would involve an appallingly complicated set of international agreements; or whether it might be possible to build up green-turtle populations throughout the Caribbean by protecting a few widely spaced nesting beaches. The answer to this, and to a great many similar questions, will come only when we know whether the fishermen are right when they say turtles make mass migrations to converge on distant breeding grounds.

I was poking about, looking for the facts of this matter, when I began to take note of recurrent rumors of marvelous feats of homing by green turtles. Mostly these tales came to me deviously, and were much twisted along the way; but I heard them in so many places that I began to wonder what lay behind them. If it was true that greens were able to find their way home through long distance or through unfamiliar waters, then the notion that they were a migratory animal carried more weight. Finding your way home is much the same problem whether you have left it under your own steam or on your callipash and against your will. This is to say, I had gathered a lot of inconclusive evidence that greens made long-haul junkets of one sort or another and were probably gifted navigators, but nobody had ever traced one through such a journey. The question was still open, and any information bearing upon it was welcome.

Every time I dug into the homing rumors I found the Cayman turtle men back of them. All the people who told me the stories turned out to be quoting, or misquoting, the stanch professionals of the Cayman Islands. The reason for this was that Caymanians not only catch more turtles than everybody else put together, but they haul them all over creation, all the way from Nicaragua to Florida, for instance; and besides this, they brand every one of them with a long-lasting incised monogram of a particular ship or owner. Thus, it only takes some catastrophe—a hurricane is the most popular sort—coming along and smashing things up and releasing captive turtles somewhere far away from home to set up ideal conditions for an informal experiment in animal orientation.

Because the Caymanians have a great horde of such tales to tell and because they generally know more about sea turtles than anybody and because since I was six they have appealed to me as mysterious and colorful people, I decided to go to Grand Cayman.

It is not easy to get to. You can go by little motor ship from Tampa, but not just any time and not in luxury. You can go by British West Indian Airways plane from Miami or Kingston; but here again, in my experience, following any sort of a schedule requires a certain rare prescience on the part of the traveler, as the flights and routes have so far maintained a steady rate of flux and revision. When I went I flew up from the south by way of Jamaica. I tried to time my arrival to coincide with that of Coleman Goin, a friend of mine who was coming down from Florida. It was a fantastically complex venture, and when we managed to get to Georgetown within the same week we were pretty proud.

Looking at the Cayman Islands on the map—or looking *for* them on the map—you might think I was going to strange lengths to collect turtle stories. The islands are not cartographically impressive. They are away out in a part of the Caribbean where nobody goes—150 miles south of central Cuba, 180 miles northwest of Jamaica; of neither the Main nor the Antilles, of only the sea in its deepest part—three little lonely islands visited only by hurricanes. The three islands of the group—Grand Cayman, Little Cayman, and Cayman Brac—are the exposed peaks of a submarine range of mountains said to be continuous with the Sierra Maestra range of Cuba and running westward through Misteriosa Bank toward Central America. The islands are a dependency of Jamaica and have a population of 7,600—most of it on Grand Cayman. A thousand fifty-two Caymanians are classed in the census as "African"; there are 3,518 people of mixed extraction, and 2,100 are of "European" descent. All this means less in the islands than in some places. There are 79 horses; 101 asses (donkeys); 1,858 head of cattle; 397 swine, or porcine cattle as the Spanish say; and 118 goats. The chief exports are turtles, thatchrope, and shark skin. The chief source of income is seamen's wages—Caymanian seamen sail the ships of the world; and the chief plague of the islands is emigration. The fishing is superb. There is not only the standard welter of reef fishes to stick or admire, but the pelagic game is there too—kingfish, sailfish, marlin, wahoo, and all the rest, all as abundant and as available as anywhere I know. And tarpon stop by and bonefish abound.

"The islands are clean and tidy," the Commissioner writes in his notes. "There is very little crime and the jails are empty. There are few rogues and no beggars, and all around a sparkling sea."

It is really distressing how pleasant the islands are, and how good the fishing. It is only a matter of time before the visitors come. It is only a matter of time before there are no places anywhere that are both wild and pleasant.

Well, as I said, the thing that drew me to the islands was the rumored lore of the turtle captains, the men who have gone with the fleet since boyhood and who learned the natural history of the green turtle from their grandfathers. These men are specialists in an exacting fishery, and they learn things no zoologist knows because it is the only way they can succeed in their calling. To a man the Cayman captains believe that green turtles make long-distance migrations at breeding time. To see why they believe this, and to see why their opinion must be respected, we should examine the operation of the turtle fishery.

The greens Caymanians take to foreign markets are not caught about the islands, as the last chapter will show, but at Mosquito Cays, a group of low islands on Mosquito Bank off the coast of Nicaragua, some 350 miles from Grand Cayman. The turtle schooners go to the cays in the fall and establish headquarters at one of the islands on which fresh water is available. Here they build a communal crawl of mangrove piling in shallow water to hold the accumulating catch of the season. The schooners go out to the banks on Monday morning and return to the cay on Saturday. The turtle ground is a broad tableland under shallow water, with sandy bottom, with vast fields of long, narrow-leafed Thalassia or turtle grass, and with rocks, bars and coral heads scattered all about. These last are important features of the turtle landscape. The turtles sleep on or under them, each morning going out to the grass flats to feed and each evening returning to a special home rock to pass the night. In some cases this daily sleeping-feeding regimen involves a round trip of four or five miles. This is not a thing you can read about in the zoology books. Seeing the turtles thus casually commuting predisposes the turtle captains to believe that they are capable of purposeful, controlled migration journeys.

Once out on the banks, the schooners divide up the territory among themselves and then carefully cruise among the heads under sail, by some hidden craft slipping past the gutting spires of rock and locating the turtle dens by the patches of clean sand the greens sweep out around them. The schooners mark these places by dropping anchored wooden buoys.

Late afternoons the catboats—seventeen-foot sailing dories or double-end whaleboats—put out from the schooners and set nets over the marked rocks. The nets, which are eight to fifteen fathoms long and two or three deep and have meshes ten or twelve inches on a side, are stretched over the turtle rock between anchored floats. When the greens come up to breathe (as they must, of course, even when sleeping), they hit the nets and tangle themselves hopelessly. Each morning the catboats come and take out the tangled turtles and transfer them to the schooner; and on Saturdays the week's catch is taken to the big crawl on the cay.

Turtling on the bank is not a year-round operation. Something happens to the turtles in the early summer. In April, when the females grow heavy with leathery-shelled eggs, a vague restlessness spreads among the herds.

Their behavior becomes unpredictable and the catch starts falling off, and by late May or early June most of them have gone from the bank. They stay away through July, and it is not until some time in August that the schooners find it profitable to return to the cays. The captains say the disappearance of the turtles means that they are off on a breeding migration. Here again you cannot corroborate the assumption in the literature of science; but the operations of the ancient and successful Caymanian turtle fleet are geared to it, and the captains don't worry much over the lack of support their ideas get from professional naturalists.

The place the captains say the turtles go to is Tortuguero, some three hundred miles south of Mosquito Cay on the coast of Costa Rica. The Caymanians call the place Turtle Bogue. They say it is not only the Mosquito Cay schools that go there to nest, but greens from all about the western end of the Caribbean. The Costa Ricans down at the Bogue say the same thing. They are all making assumptions from purely circumstantial evidence; and they are all probably right.

The Caymanians see their turtles leave the banks and at the same time the Costa Ricans see hosts of greens gathering off their shore and coming up on the Black Beach to lay their eggs. The *flotas*—fleets—as they call them, arrive in loose schools and gang up and loaf about, a few hundred yards outside the breakers, to wrangle and woo and tend to the chore of fertilizing turtle eggs for another season. The laying season is the mating season, too.

The *flotas* you see at the Bogue in July are too big to be simply gatherings from local waters. They clearly come from somewhere else. The Cayman captains and the Costa Ricans have figured it out between them that the June exodus at Mosquito Cay and the massing at the Bogue are

parts of the same phenomenon. Their case seems so clear
that mentioning the lack of experimental proof sounds like
quibbling. Nevertheless, proof is lacking, and getting it is
one of the things I am determined to do. I want to go
down to the Bogue again and meet the fleet and mark hundreds of nesting greens with monel metal tags, stamped,
in Spanish and English, with my address and with the
offer of a reward to whoever returns a tag to me with full
details of its recovery. I am as sure as you can be in such
cases that tags will be picked up at Mosquito Cay.

They will probably be recovered in other places, too.
The turtle captains and the Costa Ricans believe that the
Bogue rookery is a rendezvous for schools from places
other than Nicaragua. While there are certainly a few
other breeding centers between Mexico and the Windward Islands, it seems unlikely that any of them compares
in importance with that at Tortuguero. Just watching the
assembling of the fleet there, you build up a strong impression that parties are arriving from both north and
south. Moreover, the local people all tell you that the
northern contingent, from Mosquito Cay and beyond, and
the schools from Panama and northern South America,
come in separately, with those from the south always arriving first. The people say this because the southern end
of the beach comes into use a few days ahead of the
northern end. They believe this is because the South
American *flotas* get there first.

I was on the Black Beach at the beginning of two nesting seasons in late June. Both years, when the turtles
were just beginning to arrive, there was noticeably more
nesting activity toward the southern end of the beach than
at the northern end. During my second visit to the Bogue,
when there was still only a trickle of nesting under way,
I chartered a little airplane and scouted the whole coast

from Tortuguero to Limón, flying at under a hundred feet and counting turtle tracks on the sand the whole way. On the twenty-four-mile section of the Bogue itself only twenty-five turtles had come up during the three preceding nights. On the eight-mile stretch from the mouth of the Reventazon River to the mouth of the next river to the south there was little or no sign of nesting. But from there on there were suddenly too many tracks to count. On a six-mile piece of beach there were hundreds—maybe thousands—of tracks, lying one over the other so thick that even climbing and circling I could not keep them tallied. Most surprising of all, there was no sign of a nest anywhere. Each of the countless round-trip tracks was a simple arc or angle above high-tide wash, with no scuffed place, no covered, nearly concealed egg pit at the apex. Even from the airplane it was clear that all that multitude of turtles had done nothing more than go up out of the surf to dry sand, and then go back again.

Because I had talked to turtle captains and walked the Bogue and waited with the people there for the *flota del sur*—the southern fleet—to arrive, I interpreted what I saw as sign of a vast shoal of greens just in from the south and on its way to Tortuguero. The trial strandings seemed to mean that the school was prospecting—was somehow aware that the voyage was near an end, but could be sure only by testing the sand for whatever mystic properties they are that call the fleets to Turtle Bogue.

So my own snatched observations fit in perfectly with the folk-beliefs, and I was tempted to call the matter established fact. But a little thought showed that even then nothing had been really proved. It was a good thing to have seen, what I saw from the airplane, and it certainly added weight to the deductions of the people on the Bogue. But attributing to a reptile an ability to carry out long-distance, open-water migrations is a serious thing. It is serious because you are attributing to him powers of orientation which are not prevalent among his kind and about which we understand next to nothing where they do occur. It is true that a lot of different kinds of animals have such powers, but adding a turtle to that gifted list is not a thing to do lightly or without impeccable grounds.

In casting about for other kinds of evidence to bring to bear, I began to wonder about the pan-Caribbean gossip that seemed to show that green turtles have strong attachment for some special parcel of terrain and a mystic ability to get back to it from just about anywhere, through waters known or unknown. If they actually could do this, it meant that they have some sort of built-in equipment for navigation, for locating an unseen goal, for locating themselves and for laying and holding a proper homing course; and such equipment would obviously serve just as well for migrations as for homing journeys. The problem is the same in both cases. Thus it was that I began trying to trace the stories to their sources; and though I heard them all the way from Florida to Venezuela, they could, as I said, always be backtracked to the Cayman turtle fleet.

So I went to the Cayman islands and talked and listened; and I found that everybody there knew about the wonderful homing instinct of the green turtle. Sure, mon, I was told on every hand, turtle can go home from anywhere—just like a pigeon. Caymanians are brought up knowing this. When they hold a turtle derby on Grand Cayman to celebrate the end of a good season, and tie colored balloons to the flippers of culls left in the crawls, and let them go in the Sound, and the turtles all move out into open water and head south without a hitch—nobody is surprised. South is the course to Mosquito Bank, and that's where the creatures came from. Ask an islander

Left: the late Captain Allie Ebanks, Grand Cayman, the most famous of the old Cayman turtle captains. *Below*: turtle camp at Tortuguero, Costa Rica.

Above: female green turtle, Ascension Island. *Below*: Bertie Downes, champion *careyero*—hawksbill turtle hunter—waiting for a turtle to blow. The picture was not posed—the *careyeros* stand for hours with poised harpoon. (Photo by Jo Conner)

how he knows turtles go home and he may ask you how you know a dog will chase a cat. You may call it folklore, but it's a kind that has to be mostly right or somebody will starve. To understand the confidence of the Caymanians in their turtle lore, you must realize how intimately they have lived with the beasts and how closely they study their ways and wiles on the fishing banks.

I mentioned earlier that each of the turtle schooners fishes an allotted section of the bank during a season—sometimes for successive seasons. To make good sets the captains have to know the routine movements of the turtles and the topography of the bottom, and they spend a lot of time studying both with their water glasses. They learn a great many subtle things about the features and occupants of the various rocks, reefs, bars, and grass flats in their territory; and through years of watching and outwitting turtles they come to note individual variations—different combinations of size, sex, shape, scarring, and coloration—that a landsman would miss completely. It is because they recognize the animals as individuals, and because they know the bottom like the decks of their ships, that the captains have learned of the daily movement to and from rocks and pastures. As this routine travel may itself involve round trips of several miles, it is easy to conclude that turtles can tell one direction from another and can feel an urge to go home. There remains, then, only the need for proof that they are able to establish and follow a course through the open sea, guided only by such hidden beacons as guide salmon and seals and widgeons and eels.

Another step toward proving this would be seeing a turtle return home over a distance through which it had been carried on the deck of a ship; and out on the banks the captains have seen many such cases when turtles have made ten- to thirty-mile returns after escaping from the pens on Mosquito Cay. Since the catch of several schooners is mixed in the crawls, each turtle is branded with the mark of the ship that caught him. The mark is usually a monogram cut deeply into the cartilage of the under shell and is designed to serve for the final accounting at Key West, sometimes four or five months later. Through the years the storms come, and time after time the pens have been flooded or destroyed. At these times the turtles get out; and some of them, at least, go home. They don't just go back to the banks—they often return to the very same rocks they came from.

Even before I went to Grand Cayman I had heard dozens of tales of such short-range returns, and I was pretty sure that there was fact behind them. But actually there was nothing in these stories that strained your credulity much to start with. A turtle might grope its way across the bottom for thirty shallow-water miles and find home by trial and error. What I was after was the firsthand experiences behind the tales of homing trips from hundreds of miles away, across contrary currents, toward landless horizons, over liquid ocean, amorphous and abyssal. It was no mistake, as I said, looking up the Cayman captains. It is they who see the things and tell the rest about them.

There are not as many captains as there once were. The fleet has shrunk in the past four decades and the captains are mostly old. There are more old ones than young ones. But there is not much senility among them; and they never tell you their stories just to get your sympathy or admiration, or to entertain you. They tell them mostly, it seemed to me, to show the incomprehensibility of nature. The captains are of all shapes and sizes, but all are men of sense—simple, sea-worn, intelligent men in or near their eighties, practical naturalists from a school in which irresponsible thinking or reporting could result in disaster. They are men who could forget a detail; but they would not embellish a story.

Captain Charlie Bush was one of the old seamen I talked with, on a blazing day in Georgetown, and he told about the notch-fin turtle, as I told about it earlier.

Captain Teddy Bodden was another, and Captain Gene Thompson another. They were eighty-two and eighty-three, as sound old pods as you'll ever see; Bodden was a bit deaf, but other ways both men were alert and cheerful and full of things that happened in the past but are still valid today. They were sitting together on the porch of Captain Teddy's house when I found them. It was a white house on a side street making off away from the shore, under shady breadfruit and woman's tongue. Captain Teddy sat in the swing and squeaked it through a short arc, pink-faced and happy to be there, happy to see me there before he ever knew my errand.

"Come in, come on up," he called out to the street when he saw me pause at the white picket fence and eye the house for sign of captains. "I'm happy to see you," he said. "Now what is it you want?"

I went up to the steps and told him, and he didn't even come close to understanding. But Captain Gene got it. "He says he wants to talk about green turtle," Gene said.

"About what? About turtle? Is that what he says? Is that what you want, young man?"

I told him that was right. The two of them looked at each other, and the two sets of eyes sank into wrinkles, and they both began to chuckle. I figured they were chuckling about two things. One was the appropriateness of my coming to them for such talk; and the other was the thought of trying to talk out so vast a subject in a casual chat on a hot afternoon. They chuckled quietly for a little while, no doubt thinking things like those.

"He's been well directed," Captain Teddy said, finally. "Sit down, young man, we can talk a long time about turtle."

We did. It was not easy getting them to talk about the exact things I had time to hear. By every subtle ruse they kept leading off into other things they thought I should be told. Their both being over eighty and together there in the shade with so much to remember, and my being there with the stated purpose of listening, made it easy to get turtle stories but hard to keep them channeled. But, Lord, it was worth it, hearing about the old days with the fleet when the old men were boys and after a while captains; about good ships and bad ones; about good years and bad years, and old storms that made no choice between good ships and bad and left the women crying on the iron shore. Only, skimming through the years the captains told so much that my time wasted pleasantly away and it took will power to accumulate what I was really after.

But in the end the relevant tales came out, piecemeal and with many a zestful digression; and I made the notes I needed. For one thing, both men recalled several instances of turtles escaping from the Mosquito Cay crawl and swimming the twenty or thirty miles back to their home rocks. And Captain Teddy, who had done a great deal of deep-water sailing between turtle seasons, remembered two times meeting with westward-moving schools of greens in the open sea off Colón.

"Headed for Turtle Bogue," he said. He said it casually, as if it were something understood.

After two hours of talking I had picked up an amazing lot of odd information and along with this had heard what the captains could remember of two long-range homing journeys by green turtles. They followed the same general pattern as Captain Charlie Bush's yarn about the notch-fin turtle.

It was Captain Gene's story that took shape first. It happened years ago, he said—no use trying to settle on the exact year. At the end of the season he brought a load of Mosquito Cay turtles, forty or fifty of them, to Georgetown to be held for shipment to Key West. Meantime, a man named Thomas Eden came over from Jamaica looking for turtles to buy, and Captain Gene let him have the Mosquito lot. Eden moved the turtles to Kingston and put them in a pen in the harbor there. There was a storm and high water with it, and the waves broke out piling in the pen and some of the turtles got away. Between two and three months later Captain Gene was back at the Cay fishing the same territory as the season before when one of his catboatmen brought in a marked turtle from the lot that had gone to Jamaica. It had returned to its old sleeping-rock and had been caught by the same boat that took it the first time. The shortest course it could possibly have taken going home was 425 miles.

That was the essence of the story. Captain Gene did a lot of unhurried meditating telling it and you could see it hurt Captain Teddy to wait it out. But at the end Teddy beamed over the talent of the turtle and said now let him talk for a while. He said if I would give him a few days to think out details and check them against old logbooks and ledgers he could tell me several stories like Gene's; but there was one he could tell me right then, without delay, because it was very strange and he had told it many times. It involved the return of two greens from a single lot, and it was the only case of the sort he had ever heard of.

It was the summer of 1915 that it happened—'15 or '16, more like '15. Some time during late summer Captain Teddy sent a cargo of branded Nicaraguan turtles to market in Key West. The sloop carrying them never reached Florida. It ran into bad weather—not a hurricane, but some kind of quick, vicious squall—off Isle of Pines, near a little place called Carapach Key, and was wrecked. Some time during the following year—as well as Captain Teddy could recall, about nine months later—his catboatmen brought in two of those shipwrecked turtles from the bank where they had been caught in sets no more than a mile apart.

The statistical improbability of a double return through at least 725 miles ending in a double recapture is unsettling to think about. It will seem only a little less wild if you keep reminding yourself that the boats work the same ground year after year, and that homing to a turtle is not just going back to town but back to the same old street and number.

I am setting down these things we talked about in a couple of pages. I get the facts before you, but you miss the fine flavor of the slow talk, with one old man nodding or smiling over the careful words of the other, or reaching out a hand to correct a point or bring back a recollection. You miss the slow creak of the swing in the deep shade and the filigree of breadfruit leaves against the hot sky and the two old captains there on the porch after all the long calms and the raving winds; after the empty charts and the clawing reefs; with the call for courage answered and the hard days done and the courage still there in the quiet captains like rib-crooks of sound mahogany in a long-stranded hull.

There are a thousand tales to tell of the islands and the fleet. They are all worth hearing, too, and the captains were setting out to tell them and I, in spite of myself, to listen. But then I saw Coley down at the end of the street, peering about in the sun, looking to tell me he had found George and his car to take us to West Bay. I broke into Captain Teddy's monologue. I said it was a fine thing sitting there hearing the things they told about; but there was more of my round to make before dark, I said. There was Captain Allie to see, and he lived at West Bay and the afternoon was nearly gone.

Captain Allie was unlike the run of Cayman captains in being not old and retired but in the prime of life. Only a few years before we went to see him he had made the all-time record catch of green turtles when he brought away 725 in a twelve-week season. He had just come in from a trip on his schooner, the *Adams,* when we went to West Bay; and, for all his prime, we found him sitting on his porch, rocking in a chair and smoking his pipe—a big solid man with a fullback build and a square face full of patient competence, like all wind captains.

You might think he would have been glad to be shut of turtles for a while, having just returned from the banks; but he seemed pleased to talk about them, and when he learned what special kind of story I needed he said he could vouch for the truth of that general kind of story, that the things such tales tell about have happened to everybody in the turtle fleet. He rummaged among his recollections for a little while and then said he probably could put together the facts in a couple of examples of his own.

For the first he went back to the summer of 1948, when he had gone to pick up a cargo of turtles at an island off Quintana Roo, on the windward side of the Yucatán Peninsula. The place is called Isla de Mujeres—Woman Island—and what zest or lechery or wistful honing went into the naming of it would be worth knowing. This is one of the only places besides the beach at Tortuguero where there is definitely known to be a green-turtle rookery. The turtles taken there are thought by the fishermen to come from the Gulf of Mexico. I don't know about this; but I have seen some cargoes of them and can say that they run bigger than the ones that come up on the Bogue. Down there the average weight is somewhere between 150 and 250 pounds, while the average for breeding adults of the Mexican strain is closer to 350 pounds, and 400-pounders are not uncommon. Besides this difference, the Woman Island turtles are less well thought of in the market because of a so-called musky taste to the meat; due, the theory is, to their eating sponges instead of a straight turtle-grass diet like the succulent Costa Rican greens. I don't know about this either. It is true that stomachs of butchered Mexican turtles usually contain more animal food than you find in those from Florida or Nicaragua, but attributing the flaw in the flavor to this is just a guess. And anyway, the Mexican greens are salable, and when the Mosquito Cay catch is poor the Cayman schooners go by Woman Island to piece out their cargoes for Key West.

So it was with Captain Allie. The turtles he picked up there were the typical big ones, all caught locally and marked by the men who caught them, in characteristic Yucateco fashion, with a letter or monogram punched out on the plastron with a spike or knife point. He took them to Key West, and there they were put in a crawl with some greens from Nicaragua. Before the lot had gone into soup a storm smashed the pen and let all the turtles out.

This happened in October. Toward the end of the following season—some time in May, the captain thought—one of these Mexican turtles was caught in a net set over a coral head on Mosquito Bank. There was no doubt about it—the Yucatán brand was there, the private mark of a boy Captain Allie knew well back at Woman Island; and beside this there was the *Adams's* incised counterbrand. There could be no doubt about the origin of the turtle.

The only question was, why would a Mexican green turtle go so directly to the Nicaraguan banks. You might be tempted to say he was simply on his way back to Woman Island, but a look at the map will show the weakness there. Why go home by way of Mosquito Cay? Why go so deviously to the only place in all the Caribbean where Captain Allie Ebanks would be waiting to catch him again? There is too much coincidence in that explanation. Captain Allie had a better one.

Captain Allie and his crew decided, after a lot of wondering, that the Yucatán turtle went to Nicaragua in company with returning residents of the Mosquito Cay ground. As I said before, there were Mosquito Cay greens in the same pen with the lot from Mexico, and they all got away together. Maybe they stayed together, for comfort or company, or from plain inertia; and maybe the homing Mosquito Cay residents were the more numerous or the more persuasive—or got a stronger call—and set the group course for the banks instead of for Woman Island. It's just a guess, but it's the best one I have heard; and without it you have a real enigma. The notion would of course be strengthened if one of the Nicaraguan turtles had been retaken, but none was, and the real answer will never be known.

That anecdote was just a teaser, of high interest as a riddle, but not much good as evidence that green turtles have navigation equipment. I told Captain Allie that, and he said he agreed with me; but then he proceeded to tell me another story, and it was a good one. In fact, it was in some ways the best of all the homing stories that any of the captains told.

It happened in 1942, in midwinter, when the *Adams* was working the ground around Dead Man Bar, about eleven miles northeast of Mosquito Cay. One early morning a man came in to the schooner in a catboat heavy with a load of greens. He yelled up at Captain Allie, who is an expert at judging and grading green turtles, to ask if the captain would help him select a few out of the batch to send home for his own family's use. Captain Allie jumped down and prodded and hauled the lot about and in the end chose what seemed to him the five best turtles; and then he sat on the rail and watched as the man cut his recognition mark in the belly shell of each of them.

Three days later the five branded turtles were put aboard the schooner *Wilson*, homeward bound for Grand Cayman, and it is noteworthy that the *Wilson* was not taking back a regular cargo of turtles, and that the five marked ones were thus not trussed up and stowed under hatches but were merely set aside on their backs on deck. This is a thing to remember.

The voyage to Grand Cayman was quick and uneventful. On reaching Georgetown, the turtles were turned over to Roy Arch, who put them in a little rock crawl near the shipyard to be held against the return of the owner. Almost at once a heavy northeaster came up and drove the sea over the crawl and the five choice greens disappeared.

Twelve days passed—and the first three were stormy all about the western end of the Caribbean. Out on the banks Captain Allie waited out the storm at Mosquito Cay and then moved back to the turtle grounds to fish in the good weather that came after the squalls. On the morning of the twelfth day after the storm hit Georgetown, Captain Allie heard a boat bump the side of the *Adams*, and a voice called up to him, low, anxious, and excited. It was the catboatman who had sent the five turtles home, and he was worried. He was worried in a confused sort of way, like a person who felt he was making some sort of big mistake but couldn't see how. When Captain Allie leaned on the rail and asked the man what ailed him, he looked away at the sea and spread a look of deadpan detachment over his face, as his kind of people do to hide emotion.

"Something dom funny, Cop'm," he said. "You know wha hop'm *Wilson*?"

The *Wilson*, recall, was the ship the five turtles went away in. The captain knew nothing about it. Things were different then, even only fifteen years ago, when the fleet worked without ship-to-shore radio. There was no way for anybody to know anything about the *Wilson*. But in spite of his crabwise approach to his dread, it was clear what the dread was. The man thought the *Wilson* had been lost.

Captain Allie pressed him for a complete story—for the source of whatever news had moved him so. The man said it was a turtle that brought it, in a manner of speaking—one of the five sound greens sent back to victual his family at the start of the week before. One of these turtles had come back to the banks and he had caught it at daybreak. He had taken it with his own net set by the same rock tower the turtle had slept on before the *Wilson* carried it away.

The captain quickly thought back through the days, and they came to twelve. He must have looked dubious, because the man dropped down into his boat and jerked aside a mat, and the turtle was lying there, real and unmistakable, its size and shape right for one of the five, and the unique private brand of the catboatman on its

calipee. It lay there slapping its belly in mindless dejec-
tion over its plight—too dull to see the irony of its being
caught again; too single-track to know the bad meaning
the men saw in its being there.

Captain Allie looked at the turtle very carefully for
some way he could be mistaken. When finally he had finished he knew he must believe one of two things. Either
the turtle had swum a rigidly directed course of 350
miles, the gull-flight distance back to the banks from
Grand Cayman; or the *Wilson* had been lost in the storm,
partway home to the islands. Captain Allie said it made
him very sad to decide that of the two explanations the
latter was the more reasonable.

The story quickly spread about the banks, and as each
schooner heard it the melancholy grew, because the fleet
is a closely knit company and nearly every man in it had
some sort of kin on the *Wilson*. For a week the worry
lasted. The turtling went on, but there was no zest in the
good catches. Then one fine morning a schooner came
foaming by in front of the trade wind, outbound and
fresh from Grand Cayman. Captain Allie hailed her and
asked about the *Wilson* and the schooner said what about
the *Wilson*, the *Wilson* was anchored back home at West
Bay. As she drove by on the course to Mosquito Cay her
captain, home-fed and in a hell of a hurry to get to work,
shouted out the short story of the northeaster and the
flooded crawl and a lot of other details that made no difference at all.

So the story changed quickly from tragedy to just a
marvel of nature. Looking at the map, you see that when
the turtle got out of the pen in Georgetown there was
no coastwise shallow-water course home that he possibly
could have traveled in twelve days. Even if he went
straight across the western end of the Caribbean he made

the trip at a rate of thirty miles a day. Allow for any mis-
calculation or random wandering at all, and the distance
grows so fast the twelve days begin to seem impossibly
short. Thus, the anecdote appears to show more than a
mere urge and ability to move in the general direction
of home. In this one case it would seem to be the shortest and best route that the animal somehow chose and
followed. If this actually is what happened—and, knowing Captain Allie, it is hard to question any of the facts
of the story—it is safe to suppose that green turtles do in
fact have some sort of extra sense, or some clever way of
using the ordinary senses, that lets them make long, controlled journeys in trackless seas. This ability is what we
were looking for. It is support for the assumption that
green turtles make overseas migrations to distant breeding
rendezvous.

So, in spite of the lack of final experimental proof, there
can remain little serious doubt that the fleet that comes
to Tortuguero in June is made up of migrants from Mosquito Bank, and perhaps from many other points in the
Caribbean as well.

The night I finally met the fleet at the Bogue, after a
week of waiting and walking the black sand, Cachuminga
was with me. He was a thin, untidy little fellow; a hopeless alcoholic, dry as a boat louse, light and meatless as
a crow quill. He was steeped in strange esters and he
effused them constantly; and he was full of improbable
lore, and of the wish to please. I don't know why he went
with me—he was no asset to me, and it took him away
from the *guaro* he might have begged back in the village.
I think he came mostly because he clung to a beaten urge
to be of some use somehow. When we began to come upon
the big greens, lumbering up from the wet or scooping
the sand up where the bushes began, Cachuminga's stat-

ure grew in his own eyes because he had said the fleet would be in soon. He ran from one turtle to another, gliding across the sand like a ghost crab or like something blown by the wind. He slapped a smooth carapace and made an expansive gesture and said: "There, you see. It is the fleet. The fleet is in."

I had no heart for showing him I figured the fleet would have got there without him; and anyway the question was burning me and I asked, just as if I expected an answer: "Where do they all come from, Cachuminga?"

He waved a hand toward the sea in a slow half-circle, then sank his chin to his breastbone and closed his eyes over the remoteness of where the turtles came from.

"*OO-oo-oo,*" he marveled. "*De alla-a-a-. De alla le-e-e-jos*—from out there, away off somewhere. From everywhere."

I don't know where Cachuminga got his information, but I think there was something in what he said.

The Passing of the Fleet

I T WAS THE first of May, 1503. It was the homeward leg of the fourth voyage, and the blue line of the isthmus fading astern was the last Columbus would ever see of the New World mainland. At odds with his pilots over the course to Hispaniola and with too little easting to hold it anyway, he turned his ships as near north as the wind would let him. The May trade was fickle and the current slipped steadily westward, and he missed his goal by three hundred miles. He missed Jamaica, too. But on the tenth he raised two low islands and ran down the channel between them; and his grumbling crews were cheered by the sight of great numbers of turtles about the shores and cluttering the seaway, the chronicle says, like little rocks. Columbus named the islands Las Tortugas, and then sailed on across to Cuba—or, as he still believed, Cathay—and anchored his rotting ships in the Gardens of the Queen.

The Turtle Islands did not keep the name Columbus gave them. Fifteen years later Ponce de Leon took it for a group of keys off Florida, and this confused the groping mapmakers. The Tortugas of Columbus became the *Caymanes*—the Cayman Islands—and for three hundred years the vast *"flotas"* there—the fleets of breeding green turtles—were a prime factor in the growth of the Caribbean.

The turtle schools came in, the old writers tell us, from hundreds of leagues around; from Hispaniola and the Lucayos, from the Channel of Yucatán and the shores of the Main itself, to mate in the Cayman Sea and lay their eggs in the honey-colored sand.

As the settlements grew and got hungry, ships of half a dozen flags converged on the untended islands in June: forty sloops at a time from Port Royal in Jamaica—craft from all down the turtle-poor volcanic islands of the Caribbee arc. They took away as many as their holds and decks would carry. The turtle *flotas* were infinite as herring schools, or so it seemed.

But when Coleman Goin and I pushed through the sea grapes at the edge of a ten-mile beach on Grand Cayman and walked till we were tired, we saw the trail of one sea turtle. It was the sixth of July—dead center in the turtle season—and there was one wind-dimmed track twenty-four hours old, and probably a loggerhead track at that.

Perhaps the story behind this change is not as dramatic as the story of the bison on our western plains. The bison was in the public eye from the start. It cluttered land now Illinois real estate. It gave comfort to difficult red Indians and blocked the scant traffic on proud new railroads. The bison passed in a blaze, watched by everybody—not without lamentation here and there, but with little interference. It had to go, in the mind of the day, because it hindered progress. The green turtle, on the other hand, hindered nothing. The turtle fleets passed secretly and without commotion. They were just too good to last.

When the charts of the Caribbean were being roughed in, the great motive of the voyagers was the search for a seaway to China. The great obstacles were the old mindless fear of the Burning Zone and the slow vitamin hunger —the sickness that came from nowhere and made men's gums grow over their teeth, and could send a corpse a day sliding over the rail. One great natural asset was the trade wind; and to that I am going to add—Chelonia, the green turtle. It's barely possible that the juxtaposition is hyperbole. I'm not sure.

The point is: while there were other sources from which to replace exhausted ship's stores, none was as good, abundant, and sure as turtle; and no other edible creature could be carried away and kept so long alive. Of breadkind there was only the sparse and perishable stuff that could be taken from the Indians. There were fish in the sea, but the reef and deep-water fisheries of the tropics were a puzzle to the banksmen and trawlers of Europe, as they still are to many of the Caribbean peoples today. There were at first herds of manatee, almost as savory meat as green turtle and even bigger, but too sensitive to persecution to remain a sure source of food in quantity, and indeed soon wiped out over most of their range. Ashore, on the islands, the overgrown rats the Arawaks called *jutias* abounded and could be salted down, and for a time they provisioned many a distressed ship; but they disappeared from island after island in the process; and Cyclura, the rock iguana, did the same. Along the Main, in the rain forest and palm jungles, there were tapirs and pacas and peccaries, but these were all too wary to swell ship's stores. There were any number of things a clever lone man could find to eat, but it was all piddling stuff. You couldn't victual a ship with it.

It was only the green turtle that could take the place of spoiled kegs of beef and send a ship on for a second year of wandering or marauding. All early activity in the New World tropics—exploration, colonization, buccaneering, and even the maneuverings of naval squadrons—was in some way or degree dependent on turtle. It was quick rescue when scurvy struck, and shipwrecked people lived on it for months or even years. Salted or dried, it everywhere fed the seaboard poor. It was at once a staple and a luxury—a slave ration, and in soup and curries the pride of the menus of the big plantation houses. When the Spanish *flota* from Porto Bello and the galleons from Cartagena converged at Havana for the voyage home, they took on turtle there. Pickled or stowed alive on deck, it was a standard item in British naval logistics. More than any other dietary factor, the green turtle supported the opening up of the Caribbean.

It had all the qualities it needed for a role in history. It was big, abundant, available, savory, sustaining, and remarkably tenacious of life. It was almost unique in being a marine herbivore—an air-breathing vertebrate which grazed submarine beds of seed plants as the bison grazed the plains and which, like them, congregated in tremendous bands. It was easy to catch with simple equipment because its pastures lay under clear shallow water; and, moreover, each June it came ashore wherever there was sand, and you had only to walk the beach and turn on their backs as many as you could use.

The abundance of Chelonia expressed a straightforward ecology, a simple way of life. It ate one kind of plant that spread continuously over great areas and that recognized no seasons in the underwater climate. This was an utterly practicable way to live, the classic way to live, and the only sure way to be abundant; and as the grown-up greens were too big and hard for most predators and too fast and wary for the rest, the schools grew to limits set only by the area of the feeding space.

There were other kinds of turtles in the sea, but the rest you found only here and there—only one-one-one, as they say in Grand Cayman. All the others gummed up their energy cycles by eating animals, which of course had their own complex problems and uncertainties. The carnivorous turtles had to keep moving to forage, and they wound up solitary and scattered. You couldn't even depend on their tasting good. The green turtle, on the other hand, stayed in one place and grazed all day, unhurried and untroubled in the rich pastures, only one link down the feeding chain from the sun itself. It grew fat and numerous and succulent, and in every way a blessing. It was, as I said, too great a blessing to last.

Today the Atlantic green turtle can no longer be reckoned a major asset. And, worse, I believe that if it is not effectively protected, it must soon be extirpated as a breeding resident of American waters.

I find little sympathy for this pessimism, I must say, among the people who hunt turtles and operate the industry. They feel no alarm over its future, because they have seen no reduction in the turtle populations of their time. They are more concerned over unstable markets—over the fact that, away from its home shores where it is a staple, green turtle is in demand only among gourmets. They are plagued by lack of transportation for their catch and over England's disinclination to squander dollar credits for the makings of aldermanic soups. It is the exceptional turtle man who worries about turtles for the future.

What they all overlook is the fact that they came to know Chelonia long after it had been cut down to a mere trace of its primitive abundance. They either hunt it today in the few places where schools hold out, or they take the trickle of waifs and stragglers that still faintly outline the old great feeding range of the species. The young men of today catch about as many turtles in a season as their fathers did, and so see no cause for alarm. What they do not know, though, is that the scattering of schooners and canoes that hunt Chelonia in the 1900's is picking about among the ruins of the great turtle fishery of the centuries before. But that is what it is doing. The documentation is voluminous and clear.

One by one the famous old rookeries were destroyed. The first to go was Bermuda and next the shores of the Greater Antilles. The Bahamas were blanked out not long after, and boats from there began to cross the Gulf Stream to abet the decimation in Florida, where the crawl was once more common than the hen coop—where Charles Peake caught 2,500 greens about Sebastian in 1886 and in 1895 could take only 60; where vast herds foraged in the east-coast estuaries and on the Gulf flats of the upper peninsula and a great breeding school came each year to Dry Tortugas.

One nesting ground stood apart from all the rest and in its fecundity stirred the wonder of all who saw it. This was the Cayman Islands. The breeding aggregation there supported the biggest turtle fishery in America and had traceable effect on the course of colonization. The history of this fishery—its burgeoning and exhaustion, the wrecking of the rookery by heedless killing of females that came ashore to lay, the plight of the people who had no other way to live and their tenacity in following the declining schools from one remote shore to another—is as extraordinary from the standpoint of human ecology as from that of resource depletion.

Bernard Lewis of Jamaica has told the melancholy story of the recession into foreign waters of the Cayman fishery. The sloops worked for a while off the south coast of Cuba, but the schools there soon dwindled and they had to look farther still. They built bigger boats and scouted ever more distant shores, and finally they stumbled upon a vast new turtle ground on Mosquito Bank just off the coast of Nicaragua, some 350 miles over open sea from Grand Cayman. There was a cluster of keys where fresh water could be got, a shallow sea set with bars and rocks, miles and miles of blade-grass flats, and turtle herds that looked to the Cayman captains like home in their grandfathers' day.

That was more than a hundred years ago. The Caymanians are still the only important export turtle-hunters in the Caribbean, and the Mosquito Cays are still the main source of green turtles for the American market. The need for fast, seaworthy schooners bred superb shipwrights, and the need for men to sail them bred the Cayman tradition of seamanship. The fleets that go out each year have shrunk from thirty graceful schooners to five or six; but there in the islands is a people whose way of living Chelonia set a hundred years and more ago. And there on Mosquito Bank is a creature with its back against a wall.

I do not mean by this direful figure that it is the Cayman people who will deliver the last blow from which the green turtle will not recover. They, and the harpooners, who take the turtles on the grazing banks, are attacking the species where it is most resilient. It could almost surely stand many times more of that kind of pressure. But what it cannot stand is being deprived of the benefits of reproduction. The green turtle seems to have an innate biological toughness that lets it withstand heavy natural predation on its immature stages and thrive equally in big schools and in small colonies. Primarily adapted to herd grazing of stands of a single plant, it nevertheless can make shift on other food: manatee grass or algæ or, more rarely, even animal food—jellyfish and sponges and, in captivity, cut fish. Young green turtles survive long involuntary trips in the global currents and, like ridleys, sometimes reach England in good shape after crossing with the Gulf Stream. They are tough, and, if allowed to breed, I think they can hold on in the face of everything—but they must be allowed to breed.

That much of the general course of conservation is self-evident. But from there on the procedure is blocked by our astonishing ignorance of the biology of the animal. How do you let green turtles breed? What moves are required, and what possible? Would better protection for beaches on the Florida west coast restore the colony there, where only half-grown turtles are caught today and where none has laid for fifty years? Most of the countries and peoples with a stake in the Caribbean littoral would be in sympathy with the idea of saving the green turtle. But, once persuaded of the necessity to do something, they embarrass you by insisting that you tell them exactly what to do.

Until quite recently the problem was not critical, or did not seem so. There were hundreds of islands and keys and mainland beaches where nobody lived and where you could comfortably imagine thousands of safe nests erupting yearly multitudes of little turtles to repair the inroads of the season. But since the war the wild beaches are shrinking. The Caribbean people are among the most prolific strains on earth, and they are breeding fast. There are outboard motors on the dugouts, and little airplanes will set you down nearly anywhere. Where twenty years ago most Caribbean shore was wilderness or lonesome cocal, aluminum roofing now shines in new clearings in the seaside scrub. The people are breeding too fast for the turtles. The drain on nesting grounds is increasing by jumps. It is this drain that is hard to control, and it is this that will finish Chelonia.

From such evidence as was examined in the preceding

Above: Green turtle, Tortuguero, digging the "body-pit," in the bottom of which she will dig a smaller urn-shaped cavity to hold the eggs she lays. *Below*: immature tagged loggerhead turtle, Cape Canaveral, Florida.

Above: leatherback (trunkback) hatchling, Tortuguero, Costa Rica. *Below*: Archie Carr and a Miskito Indian with hawksbills, Miskito Cays, Nicaragua. (Photo by Anne Meylan)

chapter it seems that there must be some substance in the
tales of Chelonia's long-haul migrations. Perhaps the beach
at Turtle Bogue really is a breeding center of vital importance to the maintenance of the Caribbean stock. If so,
then I wonder what it is about this strip of sand that at-
tracts the fleets to such distant rendezvous—that brings
the thousands to these two dozen miles and leaves only
stragglers to dig in other shores.

It could be, I suppose, that certain routes are feasible
for migration and others not, and the Bogue is the only
long stretch of unsettled shore and proper sand accessible
to good seaways. Or perhaps the convergence there ex-
presses ingrained patterns of response that once made
sense but now, no longer of any special survival value,
are adhered to through evolutionary inertia, as birds are
said to cling to outmoded patterns of travel.

You have to look for some such recondite explanation,
because there is nothing evident in the lay or structure
of the beach to account for its appeal. To a man's eye, it
is just twenty-four miles of black sand—fine-grained obsidian and pumice—swept by heavy surf with strong longshore currents and no protecting banks or reefs out front.
It's an unimposing shore—low dunes covered with sea
oats, sea grape, and cocoplum, and back of these strand
scrub grading into swamp or fringe forest along the slow
river. In places the shore is eroding and high tide eats at
the base of the four-foot sand bluff that sometimes is too
steep for a turtle to climb to a nesting site.

A thousand beaches are like that. Tortuguero has one
feature that sets it apart from most—its black color. The
sand is a pepper-and-salt blend of black glass and explo-
sive rock, more pepper than salt, and almost an even black
when wet. Unlike beaches of quartz grains, on which the
wave-laid flat is hard, the Bogue fluffs up like egg icing

when the wash passes over it, and though it settles smooth as asphalt it lets you down ankle-deep in mush when you walk at the surf edge.

It is possible that the color of the sand may influence its properties as an incubating medium, even at the depths at which turtle eggs are laid. At noon the surface gets too hot to walk on barefoot and at night it must cool off more rapidly than beaches of white or yellow sand. These qualities would seem offhand to be unpropitious for turtle eggs; but then nobody really knows much about the requirements of green-turtle eggs, and the blackness of the sand might even be some sort of an attraction.

Chelonia is not the only turtle that nests on the Bogue. As we saw in earlier chapters, in May and early June before the fleet of greens arrives, hawksbills and trunkbacks come in, sometimes three or four in a mile. As a trunkback resort, it is as good as any place I have seen. As a hawksbill rookery, it is only second-rate and does not compare with such places as Chiriquí Beach to the south or with the little islands and breaking bars southwest of San Andres. Rarely, a wandering loggerhead lays there, they say, although I never saw one there, and where the river runs near the sea, as it does for several miles, iguanas come across from the big trees and lay their eggs in the sand among the turtle nests.

The place offers no special immunity from natural enemies. You find the same gangs of egg-hungry marauders there as elsewhere, and the beach is often strewn with crumpled shells from ravaged nests. Coons and pisotes make a business of egg-hunting, and when the fleet is in, ocelots, snakes, and even jaguars may come over from the inland forests. As in many places, the worst scourge of the rookery is dogs. I told earlier how, when late June comes, the dogs of the towns on the high ground miles back inland, beyond all kinds of rough terrain, come over in packs, their migration timed by who knows what insight to the migration of the turtle schools. They smell out and dig up each fresh nest they come across, sometimes before the female turtle has returned to the sea. Except for man, they are probably the most potent enemy up to the time the eggs hatch.

Even the nests overlooked by the dogs and coons and concealed by hard rain are not in the clear. If the little turtles emerge by day, the buzzards learn of it and sail in from all around to flop about the nest and struggle among themselves over the stream of hatchlings. The dogs come back, and the buzzards fight them, standing their ground, black and toothless but full of menace as any cur, giving ground only when outnumbered. It's a mess there on the Bogue when the fleet leaves turtle eggs in the sand, I'm telling you.

Most of the nests hatch at night. The buzzards are asleep then, but the jackfish and their kin are not; and out beyond the breakers a strong flashlight will show the slashing line where the crescent-tailed killers scoop and cut at the paddling hatchlings, yolk-buoyed, helpless, still running the gauntlet, toward a goal nobody knows. It is clearly no lack of enemies that explains the pilgrimage to Turtle Bogue.

In fact, I can see nothing extraordinary about the place. It is a good beach. It is long and easy to dig in, and hardly anybody lives between the two settlements at the ends— no street lights shine behind it, no jook organs sound above the surf. The hazards there are the usual ones an aquatic animal that goes to shore to lay must always face. I don't know what it is that makes the *flota* go there.

But the fact remains that, in spite of the dogs and the natural predators, the Bogue is the best nesting beach in its half of the Caribbean, and this suggests its potential role in a plan to save the green turtle. The Cayman captains believe their industry is wholly dependent on this breeding ground. They are certainly at least partly right; and, as we have seen, the importance of the rookery may be far greater than that. How then, it is natural to ask, is Chelonia faring there; and if the Bogue is in its future, what does the future hold?

As near as I can make out, it holds extinction.

Not extinction of the worldwide species, or of the Atlantic race, or even possibly of the stock in the western Caribbean; but a sure obliteration of that element that inherits or acquires a drive toward nesting in Costa Rica. Reproduction of the Tortuguero schools can at any time be cut off by an existing commercial system so organized that every female that comes ashore can be turned and taken away without being allowed to lay her eggs. The organization works like this.

All along the Central American coast the governments own a strip of the land-edge, the *Milla Maritima*, extending inland for a mile from the breakers. There are two chief sources of revenue in this strip: the *cocotero*, as they call the extensive coconut fringe, and the *tortuguero*—the turtle rookeries, hawksbill and green. In Panama and Costa Rica coconut and turtle rights are each year leased at public auction. The most valuable turtle beach on the Main, from Yucatán to the Orinoco, is, of course, the Costa Rican section from the isolated hamlet of Parismina at the mouth of the Reventazon River to the little sawmill settlement of Tortuguero at the mouth of the river of the same name. The only eminence on all this coast is a low, domed massif rising from the plain behind the dunes just across the river from Tortuguero. This is called Cerro de Tortuga, because to ships at sea the lone mound suggests a turtle, and because those who know this shore know that it marks the north end of the home of all the turtles.

Every year the Tortuguero beach is rented like the rest. Recently the high bidder—the *contratista*, they call him— has been a man who lives in Limón. He rarely sees the beach himself. He appoints a *capataz*, a manager, who is in direct charge of the corps of *veladores*, the stayers- awake, who patrol the beach from June 15 through the summer and turn the turtles on their backs as they arrive. The miles of the beach are numbered from the point at Tortuguero southward, and each *velador* is assigned a mile —except for an occasional energetic man who may get two miles. Each man is furnished with provisions, a blanket, a lantern, and a coil of rope. If his mile is near the end of the beach, he may live in one of the settlements; but most of the *veladores* build thatch *ranchos* and move to the beach for the season, often taking their families with them.

At sundown the *velador* begins his patrol, dividing the mile among whatever children or relatives may be on hand, and intercepting every turtle that comes ashore, either meeting her on the way up the beach or crossing her trail between the surf and the grass edge. By Costa Rican law he must wait and let her dig a nest and lay; but this would cost him at least half an hour, and as there is no one there to know, he turns the turtle where and when he finds her and hurries on to find another. During the height of the season—usually two or three weeks in July—he may turn thirty or forty turtles between sunset and dawn. His average for the three-month season is be- tween five and ten a night. He gets three and a half colones—fifty-odd cents—for each of his turtles, provided they get picked up at all.

This is a remote and dangerous coast, blocked behind by swamp and aimless rivers and with no barrier shoals to hinder the high seas that come in under the trade wind. There is no way for the *velador* to deliver his own turtles to market, or to do anything other than let them lie where he finds them and wait for the launch from Limón. He drags each turtle up just beyond the reach of high-tide waves and, because the sun on its belly would kill it in a few hours, builds over it a little shelter of coco thatch. He accumulates turtles for two nights; and then the launch is supposed to come. There is a law that says the launch must pick up turned turtles every two days. It says that if the launch has not come by the end of the second day the *velador* must turn all his turtles right side up and let them go. Well, obviously, since there is only one launch, and since there is often a continuous string of squalls churning into the coast from Cape Gracias to the Canal, there will be times when no launch comes after two days, or after three, or after a week. A few years ago the turtles simply lay there, every new day dying by the dozens. But the Ministry of Agriculture learned of the waste and, to control it, set the two-day limit. But it is really expecting too much of the lonely *veladores* to think they should discipline themselves to the extent of absorbing the loss. They think of the *flota* as inexhaustible, and anyway, except for the end miles where the *resguardo* can walk evenings without leaving the girls too far behind, who is there to know how long a turtle has been flapping under her little palm roof?

But sometimes the weather is good, even in July, and then the launch lurches up the coast from Limón, and the *velador* may suddenly sight her off his mile. He yells to his young ones, and they scramble for machetes and rope and run off up and down the beach to where the turtles lie. They topple the thatch and tie a chunk of balsa to each turtle's fin by a ten-foot line. They right the turtle and goad it into the surf, where the swish of the water brings back its spirit; and it streaks seaward, the balsa buoy trailing and bobbing behind. Meantime, the launch has moved up and lies with idling engine, a few hundred yards off the beach, just safely beyond the first breakers. It puts out dugouts, and these chase down the skidding buoys, draw in the turtles, and take them to the launch. Back at Limón they are held in crawls for shipment—once to New York and London, now mainly to Key West, Tampa, and Colón.

It's a deadly system; and similar systems exploit the lesser nesting beaches all along the coast. Operated at capacity, it would surely destroy the rookery, and the only reason it has not done so is the failure of the *veladores* to work full-time. Although all the miles are allotted, they are not always tended. A small excuse will keep a man in his shack, and because of this some turtles get by. But the apathy of the hunters is only due to the irregular arrival of the launch—to the fact that any time they spend on the beach is gambled, because their catch may never be picked up. And the unreliability of the launch is only a sign of the erratic post-war market. Any hint of stability in the export market—any increase in channels to the New York luxury trade, one big venture making frozen turtle known to inland consumers, or even any improvement in British currency relations—and the launch will come on schedule in spite of the squalls. Plenty of launches will come. And then every man on the beach will watch all of his mile every night, and the blockade will be complete. Meanwhile, the shore is settling up at a fantastic rate, local demand is growing, and the chance for Chelonia to establish rookeries elsewhere has gone. Looked at from this angle, the picture is dark.

Viewed from the standpoint of the opportunities for

intervention, the situation looks different. The very migratory habit that makes the green turtle vulnerable could be the basis for its rescue, and even conceivably for bringing it back to the abundance of former times. We are not at deadlock with the green turtle as we were with the buffalo. We are killing it out idly, aimlessly, with no conviction of any sort, with most of us not even aware that it is going. We have no need for its habitat for any of our own schemes. Territorially, its interests and ours overlap only on the sea beach, and even there Chelonia comes when we are asleep. And because the creature congregates each year to mate and lay its eggs, real protection for a few beaches not only would help save for the future a species now threatened with extinction, but might even bring back the fleets Columbus found.

Young farm-reared green turtles, Torres Strait, Australia.

Glossary

AKEE A West African tree and its fruit, introduced and now widespread in the West Indies. The fruit, red or orange in color, is about three inches long and has an edible aril that tastes like an omelet.

AMEIVA A genus of ground-dwelling lizards found about Caribbean shores.

ANI A long-tailed black bird of the cuckoo family. It has a high keel on the bill and a disjointed way of alighting in a bush as if thrown there.

AZUCARÓN Local Central American term for a white-fleshed, very sweet strain of pineapple.

BATALÍ Trinidadian name for a kind of sea turtle, supposedly the ridley (Lepidochelys).

BEACH MORNING GLORY A flowering vine (*Ipomea Pes-capræ*) that flourishes on the shifting sand of seaside dunes.

BLADE GRASS See TURTLE GRASS.

BONEFISH A medium-sized, shallow-water fish (*Albula vulpes*) rated by some as the most dynamic gamefish for its size in the world.

BONGO An Afro-Caribbean drum, played with the fingers and palms of the hands.

CALLIPASH The upper shell of a turtle.

CARAPACE The upper shell of a turtle.

CARAPASH The upper shell of a turtle.

CAREY The hawksbill turtle; also the commercially valuable shell from this animal.

CASUARINA   A genus of Australian trees, in this book *Casuarina equisetifolia,* the beefwood, or so-called Australian, "pine."

CAYUCA   A dugout canoe; also cayuco.

CEDRO MACHO   A name applied in Costa Rica to two timber trees (Carapa and Trichilia) of the family Meliaceæ.

CEDRO REAL   Spanish cedar (Cedrela), the wood of which is light, durable, aromatic, and termite-proof.

CEIBA   A large genus of tropical trees of the silk cotton family, including the giant *Ceiba pentandra* of the Caribbean border, the species referred to in this book.

CHELONIA   The genus of the green turtle.

CLAVES   Two hardwood sticks that are beaten together to piece out the curious rhythm patterns in Afro-Antillean bands.

COATI   See COATIMUNDI.

COATIMUNDI   A long-snouted raccoon-like animal known in much of Central America as *pisote.*

COCO PLUM   A shrub or small tree (*Chrysobalanus Icaco*) of Caribbean dunes and beaches. The leaves are broad and glossy, and the fruit is used for preserves.

COQUINA   A little bivalve mollusc (Donax), sometimes very abundant on Florida beaches and caught for soup there.

CORRIDO   A Mexican ballad derived from the Spanish *romance,* with a predictable but pleasant musical form and lyrics in quatrains.

CRETACEOUS   The last period of the Mesozoic Era. It ended about seventy million years ago, when, among other changes, the dinosaurs became extinct.

CRICAMOLA   Local name for a group of Indians of the Chiriquí Lagoon area of Panama.

CYCLURA   The ground-dwelling iguana of the West Indies; once widely distributed, but now extirpated from many of the islands and rare nearly everywhere.

DILLY TREE   The sapodilla (*Sapota Achras*), a tropical American tree cultivated for its rough-skinned, sugary fruit.

GARROBO   An iguana. A name variously applied in Central America to both tree iguanas and ground iguanas, sometimes to the male alone, often to both sexes.

GOATSUCKER Any of the birds of the group to which the whippoor-will and the chuck-will's-widow belong. A nightjar.

GREEN TURTLE A large, herbivorous sea turtle (*Chelonia mydas*) found in most tropical seas, and everywhere valued as food.

GROUPER Any of a large number of bottom-dwelling, big-mouthed fishes belonging to the sea-bass family (Serranidæ) and common about the coasts of Florida and the West Indies.

GRUNT Any of a group of small, mostly tropical fishes related to the snapper. They used to be to the Conchs of the Florida Keys what sow-belly was to the Crackers.

GUARO Aguardiente; rum.

GUAYABERA A long, pleated Cuban shirt, worn outside the trousers.

HALFBEAK A small, slim, cylindrical surface fish of the group to which flying-fishes belong. The upper jaw is oddly shortened, being less than an eighth the length of the lower.

HAWKSBILL The sea turtle (Eretmochelys) from which tortoise shell is taken.

HUAPANGO Mexican dance, and the accompanying music in which the beat is strengthened by a slap across the strings of the guitar for the last note of each measure.

HUISCOYOL A spiny, slim-stemmed, canelike palm (Bactris) of the Caribbean lowlands.

HYLA A genus of tree frogs.

IGUANA A big tropical lizard; as used in this book, either the tree iguana (genus Iguana) or the ground iguanas (genera Cteno-saura and Cyclura), according to the context.

JACK See JACKFISH.

JACKFISH An active, predacious, cursorial marine fish of the genus Caranx.

JAGUAR The largest American cat (*Felis onca*)—a powerful, short-legged, buff-colored animal with black spots, each surrounded by a ring of smaller spots. It ranges from Texas to Paraguay.

JUTIA One of a once varied and abundant group of heavy-bodied West Indian rodents. The largest of the group, the Cuban Capromys, has a body nearly two feet long and is sold regu-larly in the Havana market.

KAITIS Sandals made of a sole of heavy leather or tire rubber fastened to the foot by a single strap between the first and second toes.

KINGFISH   A big relative of the Spanish mackerel; a popular game and food fish once abundant off Florida and still common in parts of the Caribbean.

LAUREL   A common timber tree (*Cordia alliodora*) widely distributed in Central and South America.

LEÓN   The puma or cougar (*Felis concolor*). A big, long-bodied brown cat that ranges from eastern North America to Patagonia.

LOGGERHEAD   A sea turtle (Caretta) with a big head and crab-smashing jaws. The only American sea turtle that nests as far north as Virginia.

MADEIRA   West Indian mahogany (*Swietenia mahogani*), the wood of which is much heavier and more close-grained than that of mainland mahogany.

MANACA   A common palm (the cohune palm, *Attalea cohune*) of the Caribbean shore. The long, pinnate leaves are used as thatch and the nuts for oil.

MANATEE GRASS   A submarine plant (*Cymodocea manatorum*) of tropical American waters, with cylindrical, needle-like leaves borne in pairs.

MANGINEEL   A poisonous tree (*Hippomane Mancinella*) of tropical American coasts. The milky sap is a strong skin irritant, and the crabapple-like fruits have caused fatal cases of poisoning when eaten.

MANGROVE DOG   The common crab-eating raccoon of the coast of northern South America.

MONTE   Bush; wild, rough country.

MOSQUITO INDIANS   A tribe of salt-water Indians of the Caribbean shore of Central America. Most of the Mosquito groups today show heavy Negro admixture.

MUTTONFISH   One of the many delectable snappers of tropical American waters.

OCELOT   A spotted cat of the American tropics. The ocelot is similar in general appearance to a jaguar, but smaller and with markings different in detail.

OXBULL   The Hawksbill turtle (Caribbean English).

PACA   A large tropical American rodent of the genus Cuniculus. The paca mentioned in this book is the famed tepescuinte, or *guarda-tinaja*, a brown animal with longitudinal rows of white spots, the size of a month-old shoat and unbelievably savory when roasted.

PARROTFISH   One of many species of highly colored tropical reef and shallow-water fishes related to the wrasses.

PICCOLO   As used in this book, a jook organ—a pay-as-you-play phonograph of rococo design and gorgeous coloration.

PIMIENTA BRAVA   Black pepper.

PIPA   A drinking coconut.

PISOTE   See COATIMUNDI.

PITPAN   Carib name for a small dugout canoe.

PLASTRON   The bottom shell of a turtle.

PORKFISH   A strikingly decorated and succulent shallow-water fish of Antillean-Caribbean reefs.

QUEEN TRIGGER   The most colorful American species of the wide-ranging tropical triggerfishes. The name comes from a curious interlocking arrangement of three dorsal spines.

RABIRRUBIA   A medium-sized highly edible fish of the snapper family; usually known in English as yellowtail.

RIDLEY   The bastard turtle; a sea turtle of the genus Lepidochelys.

ROCK HIND   A handsome, small, tropical grouper of importance throughout the West Indies as a food fish.

SEA GRAPE   A small, big-leafed tree (*Coccoloba uvifera*) of the Caribbean shore. It bears grape-like clusters of edible fruit.

SEA OATS   A coarse grass (Uniola) of the sea beach—one of the first plants to establish itself on new wind-laid sand.

SPANISH HOGFISH   A gaudy and very edible Caribbean reef fish. The fore half of the body is often red in color and the back half yellow.

TAPIR   A heavy-bodied, nearly hairless ungulate mammal with a short, trunk-like proboscis. Called mountain cow by the Central American creoles.

TEPESCUINTE   See PACA.

THALASSIA   See TURTLE GRASS.

TICA   A Costa Rican girl. Feminine form of the national nickname arising from a tendency of Costa Ricans to use the diminutive suffix -*ico*.

TIGRE   Jaguar.

TORSOLA   Larva of a tropical fly parasitic under the skin of various mammals. A serious menace to stock-raising in the tropics.

TURTLE GRASS   A strap-leafed submarine plant of the genus Thalassia.

TRUNKBACK   The largest of all the sea turtles, *Dermochelys coriacea*.

VEGA   The bank or flood plain of a river.

VELADOR   A stayer-awake—one of the men who walk the beach and turn female turtles as they come up to lay.

WAHOO   A big, mackerel-like fish of tropical waters. Fast and strong, and one of the mainstays of the Miami charter-boat fishermen.

WOLOF   A dialect spoken in parts of West Africa from which many slaves were brought to America.

WOMAN'S TONGUE   An African tree (*Albizzia Lebbek*) of the mimosa family, introduced and widely distributed in the West Indies and southern Florida. The name comes from the aimless chattering of the seed pods in the wind.

Index